The Holy Trinity
and the Law of Three

ALSO BY CYNTHIA BOURGEAULT

Love Is Stronger Than Death
The Mystical Union of Two Souls

Mystical Hope
Trusting in the Mercy of God

The Wisdom Way of Knowing
Reclaiming an Ancient Tradition to Awaken the Heart

Centering Prayer and Inner Awakening

Chanting the Psalms
A Practical Guide with Instructional CD

The Wisdom Jesus
*Transforming Heart and Mind—a New Perspective
on Christ and His Teaching*

The Meaning of Mary Magdalene
Discovering the Woman at the Heart of Christianity

The Holy Trinity
and the Law of Three

*Discovering the Radical Truth
at the Heart of Christianity*

CYNTHIA BOURGEAULT

Shambhala
Boston & London
2013

Shambhala Publications, Inc.
Horticultural Hall
300 Massachusetts Avenue
Boston, Massachusetts 02115
www.shambhala.com

9 8 7 6 5 4 3 2 1

First Edition
Printed in The United States of America

♾ This edition is printed on acid-free paper that meets the
American National Standards Institute z39.48 Standard.
♻ This book is printed on 30% postconsumer recycled paper.
For more information please visit www.shambhala.com.

Distributed in the United States by Random House, Inc.,
and in Canada by Random House of Canada Ltd

Interior design and composition by Greta D. Sibley

Library of Congress Cataloging-in-Publication Data
Bourgeault, Cynthia.
The Holy Trinity and the law of three: discovering the radical truth
at the heart of Christianity/Cynthia Bourgeault.—First Edition.
pages cm
Includes bibliographical references and index.
ISBN 978-1-61180-052-4 (pbk.: alk. paper) 1. Trinity. I. Title.
BT 111.3.B68 2013
231'.044—dc23
2012049000

To Helen Daly
(1952–2012)
a true Wisdom trouvère

and

To Rafe
always and everywhere

Contents

Part Four

HARNESSING THE POWER OF THREE

Acknowledgments

A book that has occupied this much of my life will necessarily cut a wide swath of gratitude. The first draft of what would eventually become part 3 emerged when I was in residence at the Contemplative Centre on Salt Spring Island, British Columbia, during the winter of 1999–2000. The rest of the book finally came together twelve years later during a six-month sabbatical on Eagle Island, Maine. Between then and now there have been hundreds of students, teachers, casual acquaintances, chance meetings, books and conversations, and hours logged on the meditation cushion that have all had a hand in the final product. For all of this I give my heartfelt thanks.

I have been blessed to work with three of the most brilliant Christian mystics of our times — Bruno Barnhart, Beatrice Bruteau, and Raimon Panikkar — and each of them has had a significant hand in this work. Bruno Barnhart has been my mentor for nearly thirty years, and his gracious insights and lively correspondence during the formative stages of this book were an extraordinary gift.

I am grateful as well for my teachers in the Gurdjieff Work, particularly Elsa Denzey and Jyri Paloheimo, who took me under their wings with unwavering faith that I would eventually "get it" and who showed me that the Work does indeed have a human heart. Jyri was an enthusiastic supporter of this project from the outset and was actively mentoring me from his vast knowledge of both scientific and Gurdjieffian cosmology until his untimely death in 2006. To you, dear friend, I send my special gratitude and deepest confidence that you have indeed made it to "Holy Planet Purgatory."

A heartfelt thank–you to my risk–taking colleague Richard Rohr, who arranged the first opportunity for me to present these ideas publically when we co–led a conference on the Trinity in January 2005. The CDs from that conference (called "The Shape of God") are still available from his Center for Action and Contemplation in Albuquerque, New Mexico, and the enthusiastic response I continue to receive from them has encouraged me to believe that there is indeed an audience out there for what I have to say.

In a very real sense, the midwives of this book are the thirty-five students who participated in our Advanced Wisdom School in Orange County, New York, during the fall and winter of 2011–12. Their enthusiasm, energy, and deep understanding of the importance of the ideas I was sharing finally convinced me to stop referring to this as "my posthumous book" and actually get it down on paper. The curriculum we followed in our three sessions has essentially become the table of contents of this book.

With deep gratitude I honor you all: Judy Arnold, Lois Barton, Debra Brewin-Wilson, Robin Cameron, Eileen Clark, Susan Cooper, Liz Dahmus, Helen Daly, Marietta Della Penna, Helen Dunphey, Diane Elliott, Sandra Etemad, Mary Louise Fisher, Steve Fisher, Maureen Hanley, Mary Ellen Jernigan, Wendy Johnston, Carol Leach, Jane McKenna, Elizabeth Moulton, Kathleen Nelson, Barbara Osborne, Sherrill and David Pantle, William Redfield, Gina Ricciardi, Phil Rogacki, Carol Sadlek, Rosemary Shirley, Patricia Speak, Jane Waldron, Gail and Alec Wiggin, and Betsy Young. And of course, to Catherine McCarthy, who convened this Wisdom School and has hosted virtually all of my New England teaching over the past decade in her role as coordinator of Contemplative Outreach Orange County.

Special mention should be made of the extraordinary contribution of Robin Cameron. By the time I finally got around to teaching my material on the unfolding Trinity at our Wisdom School, the original draft composed on my 1999 iMac had vanished into cyberspace. Robin transcribed the material from a scanned hard copy of the original (and thank you, Gail Wiggin, for the scanning!) and re-input it in a format compatible with twenty-first-century technology. Robin is a certified teacher of the enneagram as well as a wicked–good typist and arranged for my chapter on the enneagram and the Law of Three to be carefully critiqued by two of her enneagram colleagues who are also well versed in Gurdjieff teaching. To Robin Cameron, Gloria Cuevas-Barnett, and Belinda Ashenfelter, I am deeply grateful for your helpful and unfailingly supportive comments.

A special thank-you as well to Jens Abildgaard, who reviewed my material on the Law of Three and the Law of Seven from his lifetime (literally!) of experience in the Work and corrected a few significant errors in my presentation.

Finally, I continue to be awestruck by the prophetic recklessness of my editor, David O'Neal, in his willingness to take a risk on a manuscript that is so far out of the box as to have no ready-made constituency. I know this will not be an easy sell: *way* too out there for traditional academic theology, likely too intellectual for contemplatives, too mystical for intellectuals, too esoteric for the orthodox, too orthodox for most of the major esoteric streams. His commitment to the ideas themselves and to the paradigm shift they may help to catalyze has been a most extraordinary vote of confidence, even though we both know that the fruits of this venture may not be reaped in our own lifetimes. Thank you, Dave! Thank you for *seeing* me. This has been one of those life tasks, and thanks to you I have been able to bring it to completion.

Eagle Island, Maine
September 2012

The Holy Trinity
and the Law of Three

Introduction

My first challenge in writing this book will be to persuade you that there is anything here worth considering at all. With so many urgent practical issues facing spiritual humanity, why waste time with the Trinity, a doctrine that most of the world (and even much of Christianity) regards as contrived and irrelevant? It takes a real stretch of the theological imagination to claim that it was ever a part of the original Jesus teachings or that it does a single thing to clarify or enhance these teachings. In fact, the eminent twentieth-century theologian Karl Rahner has claimed that if the Trinity were to quietly disappear out of Christian theology, never to be mentioned again, most of Christendom would not even notice its absence.

By way of a circuitous response, let me offer you a story that was told to me by my longtime friend and teacher, the Abkhazian dervish elder Murat Yagan.

In the years immediately following World War II, Murat recounts, he spent a time ranching in a remote corner of eastern Turkey. There he became friends with an elderly couple with whom he frequently shared a meal. Life had been good to them, but their one sadness was that they missed their only son, who had left some years before to seek work in Istanbul. He had indeed become a successful businessman, but they had infrequent contact with him and missed him greatly.

One day when Murat appeared on their doorstep for tea, the old couple were bursting with pride, eager to show him the new tea cupboard that their son had just shipped them from Istanbul. It was indeed a handsome piece of furniture, and the woman had already proudly arranged her best tea set on its upper shelf. Murat was

1

polite but curious. Why would their son go to such expense to send them a tea cupboard? Why, for a piece of furniture whose ostensible purpose was storage, was there such a noticeable absence of drawers and cabinets? "Are you sure it's a tea cupboard?" Murat asked them. They were sure.

But the question continued to nag at Murat. Finally, just as he was taking his leave, he said, "Do you mind if I have a closer look at this tea cupboard?" With their permission, he turned the backside around and unscrewed a couple of packing boards. A set of cabinet doors swung open to reveal inside a fully operative ham radio set.

That "tea cupboard," of course, was intended to connect them to their son. But unaware of its real contents, they were simply using it to display their china.

To my mind, that is an unsettlingly apt analogy for how we Christians have been using the Holy Trinity. It is our theological tea cupboard, upon which we display our finest doctrinal china, our prized assertion that Jesus, a human being, is fully divine. This is not necessarily a bad thing, just as it was not a bad thing for the elderly woman to set forth her prettiest teacups on the new piece of furniture. But what if, unbeknownst to nearly everyone, inside it is concealed a powerful communications tool that could connect us to the rest of the worlds (visible and invisible), allow us to navigate our way through many of the doctrinal and ethical logjams of our time, and place the teachings of Jesus in a dynamic metaphysical framework that would truly unlock their power?

It's simply a matter of turning the tea cabinet around and learning how to look inside. That's what I'm proposing to do in this book.

In a nutshell, I will claim that embedded within this theological formula that we recite mostly on automatic pilot ("in the name of the Father, the Son, and Holy Spirit") lies a powerful metaphysical principle that could change our understanding of Christianity and give us the tools so long and so sorely needed to reunite our shattered cosmology, rekindle our visionary imagination, and cooperate consciously with the manifestation of Jesus's "Kingdom of Heaven" here on earth. That principle is called the Law of Three, and the metaphysics that derive from it can be called "ternary metaphysics."

The Law of Three is, I believe, Christianity's hidden driveshaft, and its presence so far has only been intuited, never explicitly identified by theologians. It is distinctly different from the speculative formulations of patristic theology, or even from the well-worn metaphysical road maps of *sophia perennis* (the "perennial philosophy") in which Wisdom alternatives to doctrinal orthodoxy are nearly always couched. Comprehensive, profoundly original, and like all driveshafts concerned with forward motion, it is Christianity's authentic temperament, the key in which *theoria* and *praxis* come together, in which all of its teachings begin to hang together.

But this principle is almost entirely unheard of — not because it is particularly hidden or buried but because the conversation about it has so far gone on within circles that have been considered strictly off limits to traditional academic and theological inquiry. It does not belong to any body of knowledge that theologians generally consider germane to their studies. It is not a part of patristic theology or the Neoplatonic underpinnings on which that theology rests. It is not a part of classic Christian hermeticism or of the great tradition of *sophia perennis*. And while inklings of it can be discerned in certain Christian mystical streams (particularly those flowing through Jacob Boehme and Teilhard de Chardin), it was articulated only in the early twentieth century by the Armenian-born spiritual teacher G. I. Gurdjieff, and until very recently it has been studied and transmitted exclusively within that stream of contemporary esotericism known as the Gurdjieff Work.

That is about as far off limits as one can get.

Admittedly, the times are changing. Only a generation ago the term *Gurdjieff Work* would have evoked well-nigh universal blank stares. Now that the Work has finally begun to come aboveground ("outed," to a large degree, by the contemporary enneagram personality-typing movement, with which it shares a considerably overlapping body of esoteric material), people are looking with newfound curiosity at the eclectic and wildly original metaphysics that the one-of-a-kind spiritual genius G. I. Gurdjieff (1866–1949) claims to have synthesized from Wisdom schools he discovered, after a long search, in Central Asia.

The Law of Three, according to Gurdjieff, together with its compan-ion piece, the Law of Seven, comprise what he calls the foundational, "Laws of World Creation and World Maintenance." The interweaving of these two cosmic laws is depicted in the symbol of the ennea-gram, whose nine points reveal (to those properly initiated) the direction and energetic dynamism through which the world main-tains its forward motion. During the ten years I participated in the Work, we studied these laws assiduously, applied them to the solu-tion of both ordinary problems and cosmic mysteries, and danced their ley lines in the famous Gurdjieff movements. We even heard in passing that the Law of Three had had its origins deep within the oral traditions of the Eastern Orthodox Church and that the mys-terious prayer "Holy God, Holy the Firm, Holy the Immortal, have mercy on us" might indeed reflect a vestigial awareness of the pri-mordial forces in the Law of Three. But no one I met in the Gurdjieff Work seemed particularly interested in reintegrating this powerful transformative principle into Christianity (most seemed to feel that Christianity was beyond salvaging), and certainly most of the Chris-tians I knew from my daily rounds as an Episcopal priest and retreat leader were totally wary of anything that smacked of esotericism.

So, for a long time I simply kept these two streams separate, allowing the knowledge I'd gleaned from my years in the Gurdjieff Work to inform my personal efforts at inner awakening. While I wondered from time to time whether there might really be a con-necting link between the Trinity and the Law of Three, it all seemed too tenuous and fraught with difficulty to pursue.

What broke me out of this holding pattern came from an entirely unexpected quarter: a surprising discomfort I noticed myself expe-riencing around one of the more popular theological initiatives of our time, the effort to reclaim the Holy Spirit as "she." Motivated by a sincere desire to recover the "divine feminine" within Christian-ity, the groundswell has steadily built toward this feminine reim-aging, which indeed has a certain linguistic justification as well as a strong archetypal appeal. As a woman priest generally identified as being on the progressive end of the theological spectrum, I was surprised to find myself digging in my heels. But something from my days in the Work was evidently clicking in, as I kept realizing that the whole notion of a "feminine dimension of God" belonged to a binary metaphysical system, based on the cosmic balance of symmetrical opposites, whereas the Christian metaphysical milieu, by its very Trinitarian lineage, belonged to a ternary metaphysical system. I didn't know quite what that meant yet, but I knew that in this apparently harmless accommodation to gender equality, contemporary theologians were making a seriously wrong turn, risking the loss of a far greater metaphysical treasure.

My attempt to give voice to some of these concerns bore fruit in an article called "Why Feminizing the Trinity Will Not Work," which appeared in the Christmas 2000 issue of the *Sewanee Theological Review*. It is essentially the seed of this book. With heart in mouth, I formally introduced the Law of Three into the Christian theological conversation and tried to suggest a strategy by which Christianity's "missing" feminine might be found simply by loosening our fixation upon the three persons and allowing the Trinity to flow into new configurations according to the inner dynamism of the Law of Three — rather like turning a kaleidoscope. Since then many people have asked me to develop these ideas further. This book is an effort to draw together the teaching and writing I have done on the Trinity and the Law of Three over the past dozen years and to create a unified overview of how the Law of Three works, why I see it as the metaphysical driveshaft of the Trinity, and why it is so important to reclaim it.

This book does not intend to be a comprehensive study of the Trinity or an attempt to dialogue with traditional theological understandings. As our exploration unfolds, I will offer a brief survey of some of the more exciting developments in contemporary Trinitarian theology (which might indeed cause Karl Rahner to take heart), but I do not intend to build on them in any formal way. While it is indeed encouraging to see that some of Christianity's most persuasive thinkers are embracing the Trinity in terms more closely in line with the inherent dynamism of the Law of Three, my task here is to contribute the one piece that is uniquely mine to bring to the table.

To the best of my knowledge, no one has ever written specifically about the Trinity and the Law of Three; no one has yet attempted to interweave Christian metaphysics and G. I. Gurdjieff; and most certainly, no one has ever attempted to demonstrate how the Trinity, when "rotated" according to the Law of Three, does indeed yield a magnificent road map of divine becoming in which mystical vision, cosmology, evolution, history — and yes, Christianity's missing feminine — all come together in a seamless tapestry that indeed looks something like the classic archetypal vision of "the seven ages of man" but on a far vaster scale. That is what I hope to unfold here.

This book is basically in three parts. In the first, I will introduce the Law of Three (starting from that original article in the *Sewanee Theological Review*), explore its basic principles with the help of some recognized reference points in the Gurdjieff Work, and show you how to work with it on a practical basis. For the Law of Three is indeed intended first and foremost as a *practical* tool. Its domain is not just cosmology and metaphysics; it is equally at home solving interpersonal problems, affecting political outcomes, and navigating through impasses of every shape and form. We will also be learning some of the core principles of ternary metaphysics, which will come into play in part 3 of the book.

In part 2 I will tackle a more difficult question: Why do I think this Law of Three has anything at all to do with the Trinity? The case is admittedly hard to make from a historical standpoint, since Trinitarian theology predates Gurdjieff's articulation of the Law of Three by a good sixteen centuries. But I will attempt to flesh out my argument on the grounds of dynamic affinity more than linear causality. My hunch is that Christian metaphysics has always been inherently ternary (precisely because of the Christ event at its epicenter) and that the core notion of the Trinity arose out of the collective imagination of the early Christian fathers to hold the space for this realization until its actual working principles could be more fully articulated. For all of its notorious doctrinal sticky wickets, it nevertheless held the line against a certain gnosticizing tendency inherent in Christian theology from the start and insisted on the centrality of the incarnation and the spiritual principle of kenosis — self-empty-ing, or descent — as the fundamental touchstones of Christian self-understanding. In this section I will unpack some of these intuitions in more detail, then call on Jacob Boehme, that most magnificent of medieval visionary cosmologists, to help me build a bridge between the outermost known reference points in traditional Christian mysticism and the Law of Three.

The third part of my book will be the most challenging — partly because it is so very personal and partly because it is, frankly, a world unto itself. I would probably describe it as a metaphysical prose poem — more art than theology — and the best way to get into it is the way you get into a turning jump rope: you simply leap into the middle and start jumping to its rhythm. I apologize in advance if this leaves some readers behind in its admittedly eccentric conflation of mystical vision, metaphysical "math," and quasi cosmology; you may wonder what realm of reality I think I'm describing here. I wonder the same thing myself. But it is for the sake of this third section that I am really writing this book.

I have to confess that this prose poem (if that's what it is) emerged, pretty much as is, from a single, very intense spate of visionary seeing not long after I had completed that original essay on feminizing the Trinity. In the final paragraph of that article, as you will shortly see, I issued this challenge: "The solution is not to abandon the ternary principle but to apply it, permitting the Trinity to flow again." One afternoon I found myself taking myself up on that challenge. What did it mean to "permit the Trinity to flow again"? What would happen if I applied the basic tenet of the Law of Three — "the interweaving of three separate forces creates a new arising on a new plane" — to set the familiar static triangle of Father–Son–Holy Spirit in motion, generating new patterns of itself?

Whoosh! That's really all I can say. In less than an hour the conventions governing this "turning" of the Trinity all fell into place with a kind of mathematical elegance that confirmed I was on the right track. What emerged over the next couple of weeks was a breathtaking glimpse of the journey of divine love into time, through time, and out of time — from Alpha to Omega, from origin to final *"Consummatum est."* In the vastness of that canopy, I could finally taste the spaciousness out of which had emerged that profound Pauline hymn of Colossians 1:12–20:

He is the image of the unseen God
And the firstborn of all creation,
For in him were created
All things in heaven and on earth:

Everything visible and everything invisible
Thrones, dominations, sovereignties, and powers —
All things were created through him and for him.

Before anything was created, he existed
And he holds all things in unity;
He is, moreover, the head
Of the body, the Church.

As he is the Beginning,
He was first to be raised from the dead,
So that he might be first in every way;
For in him the complete being of God
By God's own choice came to dwell.

Through him God chose to reconcile
The whole universe to himself,
Everything in heaven and everything on earth,
When he made peace by his death on a cross.

At long last I could see how this great cosmological hymn was not merely an ecstatic raving or an antiquated Christocentric hymn now relegated to the status of "mythology" after the Copernican revolution six centuries ago knocked Christianity off its cosmological footings. It is our Christian charter and birthright. For truth, real truth, is seamless and indivisible. Christianity is either Christocentric or it is not; Christ is either literally the one "in whom all things hold together" or he is not. A claim *that* fundamental must be consistently and reliably true; it cannot be true in one realm (the realm of faith) and false in another (the realm of empirical reality). Modern and postmodern Christianity's schizophrenic attempt to live in both realms has gradually sapped its strength and blurred its vision. But how in the name of intellectual integrity could one do otherwise? Suddenly I could see the resolution to that impasse. It simply required the full wingspan of Trinitarian space/time — unlocked by the Law of Three — to assign each of Paul's visionary truths to their proper cosmic domain so that faith and cosmology could reunite in a single visionary whole. My map was showing me how to do it. I emerged from that period of intense "download" with my Christian mystical imagination rekindled and my confidence renewed.

For the next dozen years that vision percolated beneath the surface as I gradually found my place as a spiritual writer and teacher. It was with me as I wrote my other books: *The Wisdom Jesus, The Meaning of Mary Magdalene, Centering Prayer and Inner Awakening, Chanting the Psalms*. It was there as I led workshops and established Wisdom Schools; it was in the back of my mind whenever I found myself quoting that marvelous quip from G. K. Chesterton: "Christianity isn't a failure; it simply hasn't been tried yet." But I could never see any way to speak directly about what I was seeing — it was so far outside the usual stream of theological conversation. Who would ever have the patience as I wove the pieces together? Among my Wisdom students, we began joking about it being my "posthumous book."

And if truth be told, I was content with that verdict. But a glimmer of hope that I might yet live to see the sprouting of this vision was rekindled last year when a group of my most senior students volunteered themselves as guinea pigs to see if the material could actually be taught. So the grand experiment began, in a three-session Wisdom School following more or less the layout of this book. In the first two sessions we laid the groundwork with a thorough study of the Law of Three and the basic ternary predisposition of Christian metaphysics (including a crash course on Jacob Boehme). Then, in the third session, we began to unpack the vision.

That session will long remain in my heart, not simply as an accomplishment, but as the gift of a life task fulfilled. And it is at the urging of these dear friends and intrepid wisdom seekers that I have returned to the task of putting the material in publishable form. "If thirty-five of us can get it," one of them said, "why not the whole world?"

So there you have it. I will do my best to make the ride as smooth as possible. But in the end, my commitment is to getting there, because I know beyond all personal doubt that there is indeed a ham radio concealed inside this Trinitarian tea cupboard. And in the midst of this long winter of our Christian discontent, when spiritual imagination and boldness are at an all-time low and the church itself hovers at the edge of demise for lack of an animating vision, perhaps now more than ever the time is ripe to remove the packing boards from this tea cupboard and release its contents.

Part One

THE LAW OF THREE

1

Why Feminizing the Trinity Won't Work

This is the original article, almost exactly as it first appeared in the December 2000 edition of the Sewanee Theological Review. *Our exploration takes off from here.*

IN RECENT YEARS it has become increasingly fashionable in liberal theological circles to envision the third person of the Trinity as feminine. For many reasons both linguistic and archetypal this designation seems to fit. It can be argued that the Holy Spirit is really identical with Sophia, the wisdom of God, personified as female in the Old Testament; that the "spirit" words in our biblical tradition tend to be feminine; and that in its intuitive, indwelling perceptivity, the Spirit embodies a "feminine" way of knowing and being that counterbalances the more "masculine" knowing and being of the Logos, or "Word made flesh" in the male personhood of Jesus Christ.[1]

Certainly, from a practical standpoint, this gender corrective yields tremendous gains. If, as seems sadly true, the church's exclusively male representation of the inner life of God laid the theological groundwork for an exclusively male political hierarchy that has systematically devalued the place of both the feminine and women in Christianity, then an authentic female representation among the persons of the Trinity would seem a graceful way to redress the grievance and correct the imbalances that have distorted so many areas of the church's life.

But while, as a woman, I wish it could be done so simply, I am more and more convinced that it can't. It is "doing the right thing for the wrong reason." In this case, the extremely shortsighted metaphysical thinking it introduces is likely to do a lot more damage than the short-range good accomplished. However laudable the attempt to secure a feminine presence in the Trinity, the present strategy leads to a serious confusion of metaphysical systems whose long-range effect will be to leave Christianity adrift in a post-Jungian archetypal sea, its own intuitive genius fatally blunted.

Some of the more astute feminist theologians, such as Elizabeth Johnson, have already sensed the trap in this short-range corrective and argued the need for a more comprehensive revisioning. In her influential *She Who Is*, Johnson demonstrates how the attempt to reclaim the third person of the Trinity as "the feminine dimension of God" represents a double danger, diminishing the full range of womanhood by a gender stereotyping that associates the feminine only with qualities of nurturance, tenderness, and receptivity while diminishing the fullness of divinity by "ontologizing sex in God," extending human divisions to the Godhead itself.[2] Her solution, based on a recognition of the symbolic nature of language, is to offer a comprehensive set of equivalent metaphors, allowing one to depict all three persons of the Trinity in feminine imagery. But while her proposal is headed in the right direction, it still remains largely a surface rearrangement that re-visions the persons while leaving the concept of divine personhood itself intact. It is thus a solution at the theological level. But the real source of the conundrum — and hence, the leverage needed to resolve it — lies at the metaphysical level.

The Metaphysical Corrective

To describe the metaphysical error on which this feminizing of the Trinity rests is not so easy, however, for Christians themselves are not used to thinking of their beloved Trinity in terms of metaphysical process. They have been drilled to think that the Trinity is about "persons" — whose names are Father, Son, and Holy Spirit and who live in an eternal, self–generating, and self–sustaining community. While the complex interrelationship among these divine persons may escape all but the trained theologian, the *fact* that these persons actually exist — and that they are the three unique manifestations of the unseen fullness of God — comprises the theological cornerstone of Christian experience. I have startled several people by suggesting that the Trinity might actually be seen as the Christian equivalent of the East's symbol of yin/yang. The Trinity is primarily about how God moves and flows, how God changes from one form (or "state")[3] into another within the domain of manifestation and interpenetrates the mutability of creation with the wholeness of divine being. The idea that the Trinity might be about process rather than persons seems to be a radical notion.

It is this idea, however, that I need to start with: the Trinity is primarily about process. It encapsulates a paradigm of change and transformation based on an ancient metaphysical principle known as the Law of Three. The persons are not incidental to the Trinity, certainly, but they are derivative to the extent that they unfold and manifest according to this more foundational principle, which shows itself to be (intuitively, at least) at the heart of Christian metaphysical self-understanding. So we need to begin our inquiry by considering this system in its own right.

Binary Systems and Ternary Systems

Most of the world's ancient metaphysical paradigms are binary systems. That is to say, they function on the principle of paired opposites. Yin/yang is an obvious example. In binary systems the universe is experienced as created and sustained through the symmetrical interplay of the great polarities: male and female, light and darkness, conscious and unconscious, yin and yang, *prakriti* and *purusha*.[4]

The categories masculine and feminine also belong to a binary system; in fact, they are perhaps the primordial binary system within creation. Life sustains and expresses itself in the tension of opposites, and a slackening of this tension through an imbalance of the parts leads to a collapse of the whole system.

A ternary system envisions a distinctly different mix. In place of paired opposites, the interplay of the two polarities calls forth a third, which is the "mediating" or "reconciling" principle between them. In contrast to a binary system, which finds stability in the balance of opposites, the ternary system stipulates a third force that emerges as the necessary mediation of these opposites and that in turn (and this is the really crucial point) generates a synthesis at a whole new level. It is a dialectic whose resolution simultaneously creates a new realm of possibility.

Let's consider a few simple examples. A seed, as Jesus said, "unless it falls into the ground and dies, remains a single seed." If this seed does fall into the ground, it enters a sacred transformative process. *Seed*, the first or "affirming" force, meets *ground*, the second or "denying" force (and at that, it has to be *moist* ground, water being its most critical first component). But even in this encounter, nothing will happen until *sunlight*, the third or "reconciling" force, enters the equation. Then among the three they generate a *sprout*, which is the actualization of the possibility latent in the seed — and a whole new "field" of possibility.

Or take the analogy of sailing. A sailboat, as nearly everyone knows, is driven through the water by the interplay of the wind on its sails (first force) and the resistance of the sea against its keel (second force). The result is that the boat is "shot" forward through the water, much like a spat-out watermelon seed. But as any sailor knows, this schoolbook analogy is not complete. A sailboat, left to its own devices, will not shoot forward through the water; it will round up into the wind and come to a stop. For forward movement to occur, a third force must enter the equation, the heading, or destination, by which the helmsperson determines the proper set of the sail and positioning of the keel. Only if these three are engaged can the desired result emerge, which is the course made good, the actual distance traveled.

Later in this chapter I will have more to say about the relative strengths and weaknesses of binary and ternary paradigms on precisely that issue: forward motion. In terms of the main question under consideration, however, the point is that a binary and a ternary system cannot be mixed and matched because they stem from fundamentally different metaphors for process. It is like playing three against two in a Brahms sonata; the beats do not line up. In a ternary system the categories masculine and feminine do not strictly compute, for the ternary system is not about paired opposites but about threefold process.

Is the Trinity a Ternary System?

From a historical standpoint, the doctrine of the Trinity appears to have emerged almost ad hoc from a series of defense positions hammered out during the fourth century in response to the successive waves of Arian challenges to the divinity of Christ.[5] But when viewed phenomenologically, the Trinity is a prime example of what is sometimes called in sacred tradition an arcanum: a densely encoded symbol (image, sacred gesture, or liturgical formula) that, when read by an illumined heart, conveys objective metaphysical knowledge. In this case, the Trinity, viewed as the primordial manifestation of the ineffable divine Unity, provides the template by which all further manifestation will be made known, both as eternal principle and as temporal process. With the Law of Three as its hermeneutical key, the Trinity reveals the knowledge of how God, the hidden, unmanifest, inaccessible light, becomes accessible light, manifesting and creating love; and how love in turn becomes the driveshaft of all creation, bringing all things to their fullness not by escaping createdness but by consummating it.

Demonstrating that this is so, intentionally and anterior to the persons, is possible but not without wading into metaphysical seas that few save Jacob Boehme have been able to negotiate. Later in this book I will attempt to unpack more fully Boehme's brilliant but intricate metaphysics as he traces the journey by which the divine Unity "brings itself forth"[6] into form and diversity — insights that, to my mind, still hold the key to unscrambling the present Trinitarian conundrum.

Without diving too far into these sacred mysteries at this point, I would merely hope to convey some sense of the dynamism inherent in a ternary system. While Christianity has yet to fully tap the explosive transformative power locked up in those covalent bonds of the Trinity, the potential has not gone entirely unnoticed. As Olivier Clément astutely comments in *The Roots of Christian Mysticism*:

> A solitary God could not be "love without limits." A God who made himself twofold, according to a pattern common in mythology, would make himself the root of an evil multiplicity to which he could only put a stop by reabsorbing it into himself. The Three-in-One denotes the perfection of Unity — of "super-unity," according to Dionysius the Areopagite — fulfilling itself in communion and becoming the source and foundation of all communion. It suggests the perpetual surmounting of contradiction.[7]

Twofoldness leads to cyclic recurrence. All progression, or forward motion through time, operates under the Law of Three, its very asymmetry creating the necessary forward impetus. There is no progression apart from the Law of Three and no Law of Three apart from progression. This deceptively simple point is actually at the heart of Christian metaphysics, if we only knew how to tap it better.

The Quarternity?

The quarternity was first suggested as an "improvement" to the Trinity by C. G. Jung, who noted that the square form (or more specifically, the mandala, or square combined with the circle) has a greater stability and archetypal completeness than the triangle. He suggested that the "missing feminine" in the Christian Trinity could be found by extending the form into a quarternity, adding the feminine as the bottom, or earth pole. Jung's insight has furnished both the agenda and to a large extent the strategy for contemporary efforts toward a more androgynous revisioning of the Godhead.[8]

In a very important recent contribution to this field, Father Bruno Barnhart, in his *Second Simplicity,* enthusiastically embraces Jung's four-fold schematic while at the same time introducing a significant variation: he locates the feminine at the third (rather than the fourth) pole.[9] In this position it coincides with the traditional placement of the Holy Spirit in Trinitarian thought, emerging in this new overlay as "the immanent and unitive Spirit…the divine Feminine…the inner wisdom and power that moves the history of humankind toward its consummation."[10] Here Barnhart bridges the worlds between feminine and Jungian thought, bringing powerful new theological support to a feminine designation of the Holy Spirit.

But while the initial attraction of the principle of quarternity is strong, representing, in Barnhart's words, "the wedding of the masculine principle of structure and polarity with the feminine principle of wholeness, simplicity, and unity,"[11] in terms of the metaphysical system laid out so far, the flaw should be apparent. For the quarternity is in fact merely a double binary and hence operates under the earlier mythological law of paired opposites, in this case doubled pairs. While it does bring a "mandalic" completion to the Trinity, it has also switched tracks metaphysically and hence leads to a muddying of the waters and a weakening of the dynamic asymmetrical driveshaft of the ternary system's whole self-understanding. While binary systems seek completion in a "reabsorption into the whole," as Clément observes, ternary systems seek completion in *the drive into a new dimension.* To find the "missing fourth," according to the Law of Three, we must seek for it at a whole new level. The fourth is not a final and stable completion but the new arising that inevitably emerges from the dynamic interplay of the three.

Letting the Trinity Flow

Hence, to my mind at least, the price paid for feminine participation in the Trinity (at least by the present strategies) is far too high. The result is to collapse a dynamic metaphysic of change and transformation that we have not yet begun to fathom into a staid principle of symmetry, or balanced opposites, that can sustain at a given level but lacks the ability to drive into the new.

The real source of the present theological dilemma concerning the attempt to feminize the Trinity or "correcting" the Trinity as a quarternity lies at the metaphysical level — and it is the very problem that the Trinity, by its own inner hermeneutic seeks to avoid: the conflation of eternal principle and temporal process. The difficult seam of Jesus as human being and as divine hypostasis has bedeviled theologians for centuries and remains at the core of the present conundrum, where a male eternal principle seems to demand a counterbalancing female one. In the same way, the Holy Spirit, when the distinction between eternal and temporal realms is lost, emerges as a conflation of eternal Wisdom with the energetic presence of the risen Christ, a tension of opposites that even Barnhart cannot satisfactorily reconcile.[12]

But the solution is not to abandon the ternary principle but to apply it, by permitting the Trinity to flow again. As a metaphysical principle, the Trinity is by nature kinetic, overspilling itself into new expressions of its tremendous creative energy. In our dogmatic insistence upon only *one* triad of this eternal manifesting principle (Father–Son–Holy Spirit), we have bottled up its energy and conflated its unfolding manifestations. But the solution is not to find more–inclusive–language expressions of this one triad but to become much more fluid in our use of the Law of Three, realizing that Father–Son–Holy Spirit takes its place among many triads of God's expressiveness in a ternary metaphysical system — each revealing a different facet of the divine wholeness:

- Unmanifest/manifesting/manifested
- Hidden ground of love/Wisdom/Word
- God/Word/Word made flesh
- Mother-Sophia/Jesus-Sophia/Spirit-Sophia[13]
- Father/Son/Holy Spirit
- Affirming/denying/reconciling[14]

The great secret of the Trinity, viewed as metaphysical principle, lies in its knowledge of "the impressure of nothing into something," in Boehme's words: how eternal principle comes to manifest in time and form.[15] Time — that is, sequential process — is an essential ingredient, and it is in time that we will find the missing feminine. From the list above we can see as well how the ternary is a principle that cuts across the paired opposites and engages both the masculine and the feminine at shifting points, according to the particular triad (the feminine will not always automatically be the "denying" or receptive force but can be denying, affirming, or reconciling; the stations are fluid).[16] In this flexibility there is liberation not only from the lack of feminine participation but from the gender stereotyping so prevalent in contemporary psychological models.

If the feminist dilemma is to be satisfactorily resolved, the real task before us is to have the courage to let go of the Trinity as Christianity's theological ace of clubs (using it only to prove that a human being was fully God) and to approach it instead in its cosmically subtle role as an ordering and revealing principle, of which Christ is its culminating expression. In misusing the metaphysical principle as a doctrinal prop, we have missed the inherent energy for transformation. If we could bring a new expansiveness to our search, we might discover that the Trinity holds treasures we have not yet begun to suspect. But also, to abandon it or adulterate the arcanum out of a well-intentioned but ill-reasoned attempt to strengthen the "feminine" dimension of Christianity is to make a wrong and very dangerous turn.

2

Exploring the Law of Three

IN THE PREVIOUS CHAPTER I offered a general orientation to the Law of Three. Now it is time to fine-tune some of the details and get a better idea of its operating principles and range of applicability.

As I mentioned earlier, the Law of Three is a concept that until very recently was completely unknown outside the inner circles of the Gurdjieff Work. Gurdjieff's initial presentation of the concept to his followers was oral and experiential, and to this day that is still how the teaching is most effectively transmitted in Work circles. Nonetheless, over the near century since those first Russian groups gathered around the mysterious "dancing master" from Central Asia, the Work has developed its body of literature and recognized patriarchs, and it is these to whom I will turn to help put meat on the bones of the introduction I offered earlier.

Let me briefly introduce my expert witnesses.

While Gurdjieff is, of course, himself the court of final appeal and his own writings are there to be consulted, particularly his sprawling, magnificent, outrageous _Beelzebub's Tales to his Grandson_, most newcomers to the Work find this book simply too formidable to get on board with, with its arcane language and inimitable mixture of cosmic truth and pure blarney. The normal gate through which most people still enter the Work is P. D. Ouspensky's _In Search of the Miraculous_. Ouspensky was already an established author and philosopher when he met Gurdjieff in 1914, and his work — part biography, part exposition of the principles — is clear and meticulous, although his careful, measured temperament is so different from Gurdjieff's exuberant, mystical bravado that one sometimes feels that he has fundamentally missed the living heart of the Work. The two parted

ways in 1922, and their respective lineages still compi
different flavors of the Gurdjieff teaching.

The second major commentator I will draw on is M
(d. 1953), whose massive five-volume _Psychological Commentaries on
the Teaching of Ouspensky and Gurdjieff_ comprise a written corpus no
less voluminous than Gurdjieff's and Ouspensky's combined. (In
all fairness it must be stated that Nicoll never set out to write such
a tome; the 1,776-page text was assembled out of weekly talks he
faithfully gave during his long tenure as a steward of the Work in
Great Britain.) A doctor, psychologist (he was also for a time a student of Jung's), and lifetime student of the Christian mystical tradition, Nicoll was a careful and committed teacher. His commentaries
offer a balanced and eminently practical approach to applying the
Work principles to daily life and are still read daily by a number of
students in the Work, my own hermit teacher included.

I regret that I have been unable to include in this brief survey
citations from that other remarkable interpreter of the Work, J. G.
Bennett (d. 1974), whose influence has been particularly strong in
North America. This is not to be interpreted as any lack of confidence or respect but simply a recognition that the intricacy and
originality of Bennett's understanding of the Work make it a bit of
a universe unto itself and not necessarily the most accessible starting point for a newcomer, particularly in light of the very limited
and specific purposes I have in mind here. A few of Bennett's major
works are listed in the bibliography at the end of this book, and I
recommend them heartily. In particular, his grasp of the enneagram,
as well as his presentation of the Near Eastern and Sufi sources of
the Gurdjieff teaching, remains unparalleled.

To this established corpus of Gurdjieff literature have arrived in
recent years some welcome new additions. I would now recommend
James Moore's _Gurdjieff: The Anatomy of a Myth_ as the normative starting point for most newcomers to the Work, even before cracking the
pages of _In Search of the Miraculous_. A highly respected figure in Work
circles in the United Kingdom, with a discriminating mind and a keen
sense of irony, Moore gives a wonderfully comprehensive overview
of the Work and offers some astute comments on delicate subjects all

oo often glossed over by less independent-minded devotees. And as Jacob Needleman, long a respected voice in the North American intellectual scene, becomes increasingly willing to "own up" publicly to his long-standing involvement in the Work, a whole new stream of insight is beginning to emerge. In his recent *What Is God?* Needleman has some excellent and insightful points to make about the Law of Three and particularly about its companion piece, the Law of Seven, which I will be drawing on in due course. The recent publication of *The Reality of Being*, talks given by Madame Jeanne de Salzmann, Gurdjieff's longtime Work partner and heir, gives us yet another rich window of insight into the teachings of the Work.

My purpose in this chapter, however, is to focus on the Law of Three. My goal here is not to give you a formal introduction to the Gurdjieff Work but simply to spare you the effort of having to wade through a challenging body of literature by distilling out the major points as they bear on our topic at hand. My real concern is simply that you understand what makes the Law of Three so subtly different from other systems describing process and change, and more important, that you might even get interested in applying it to your own life situations to see what results. I'm not sure whether you might call this the "Law of Three for Dummies," but I have at any rate distilled out eight core points that pretty much cover the initial bases. I will first list these in their totality — followed by the authors and titles of the works to be cited — then come back and unpack each one individually.

THE LAW OF THREE: THE FOUNDATIONAL PRINCIPLES

1. In every new arising there are three forces involved: affirming, denying, and reconciling (or affirming, denying, and neutralizing).
2. The interweaving of the three produces a fourth in a new dimension.
3. Affirming, denying, and reconciling are not fixed points or permanent essence attributes, but can and do shift and must be discerned situationally.

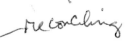*reconciling*

4. It is always at the neutralizing point that a new triad emerges.

5. Not any set of three items constitutes a trinity but only those sets in which the three can be seen to be dynamically intertwined according to the stipulations of the Law of Three.

 6. Solutions to impasses generally come by learning how to spot and mediate third force, which is present in every situation but generally hidden.

7. New arisings according to the Law of Three will generally continue to progress according to the Law of Seven.

8. The idea of third force is found in religion in the concept of the Trinity.

WORKS CITED HERE

G. I. Gurdjieff, *Beelzebub's Tales to His Grandson*

James Moore, *Gurdjieff: The Anatomy of a Myth*

Jacob Needleman, *What Is God?*

Maurice Nicoll: *Psychological Commentaries on the Teaching of Ouspensky and Gurdjieff,* volumes 1 and 3

P. D. Ouspensky, *In Search of the Miraculous*

(Note that this list of sources on the Law of Three is by no means complete. For a much more extensive compilation of teachings on the Law of Three by Gurdjieff and his students, see the bibliography.)

Now let's take each of these points in turn.

1. In every new arising there are three forces involved: affirming, denying, and reconciling (or affirming, denying, and neutralizing).
    —Gurdjieff, 687–89; Moore, 44; Nicoll, 108, 110; Ouspensky, 77–78

The essence of the Law of Three is the stipulation that every phenomenon, on whatever scale (from subatomic to cosmic) and in whatever world, springs from the interaction of three forces: the first active, the second passive, and the third neutralizing. In the language of the Gurdjieff Work, these are known respectively as "Holy Affirming, Holy Denying, and Holy Reconciling," or "affirming, denying, and reconciling (or neutralizing)," or simply "first, second, and third."

The most important thing to keep in mind here is that this third force is an *independent* force, coequal with the other two, not a *product* of the first two as in the classic Hegelian "thesis, antithesis, synthesis." Just as it takes three independent strands of hair to make a braid, so it takes three individual lines of force to make a new arising. This third force serves to bring the two other forces (which would otherwise remain disconnected or deadlocked) into relationship, from which forward momentum can emerge.

You can see how this principle underlies the examples I offered in the previous chapter. The opposition of wind and keel will not push a sailboat forward through the water; it takes the "reconciling" presence of the helmsperson to create the new phenomenon: the course made good over the water. The seed will not sprout simply by being placed in the earth (even moist earth); it is sunlight that catalyzes the action. James Moore offers a trio of other examples, all familiar to students of the Work: "Flour and water become bread only when bonded by fire; plaintiff and defendant have their case resolved only through a judge; nucleus and electrons constitute an atom only within an electromagnetic field." In the next chapter we will add to this list several additional examples contributed by my own Wisdom students through their own practical efforts to master this principle, but this present list is enough for you to get the drift.

This is not to say that third force is *completely* independent of the other two. Gurdjieff himself gave conflicting indications on this point, and his famous dictum in *Beelzebub's Tales* — "The higher blends with the lower in order to actualize the middle and thus becomes either higher for the proceeding lower or lower for the proceeding higher" — has been enough to send whole schools of Gurdjieff students off on wild goose chases. Moore sensibly mediates in this dispute by suggesting that this apparently conflicting instruction actually belongs to a slightly different domain of Gurdjieffian thought, having more to do with Gurdjieff's emphasis on interdependent arising (or "reciprocal maintenance," as he calls it) than with the actual mechanics of the Law of Three. However that may be, I can attest that the main body of Work teaching supports the idea of three independent forces, and it is here that the most stunning confirmations of both the accuracy and the utility of this principle are to be found.

2. *The interweaving of the three produces a fourth in a new dimension.*
   —Gurdjieff, 131; Moore, 44; Nicoll, 108–9

Essentially this point is merely restating the first point from the opposite direction, but the perspective gained is important enough to make the exercise worthwhile. Gurdjieff called the Law of Three "the Law of World Creation," and its real purpose is to show how new arisings — that is, new phenomena, new worlds, new outcomes, new possibilities, new "octaves" (to introduce a particularly important piece of Work terminology) — come into being. The law is all about the creation of new playing fields in an ongoing dynamism of manifestation. It is, according to Gurdjieff, "a law whose consequences always become the cause of other consequences."

When we focus on this new "something" that has come into being through the interaction of the three forces, we can see that it is not merely a continuation of a sequence; it is at a whole different level. A braid is not simply a fourth strand of hair; it is a whole new category of "thingness." A young bean sprout is no longer a seed but a *plant*, with a brand-new range of possibilities awaiting it. A child begotten through the interaction of sperm (affirming), egg (denying), and the act of lovemaking (reconciling) is not simply a continuation of its parents but a new life, with a whole new horizon stretching before her and the dynamism of manifestation imprinted within her. She is a "new triad," in Gurdjieffian language — emphasizing that she is not only a new creation but a creative force herself, containing within her the potential for the bringing into being of yet another whole new realm of arising.

"The interweaving of the three creates a fourth." In this sense Jung was right in his instinct to "complete" the Trinity by extending it into a quarternity. But he failed to realize that the "missing fourth" was not simply a fourth leg on a two-dimensional cruciform shape; it was a whole new dimension that transformed the triangle into a pyramid.

In part 4 of this book I will draw heavily on this second point in order to demonstrate how the Trinity is not simply a static, two-dimensional triangle but a genuine "triad" in the full Gurdjieffian sense of the word, bearing within it that active principle (the Law of Three itself) which imbues it with the inherent dynamism of new creation. "Every triad can give rise to another triad," Nicoll writes, "and under right conditions a chain of triads results." This is in essence the master principle by which I will expand our traditional notion of the Trinity to a sevenfold chain of Trinities bridging the gap between Alpha and Omega in a single trajectory of divine self-communication.

3. Affirming, denying, and reconciling are not fixed points or permanent essence attributes but can and do shift and must be discerned situationally.
—Ouspensky, 77; Nicoll, 109–112

This aspect of the Law of Three takes some getting used to for most Western minds, conditioned as we are to think in terms of great binary opposites with fixed archetypal characteristics. It is difficult to hear the terms *active/passive* and not immediately translate as "masculine/feminine." It's equally difficult to avoid imputing a value judgment: affirming force is "good"; denying force is "bad." But both of these well-engrained mental habits will make it very difficult to grasp the novelty of the idea that Gurdjieff is presenting here. If you fall into the trap of seeing holy affirming as the masculine principle or of equating holy denying with the obstacle to be overcome, then you will have missed the powerful new leverage the Law of Three has to bring to our traditional notions of process and change. It is precisely for this reason, to avoid old trains of association, that many students of the Work prefer to identify these three forces simply as "first, second, and third."

1) The first all-important implication to be drawn from this model is that all three forces are *equally important* participants in the unfolding of a new arising. Denying (second force) is never an obstacle to be overcome but always a legitimate and essential component of the new manifestation. In and of itself this realization brings a radically new orientation to problem solving. The "enemy" is never the enemy but a necessary part of the "givens" in any situation, and solutions will never work that have as their goal the elimination of second force. As in Jesus's famous teaching in Luke 14:28 — "For what king, going out to war against another king, will not sit down to consider whether he with ten thousand is able to oppose the one who comes against him with twenty thousand?" — resistance must be factored in: not simply to cover one's bases but because it is an indispensable ingredient in the forward motion.

2) The second, and equally profound, implication here is that "affirming, denying, and reconciling" are *roles,* not identities, and they reveal themselves only situationally. For any situation to move forward, all three must be present, and the accuracy with which one is able to assign the roles is a critical component in the solution of any problem. Often a situation that appears to be at an impasse can be shifted simply by interchanging the roles. A shift in any one of the terms will immediately affect the other two.

This point is well illustrated in Nicoll's celebrated example of "the Work as Neutralizing Force" (111–12). In the unawakened human being, according to Nicoll, personality is active, essence is passive, and life itself is the Neutralizing [third] force — or in other words, life conspires to keep a person just where he is: conditioned, superficial, and in Gurdjieff's unlovely estimate, "a machine." When that person commits himself to a path of awakening and places the Work in the position formerly occupied by unconscious living, a change begins to take place: personality ceases to run the show and the person's real but heretofore latent essence begins to emerge as the active force. As Nicoll comments: "Change in the quality of the Neutralizing Force will not only alter the relation of forces in a triad but may reverse the Active and Passive Forces." It is this flexible, shape-shifting capacity of the three forces that is primarily responsible for the Law of Three's intrinsic dynamism.

4. *It is always at the neutralizing point that a new triad emerges.*
— Nicoll, 109

Once you get used to how the Law of Three works, this point is rather obvious, since the neutralizing (or reconciling) point is where the two other forces cease opposing each other and come into relationship. But that's about the only "always" you can apply to the assignation of roles. Just because an element takes the role of active force in one triad does not mean it will continue that role into the next. Variation is always the rule.

5. *Not any set of three items constitutes a trinity but only those in which these three can be seen to be dynamically intertwined according to the stipulations of the Law of Three.*
— Nicoll, 109

The Law of Three is pure dynamism. Its purpose is to show how new manifestations arise out of old ones along a very specific pathway of interaction. Not any random group of three things constitutes proof of a ternary process at work but only three things that within a given situation specifically take on the relationship of affirming/denying/reconciling so as to catalyze a new arising. Red, yellow, and blue, for example, is not a Law of Three triad (unless the outcome you want is mud); the dynamic triad in this situation is actually red/yellow/*paintbrush* = orange. By these standards, most of the classical metaphysical triads prove themselves to be merely lists of component parts: "body, mind, spirit"; "Monad, nous, soul"; "memory, understanding, will." Even the famous Platonic triad "body, psyche, spirit" becomes a genuine ternary only when so configured as to demonstrate how psyche serves as holy reconciling between body and spirit in order to bring into being a new arising, the Self. In its usual iterations, this triad merely delineates a hierarchy of being or different psychological types (fleshly man, psychic man, spiritual man).

How about the Holy Trinity itself—"Father, Son, and Holy Spirit"? Does it bear witness to a ternary process at work, or is it merely a static list of component parts? In its traditional presentations, it certainly looks a lot more like the latter, but I believe that this is largely because the real dynamism of the Law of Three has gone so long unsuspected in Christian metaphysics. In part 3 I will attempt to bring these three components into a genuine Law of Three relationship and demonstrate how the resulting new arising does indeed conform to a specific stage in the continuing dynamic unfolding of the Trinity—in fact, the stage our era happens to be in. For now, however, it is important to keep in mind that "three things do not a trinity make." There are static triads and dynamic triads, and only the latter category fulfills what the Law of Three really means by the term *triad*.

6. *Solutions to impasses generally come by learning how to spot and mediate third force, which is present in every situation but generally hidden.*
—Ouspensky, 77–78; Nicoll, 109–110, 968–71; Needleman, 96; Moore, 44

"If we observe a stoppage in anything, or an endless hesitation at the same point," Ouspensky writes, "it is because third force is missing." From what we have seen already about the Law of Three, this point should now be obvious, since the third, or neutralizing, force is what brings the other two into relationship. No third force, no action. It is worth reemphasizing the consequences of this principle in terms of orienting oneself toward enlightened action: it does no good whatsoever simply to align oneself with one of the two opposing forces in an attempt to overcome the other; a solution will appear only when third force enters. The Gurdjieff equivalent of Buddhist "skill-ful means" implies attuning oneself always to third force and striv-ing to midwife it in the situation at hand.

The problem is that third force is not that easy to attune to; in fact, according to virtually every writer in the Gurdjieff tradition, perhaps most succinctly summarized by Needleman: "Third force is invisible to human beings in the ordinary consciousness in which they live." This is not because it is in and of itself so subtle and rari-fied (although some Work teachers do indeed tend to portray it that way) but because the default setting of our usual consciousness is skewed toward the binary, toward "either/or." It lacks both the sen-sitivity and *the actual physical capacity* to stay present to third force, which requires an established ability to live beyond the opposites. This capacity does not belong to our usual "formatory" mind, as Gurdjieff calls it — that is, our egoic operating system, with the ten-dency to think in facile and conditioned "thought bytes." It is only attained through persistent efforts toward conscious awakening, effected through practices that reorient the mind and strengthen the nervous system to be able to bear the higher vibrational frequency of what Gurdjieff calls "objective truth." In the conceptual map more familiar in our own times, the capacity to recognize and consciously mediate third force belongs to what we would now call unitive or nondual consciousness, and its stabilization in a person reflects an evolutionary advance in consciousness.

The Work tradition is by no means of one mind in its under-standing of third force. To those writers of a more mystical inclina-tion, it seems itself to be an inbreaking of a higher order of reality (akin to what Christians might call grace); to others, it appears more the case that this inbreaking of a higher reality simply opens a per-son's eyes to the third force that is actually there already but hidden. Perhaps the truth lies somewhere in between: Whatever it is that awakens the mind to this higher level of perception at the same time "draws down" third force like a lightning rod. Whatever the actual mechanics may be, the bottom line is that third force does not enter a situation automatically; it requires the conscious mediation of an alert presence and a flexible intelligence. The cultivation of these two capacities comprises the primary practical business of the Work.

7. *New arisings according to the Law of Three will generally continue to progress according to the Law of Seven.*
   —Gurdjieff, 686–87; Nicoll, 108; Needleman, 96–101; Moore, 44–45

The Law of Seven is more complicated than the Law of Three, and a full consideration of it lies beyond the scope of this book, but let me at least try to give you the gist of it. It begins straightforwardly enough with the assertion that every developing process whatsoever must pass through seven distinct stages before it reaches its completion. There is nothing particularly new here; intimations of an intrinsic sevenfoldness to process come readily to mind in all domains, from fairy tales to biology to the days of the week. But then Gurdjieff introduces his famous twist: along this sevenfold trajectory energy does not flow uniformly (as one would expect according to the law of inertia) but undergoes a constriction or loss of force at certain precise points, where an additional boost of energy must be introduced in order for the process to remain on course.

Needleman labels this phenomenon "the discontinuity of vibrations" and sets forth its revolutionary implications in a paragraph worth citing in full:

> I read [in Ouspensky's *In Search of the Miraculous*] about the fundamental notion of the inherent discontinuity of vibrations, a notion which contradicts Newton's first law of motion or inertia, which, roughly speaking, says that a body maintains its state of uniform motion unless acted on by an external force. According to Gurdjieff, on the contrary, all vibrations, and hence all individual movements of energy, intrinsically lose their force at certain precise stages in their development and must therefore receive an additional impulse of energy at certain stages or intervals in order to proceed "in a straight

line," that is, in order to reach the aim or destination of the original impulse. Gurdjieff does make passing reference to some of the newest theories in physics (this in the year 1915) where the Newtonian law is beginning to be shaken, but, he says, "physics is still very far from a correct view of the nature of vibrations…in the real world."[1]

According to Gurdjieff, this "correct" information about the nature of vibrations was deliberately embedded in what we now know as the modern diatonic scale with its signature arrangement of half steps and whole steps. As every budding pianist learns, the intervals of the scale are called *do re mi fa sol la si do* (although most would be surprised to learn why; you will discover that in Moore's account). Five of these intervals — or as Gurdjieff calls them, "stopinders" — are whole steps: *do-re, re-mi, fa-sol, la-si*. You can confirm this visually on the piano keyboard; if you play this pattern on the white notes beginning on middle C, you'll see that there is an intervening black key between each of the two whites. But between *mi* and *fa* and between *si* and *do* the white keys are directly contiguous. These are the half steps — the two "lesser stopinders" — and it is precisely here that the loss of force occurs.

While this information may be of little relevance to a piano player, once you recognize the musical octave as a symbol for the entire "ray of creation" (as Gurdjieff calls it) and begin to listen intently to the cosmic harmonies being played here, you realize the practical and even urgent import of this teaching: unless an additional energetic impulse is introduced at precisely these points, the whole line of development will tend to veer off in another direction. At each *mi-fa* and *si-do* a further angle of deflection will be introduced until eventually, over the course of several octaves, the line will arrive back where it started, carving roughly the shape of a polygon (you can see this pictured on page 128 of *In Search of the Miraculous*).

"This law," explains Gurdjieff, "shows why straight lines never occur in our activities, why, having begun to do one thing, we in fact constantly do something entirely different, often the opposite of the first, although we do not notice this and continue to think we are doing the same thing that we began to do."[2]

Then, in a comment that can only fall upon a Christian heart with a painful twinge of recognition, he adds: "Think how many turns in the line of development of forces it must have taken to come from the Gospel preaching of love to the Inquisition; or to go from the ascetics of the early centuries studying esoteric Christianity to the scholastics who calculated how many angels could be placed on a point of a needle."[3]

From here, things very quickly drop off the deep end in the Gurdjieff Work, and one can be quickly swept into in a dense cosmological jungle. Remarkably, it does, in fact, all hang together in a magnificent cosmic tapestry of divine purpose and human accountability, but for most people it is a very tough slog. Many a well-intended spiritual seeker has lost his or her way in the mazes of Gurdjieffian "hydrogen tables" or drowned in the sheer volume and eccentricity of the terminology. For those who do manage to make it through, the vista is indeed breathtaking.

Without further belaboring the point, I would again emphasize that the Law of Three and the Law of Seven are intended to work together as the twofold pillars upholding the entire system of "World Creation and World Maintenance." Dr. Jyri Paloheimo, for many years a leader of the Gurdjieff group in Toronto and my own principal mentor on this path, offers a very good overview from his perspective as a working scientist:

It is interesting in these days that physics is looking for a unified field theory that would reduce all the diverse forces and the laws governing them into one force. In contrast Gurdjieff has two universal laws, the Law of Three and the Law of Seven. He calls them the laws of world creation and world maintenance. They govern the manifestation of all phenomena, all their interaction, and all their transformation of substances. In some ways they are broader than any laws of physics in that they apply to all phenomena and not just to what we call the world of matter (the physical world). In being broader they are more like organizing principles, allowing the world to be what it is, rather than rules that can be used to make calculations as to what will happen next. Besides being broader and applicable both in the fields of psyche and matter, they also include the hazard or uncertainty in their very structure in a way that physics has never been able to do.[4]

The nature of the interaction between these two laws is powerfully encoded within the symbol of the enneagram for those with "eyes to see and ears to hear," and I will have a bit more to say about this in due course. Meanwhile, for a highly intelligible overview, one can hardly do better than James Moore's "The Revelation in Question" in his Gurdjieff biography (pp. 41–62).

8. The idea of third force is found in religion in the concept of the Trinity.
—Gurdjieff, 687–89; Nicoll, 110–11

Gurdjieff was a celebrated trickster, and much of what he says must be taken with a grain of salt. While it would be delicious indeed to be able to prove that the ancient Trinitarian liturgical formula "Holy God, Holy and Mighty, Holy Immortal One, have mercy on us"[5] has its roots in a vestigial memory of a once fully conscious knowledge of the Law of Three within early Christianity, it is hazardous to press the point historically; the supporting evidence is simply not there. It seems more than clear that the doctrine of the Trinity took shape gradually during the first four centuries of Christian identity formation in response to various doctrinal and theological challenges posed from both within and without. There is no indication that any of the great patristic architects of Trinitarian theology had any explicit knowledge of the Law of Three or derived their complex calculations of intradivine relations according to its principles. And speculations on "underground esoteric oral traditions" must remain just that: speculations.

But it is also true that history has tended to bear Gurdjieff out and that many claims set forth in his *Beelzebub's Tales* that were originally dismissed as outlandish are now finding themselves validated — among them, his proposal that the moon came into existence as a result of a comet colliding with the earth, his notion of discontinuous vibrations, and his descriptions of the "lost Atlantis" and primordial flood. One must be careful with this trickster; he is often writing straight with crooked lines!

Thus, while no hard evidence as yet has turned up to validate Gurdjieff's claim that the doctrine of the Trinity was once explicitly connected to the Law of Three, there is much to support the impression of a sympathetic resonance between them and to suggest that the real line of causality does not run through the horizontal level but through the vertical — that is, from what Gurdjieff calls "objective truth" into our own space/time continuum. If one dare take as a starting premise the wager that Jesus's human incarnation does in some particularly concentrated way mirror forth the causal principles from which he came, then it stands to reason that even in his lifetime the primitive lineaments of Trinitarian theology would begin to constellate around him and that his followers would intuitively recognize the dynamism of its energy field as an extension of his own presence and order their budding institutional life accordingly. I am aware that this may sound like circular logic; it will be my business in part 3 of this book to demonstrate why it is not.

For now, however, let us continue to keep our eyes on the Law of Three.

3

The Law of Three in Action

IN THE PREVIOUS CHAPTER we explored the Law of Three in a theoretical way, getting acquainted with its major precepts and a few of its peculiarities. We have also by now begun to accumulate a collection of classic Law of Three triads, such as

seed/earth/sun = *sprout*

flour/water/fire = *bread*

plaintiff/defendant/judge = *resolution*

sails/keel/helmsperson = *course made good*

But these are only textbook examples, while the Law of Three is all about action. It is one thing to recognize a Law of Three configuration in a theoretical exploration; it is another thing altogether to recognize it in actual life and be able to work with it confidently and skillfully. Whether or not you stay on board with this exploration all the way to its final destination in our ternary unfolding of the Trinity, the Law of Three is a valuable tool in its own right and well worth getting to know better.

To that end, this chapter consists almost entirely of Law of Three stories, many of them contributed by my own students, together with a brief commentary structured around the five or six most important practical learnings to have emerged out of our collective fieldwork with the Law of Three. These case studies and reflections are intended to help put further meat on the bones of those eight core principles I laid out in the previous chapter and to give you a better feel for how the Law of Three actually works in daily life (consider this your official user's manual to chapter 2). But as you will see shortly, they also make for a very interesting commentary on the scope and wider implications of this law.

The Opposition Is Never the Problem

The single most liberating insight to come out of our collective work with the Law of Three was the realization that what appears to be the resisting or opposing force is never actually the problem to be overcome. Second force, or holy denying, is a legitimate and essential component in every new arising: *no resistance, no new arising!*

That realization in and of itself radically rearranges the playing field, shifting the focus away from trying to eliminate the opposition and toward working collaboratively for a more spacious solution. According to the Law of Three, once an impasse has constellated, it can never be solved by going backward but only forward, into that new arising that honors all the players and brings them into a new relationship. (Einstein seems to have been on to this insight in his famous dictum that a problem can never be solved at the level at which it is created.) The three forces are like three strands in a braid; all three are required for the weaving.

One woman in our group was almost instantly able to turn around a very difficult standoff with an ultraconservative bishop when she realized that his resistance was not the problem to be solved but a given to be worked with. With an almost visceral "Aha!" she relaxed her sense of polarization and was stunned to learn the next day that he had miraculously softened his stance. While it was not clear to her who in the chancery office had actually been the broker of third force here, it was clear to her that the two relaxations were not unrelated.

One can only imagine how greatly the political and religious culture wars of our era could be eased by this simple courtesy of the Law of Three: (1) the enemy is never the problem but the opportunity; (2) the problem will never be solved through eliminating or silencing the opposition but only through creating a new field of possibility large enough to hold the tension of the opposites and launch them in a new direction. Imagine what a different world it would be if these two simple precepts were internalized and enacted.

The Three Forces Are Functions, Not Identities

As I mentioned in our earlier discussion, the aspect of function rather than identity in the Law of Three took some growing into. We are so culturally conditioned to equating words like *active, affirming, passive, denying* with fixed ontological principles, usually gender related (that is, male = active, female = passive), that it requires a real mental effort to override these preconditioned patterns. A good part of the initial learning curve with the Law of Three is around developing a capacity to look directly at a situation and assign the forces according to the role they are actually playing, not according to pre-formed judgments or expectations.

One of our group members found herself immersed in exactly this learning when she took as her area of research her ongoing struggle with dieting, particularly her attraction to a certain "rich, fatty food" that had so far bested all of her efforts to resist it.

"When I first set this up as a Law of Three triad," she reported, "I naturally chose as 'affirming force' my desire for sensible eating habits and as 'denying' the bad, fatty food. So, of course, third force was my willpower."

But, of course, willpower was not really third force at all but merely the servant of her desire for a better body image. Her conflicting desires — for the satisfaction to be had from that "rich, fatty food" and at the same time a good body image — were simply self-canceling, which is why her ongoing efforts at dieting all wound up in frustration.

Then she hit upon her brainstorm. What if she reversed first and second forces? Saw "affirming" as her body's authentic desire for a savory treat and "denying" as her personality's concern about self-image? Suddenly the whole picture shifted, and she could instantly spot what true third force might be: "I decided to enter into a conscious relationship with that rich, fatty food: not to treat it as the enemy but to honor my body's desire for it and to satisfy it — but consciously."

This shift in perspective initiated a domino chain of results as she saw her relationship shifting not only with this one particular food but with all food and with eating itself. In this more conscious relationship with her embodiment, she has so far managed to keep the weight off.

The Presence of Third Force Can Reverse the Roles of First and Second

The potential reversal of the roles of first and second in the Law of Three was particularly intriguing to Maurice Nicoll, who returned to it again and again in his teaching. His thinking here is encapsulated in his oft-quoted dictum: "When life is Neutralizing Force, personality is active in a man and essence is passive. When the Work is Neutralizing Force, the position is reversed — namely, essence, or the real part, becomes active, and personality, or the acquired part, passive."[1] While the "fourth in a new dimension" is clearly the emerging true self or "Real I," the reversal of first and second forces is both a harbinger of its emergence and a significant breakthrough in its own right.

Exactly this same reversal of essence and personality happens to be brilliantly illustrated in the short story "Good Country People" by that master storyteller Flannery O'Connor. This sardonic variation on the classic theme of "the trickster tricked" is virtually a Law of Three teaching tale (no doubt totally unsuspected by O'Connor). Its main character, Joy, is an intellectually brilliant, aggressively angry woman who lost her leg in a childhood accident and has since perfected the art of victimhood — even to the point of legally changing her name to the singularly ugly "Hulga." Into her life steps a young Bible salesman, a cad and a con artist, who plays her like an ace up his sleeve. In the story's final scene he leads her up to the barn loft, seduces her, then steals her prosthetic leg and runs away. She is left alone, exposed, and disarmed.

At first it may be hard to see what this tale of double manipulation and chicanery has to do with the Law of Three, but on closer analysis it becomes evident that the story's deeper meaning is powerfully revealed in its light. As the story opens, first force is played by "Hulga," the angry victim personality. Second force is the passive essence — Joy (seeking exactly what her true name indicates). Before the arrival of the Bible salesman, life is indeed third force, Hulga's perfectly orchestrated vicious circle. When the Bible salesman shows up as the new "neutralizing" force between these two warring opposites, he manages to snatch away Hulga's badge of victimhood, thereby reversing the polarities of first and second force in her life. In the classic Flannery O'Connor way, he does, in the end, turn out to be a very good Bible salesman, announcing the good news of healing and liberation.

The New Arising Is Not a Compromise but a Whole New Ball Game

Another major step on the Law of Three learning curve is to begin to taste the difference between a traditional negotiated compromise and an authentic new arising according to the Law of Three. Surprise is almost always an element in a genuine Law of Three unfolding: a person who walks in off the street, a sudden synchronicity, or a sudden complication that throws the whole situation into a new ballpark. But a new ballpark it is, and its most powerful telltale is the sense of satisfaction attending it. Unlike a compromise, which so often leaves both parties feeling unfulfilled and still polarized, there is an "aha" quality to a Law of Three solution that allows first and second forces to relax their grip and quietly retire from their respective posts. The new triad is free to arise.

One of my all-time favorite Law of Three true stories illustrates exactly this signature Law of Three mix. It happened quite some time ago now, at a small, ultraprogressive liberal arts college in a corner of rural New England. As the search got under way for a new president, a very vocal feminist element within the college community successfully imposed its demand that only women candidates be considered. After a high-profile search marked by legal challenges and bitter controversy, a woman was indeed called to the post, but in an atmosphere by then so badly polarized that she was unable to establish a governing presence. As the situation rapidly deteriorated, she tendered her resignation after less than a year.

As the board regrouped for a new national search, it was clear that an interim president needed to be appointed as quickly as possible to contain a situation now verging on chaos. The board hastily went through the roll call of present and former trustees and offered the job to the first one to say yes. That is how P., a retired banker and an unassumingly but also unmistakably alpha male, "temporarily" assumed the helm at this embattled little institution.

Ten years later he was still there. How it happened nobody exactly knows. But little by little battle lines softened, the rhetoric grew less shrill, contentment returned. The official search for a new president was never formally abandoned; it just kept slipping further and further down the priority list. Under P.'s low-key but astute nurturance, a new vision began to emerge, and with a newfound energy behind it, the college again began to grow. That "interim" presidency is now fondly remembered as a decade of unprecedented prosperity and goodwill.

Surprise, satisfaction, elegance: the signature Law of Three mix. Perhaps it was simply luck that landed the right person in the right place at the right time. But it may also have been an alert board member who recognized that the real qualities needed for healing a seriously broken situation had nothing to do with either gender or ideology but with the capacity to take oneself lightly.

A New Arising Is Not Always the Same Thing as a Solution

But wait a minute! Didn't I list as our leading Law of Three principle, "When three come together, there is a fourth in a new dimension"? Yes, and that is so. But the catch here is that this new dimension is not always a physical solution to the problem at hand — a deus ex machina or rabbit out of the hat. Sometimes it is simply the infusion of a more subtle quality of aliveness in whose light the real meaning of the situation is transfigured (or at least made more clear). It is a resolution at a more subtle level, an imaginal resolution.

This important nuance is perhaps best demonstrated in another of those incognito Law of Three tales, "The Gift of the Magi" by O. Henry. This well-loved Christmas story tells the tale of two newly-weds, poor as church mice but madly in love, who, unbeknownst to each other, sell the one precious thing they own to buy a Christmas present for the other. He pawns his valuable antique pocket watch to buy her combs for her beautiful long red hair; she shaves her head and sells the hair in order to buy him a chain for his antique watch. On Christmas Eve the newlyweds stare at each other blankly, almost numb with shock, it would seem, trying to compute the meaning of the "useless" presents they have just exchanged.

The story proves to be a classic Law of Three triad leading to this more subtle resolution. First force (holy affirming) is the couple's love for each other; second force (holy denying) is their poverty. Third force (holy reconciling) is contributed by their willingness to sacrifice their most precious possessions for the sake of that love (those of you who are familiar with my work will already have spotted this quality as kenosis, or self-emptying).[2] The new arising is indeed "the gift of the magi" — as the story is so appropriately named — the reality of their love for each other transformed into pure agape and made manifest in a whole new way.[3]

Third Force Is Best Accessed through an Alert, Flexible Presence That Can Hold the Tension of the Opposites

Work teachers are unanimous in their assessment that human beings tend to be third-force blind. Jacob Needleman puts it very directly: "Third force is invisible to human beings in the ordinary state of consciousness in which they live."[4] This is not only because our "ordinary state of consciousness" is summarily dismissed by most Work teachers as "sleep" but specifically because our ordi-

nary consciousness is hardwired toward perception by differentiation — that is, toward either/or thinking — while detection of third
force requires a finely developed sense of both/and.

With that challenge set before us, our group was quite naturally
intrigued by what qualities or manner of presence seemed most
conducive to the emergence of third force in a situation. Virtually
everyone was in agreement about what does not work: judgment
and a rigorous adherence to a desired expectation or outcome. But
from there opinions divided (as they do in the Work as well): is third
force *discovered* in a situation or is it *created*? Or is it *invoked*? Is the
missing piece already right there under everyone's nose, or is it specifically catalyzed by the infusion of a particular kind of conscious
energy?

Perhaps these alternatives are not as different as they seem. A
lost earring can be lying in plain sight in a dark corner of a room
but will show up only when a light is shone on it. That, at any rate,
seemed to be the conclusion emerging out of our rich and often surprising explorations around this point. As the old Sufi maxim goes,
"You can't catch the wild horse by running, but nobody who is not
running will catch the wild horse." Perhaps the most accurate word
to describe the delicate symbiosis at work here would be to say that
third force is *midwifed*, and the midwife is our conscious attention.

A remarkable example of this kind of midwifing was contributed by a member of our Canadian Wisdom circle. As the director of
a small, government-subsidized service agency, she steeled herself
each year for the dreaded spring ritual when the heads of all such
agencies were required to appear before a board of provincial adjudicators to orally defend their budget and make their request for
next year's needed funds.

As she waited her turn in this seemingly endless litany of peti-
tions, she pictured the situation according to the Law of Three. First
force was clearly held by the presenters, with their legitimate need
for funding and equally legitimate sense of desperation. Holy denying was quite literally held by the adjudicatory board, which seemed
increasingly of a mind to throw out a certain number of requests
altogether and substantially trim back the rest. She realized that in

the situation as presently configured, the two opposing forces were simply colliding on an energetic ground of scarcity, the assumption that there was not enough to go around. There was no third force. Could she do anything to create it?

Suddenly an inspiration arrived. In an instant she threw away her prepared speech, and when it came her turn to speak, she smiled warmly and began, "I want to thank you all for the generous funding we received from you last year. Here's how we spent it." She then went on to detail all the good work they had managed to accomplish on what was actually a very small subsidy. As she spoke, she could sense the adjudicators visibly relaxing and her colleagues staring in wide-eyed amazement. She concluded, "We are not asking you for a single additional penny this year, and if we need to cut back, this is the strategy we've put in place to do so with a minimal impact on our service."

It almost goes without saying that she received the full amount requested. By introducing gratitude as the missing third force, she managed to shift the energetic field from a sense of scarcity to a sense of abundance. And from that field of abundance she did indeed receive her daily bread.

Sometimes this infusion of third force arrives even more directly. Two of my students recounted how under quite different but parallel circumstances — calming a crisis on a subway and in a heated business meeting that was spiraling out of control — they were able to open themselves directly to a Wisdom that seemed to come from beyond them and speak through them.

"I stepped onto air, and it held me up," T. said, recalling the moment in that business meeting when he knew intuitively that the baton had been passed to him. Up to that point, he had been watching almost as a spectator, with an unusual sense of detachment. He was prepared in the sense of an inner openness but not in the sense of having cognitively prepared anything to say.

What followed was pretty much a third force classic: "I spoke for a few minutes. The words came out. Everything shifted in the room. Anger left. Opposition left. Others began to make comments, and we left with the creative proposal intact but, more importantly, with the client relationship restored. A complete impasse had become a doorway.

"This may have been third force," he reflected later. "Why? Because the words supplied were objective. What I mean is that the words were not mine. Not mine in the sense that they seemed to be devoid of a need to win an argument. They were not combative. Without denying or amending anything that had been said earlier, they ushered in something new.

"This idea of 'objective' seems to me a useful field mark for identifying third force. Third force contains transformative power because it does not take sides. It doesn't have a dog in the fight. Could it be said to be compassionately indifferent?"

T.'s thoughtful reflections are a good note on which to bring this chapter to a close. Whether it's a matter of salvaging a client relationship, shedding unwanted pounds, analyzing a piece of literature, or exploring the mystery of the Trinity, the Law of Three is applicable across such a wide range of disciplines simply because it *is*, in fact, a cosmic law — an organizing principle "allowing the world to be what it is," in those words of Dr. Jyri Paloheimo cited in the previous chapter. The fact that it is equally adept in the domains of psyche and matter (it applies to all phenomena and not just the physical world, Jyri reminds us) may contain an important clue toward the healing of that split field of reality (science versus religion) that has tormented the Western mind for more than five hundred years. I will return to that possibility in the final section of this book. But for now, on a more practical note, the Law of Three is good to know about simply because it's such a damnably useful tool. Once you get the hang of it, it has remarkable leverage to bring to bear on any situation where process and change are involved, and it is particularly brilliant in situations that appear to be at an impasse. As I mentioned earlier, you might consider it the Gurdjieff equivalent to what the Buddhists call skillful means. Learning to wield it is in itself a path of conscious transformation, and the conscious energy that it seems to infuse into any situation it touches is itself a precious energetic boost to a world dashing itself to pieces on the rocks of either/or.

4

The Law of Three and the Enneagram

THE INTERWEAVING of the Law of Three and the Law of Seven is the great cosmic Mystery embedded within the symbol of the enneagram. Gurdjieff was the one who first brought this symbol to the West. He never exactly divulged its source; it seemed to belong to that great treasury of esoteric knowledge he acquired during his travels among the hidden Wisdom schools of Central Asia. With its striking nine-pointed "grasshopper" configuration, it quickly became the logo of his Fourth Way school and the cornerstone of its entire curriculum. So great was the power locked within this symbol, Ouspensky used to claim, that if one could only read it properly, it would make books and libraries entirely unnecessary—for "*everything* can be included and read in the enneagram."[1] It has been a cherished and closely guarded secret within the Gurdjieff Work for nearly a century.

Beginning in the early 1970s, the symbol was reintroduced into Western spiritual consciousness, this time with a very different spin to it. Again claiming secret esoteric sources for their teaching, Oscar Ichazo and Claudio Naranjo rebooted the enneagram as a tool for personality typing. In a new layer of meaning apparently missed by Gurdjieff, they discovered that each of the enneagram's nine points yielded a remarkably precise description of a distinct personality type.[2] If you're at all familiar with the material, you probably already know the types: one, the perfectionist; two, the giver; three, the performer; four, the romantic; five, the observer; six, the loyal skeptic; seven, the epicure; eight, the protector; nine, the mediator.[3] The types were claimed to be universal and exhaustive; *everybody* could eventually find himself or herself in one of these vignettes, and once one's inner type was correctly identified, the tools were at hand for tremendous growth in self-awareness and inner freedom. The movement took off, and today it's fair to say that the enneagram is far more widely known as a tool of personality typing than as the cosmological arcanum it was originally construed to be.

Old-school Gurdjieffians responded to this new development with virtually unanimous horror. James Moore's caustic dismissal of the entire movement in a brief note at the end of his Gurdjieff biography is for better or worse an accurate reflection of the prevailing sentiment: "No light is shed on Gurdjieff's teaching by the pastiche version of the enneagram — a sort of facile psychometric typology — which in the 1980s began to percolate from the 'Human Potential Movement' into universities and Roman Catholic retreat centers. Those associated with this phenomenon…appear to have borrowed the exterior form of Gurdjieff's symbol without grasping its interior dynamic."[4]

In turn, most of the good souls I have met in the enneagram of personality movement are sincerely bewildered by this negative reaction. With such an elegant new tool in the spiritual tool kit, which has already more than proved its worth in the psychological breakthroughs it continues to deliver and the excitement it continues to generate, what, pray tell, is the problem? There is little argument that far more lives have now been transformed by the enneagram of personality than by its Gurdjieffian prototype. In fact, if people have heard of Gurdjieff at all nowadays, the chances are that most of them first encountered his name through the enneagram of personality.

Whatever irony — or perhaps third force — may be at play in all of this, I believe that as a starting point for honest and helpful conversation (and I hope that much more of this will be forthcoming), it is important to be very clear about the differences between these two systems. All too often in modern enneagram circles, the teaching is depicted as continuous with that of Gurdjieff. It is not. The enneagram presented within the modern enneagram of personality movement is not the same enneagram that is taught and studied in classic Fourth Way schools. There are overlaps, to be sure, but the differences outweigh the similarities, particularly when one moves on from personality typing into the more fundamental spiritual principles at stake. In general, I share many of the same concerns as those "hard-line" Gurdjieffians that the personality-typing component is at best a distraction and at worst an outright distortion of the real truth the enneagram has to reveal. But at the same time (perhaps paradoxically), I believe the enneagram of personality is a valid and important new expression of this tradition, acutely attuned to the temperament of our own times and offering real possibility for our new growth and insight. Thus, my comments here are offered not so much as a critique as for the sake of clarity, so that all concerned can work together more productively to midwife the third force that may be coming to us here.

Not Nine, Only Three

The most immediately noticeable difference between these two schools of thought is that for Gurdjieff there are only three "personality types," not nine. You are either a moving center type, an emotional center type, or an intellectual center type, depending on which of these three distinct systems of embodied intelligence is your default starting position. And take note that these three types do not quite line up with the "head types, heart types, and gut types" of modern pop psychology, for what Gurdjieff means by a moving center type is not what most people nowadays understand by a "gut" type. The moving center is not about primitive instinctual emotions like anger or shame. In Gurdjieff's system it designates "intelligence in movement" — as is reflected, for example, in the capacity to learn a dance pattern, ski down a hill, imitate an accent, or master a new language. It refers to a person's capacity to explore the world, gather information, and synthesize the pieces through the modality of movement.

Nor are these three in fact "personality" types in Gurdjieff terminology. Strictly speaking, they are *essence* types. For Gurdjieff, essence

Essence

is what you're born with; personality is what you acquire through external conditioning. Essence might be seen as something akin to the hand of cards you're initially dealt as you come onto the play of life: it includes such factors as your gender, heredity, astrological influences, and basic biological temperament and predisposition. It does not represent a primary set of defensive or compensatory behaviors, as is so often the case in modern psychological models. It is not a false self. You cannot be born without an essence type any more than you can be born without your skin. And you will never leave it entirely behind, for it will always be the physical mooring ball for your incarnation here on earth.

That being said, the essence type in Gurdjieff teaching is not intended to be the permanent home of your identity. You can never be a "redeemed moving center type" in the way that contemporary enneagram people sometimes speak of themselves as "redeemed fours"—that is, realizing themselves within the highest attributes of their given personality type by overcoming their preassigned "chief feature."[5] For Gurdjieff, the essence type is merely the starting point for a pathway of transformation that itself unfolds according to the Law of Three; essence is plowed back into the interweaving and emerges at a whole new level, as "Real I."[6] Whether you begin the journey as "man" number 1, 2, or 3 (corresponding to the three essence types), the goal is to strengthen and balance these three lower centers so that you can move on to man number 4—"balanced man." For only here can personhood in any true sense be said to begin. A person identified entirely with his or her type (whether you consider this to be an essence type or a personality type) is in Gurdjieff's estimate simply "a machine."

The Cosmological Laws

But, of course, the fundamental issue is whether the enneagram is to be understood as a tool of personality typing at all. And to this, most Gurdjieffians would answer with a resounding no—not because the model doesn't work but because the real original purpose for which this esoteric tool was given was to portray the interweaving of the Law of Three and the Law of Seven. The esoteric knowledge encoded in the enneagram is cosmic in its scope and far-reaching in its force. It is *this* knowledge that Ouspensky has in mind when he writes, "The understanding of this symbol and the ability to make use of it give man very great power."[7] At the junction of three and seven lies a geyser of cosmic wisdom. But it is precisely this wisdom that the contemporary enneagram of personality movement has not been able to access because of its preoccupation with the exoteric function of personality typing.[8]

This "failure" (as Gurdjieffians would see it) is not at all surprising, because from a Work perspective, the focus has been upside down from the start. By concentrating its attention on the individual points (the nine personality types themselves) rather than the circulation among them, the modern enneagram movement has already substantially lost touch with Gurdjieff's core understanding of the enneagram as "a perpetual motion machine."[9] And while the more spiritually oriented of contemporary enneagram teachers have begun to correct that impression and now emphasize transformative movement over diagnostic typology, it is only in the light of the *entire* circulation (not just back and forth within each type's three-point range) that the pattern can be read.[10] That is essentially the gist of James Moore's complaint about "borrowing the exterior form of the symbol without grasping its interior dynamic."

Even within the givens of contemporary enneagram pedagogy, this conceptual weak link (if that's what it is) has immediate practical consequences. As a beginning enneagram student quickly learns, the three pattern and the seven pattern do not interact. If you identify yourself as a one, two, four, five, seven, or eight, you will "progress" or "regress" among these points according to the line of direction 1-4-2-8-5-7 (for an explanation of this numerical pattern, see note 10, above). If you are a three, six, or nine, you take up your position on the inner triangle, cycling through only these three points. There is no place that these two sets directly interact. While it may be *called* an enneagram, for all practical purposes it is two concentric circles whose gears do not intermesh. The lines symbolically cross on the diagram itself, but they do not cross in the accompanying psycho-logical teaching. If you are a six, you will never move to two; if you are five, you will never become a nine.[11]

From a Gurdjieffian perspective, this failure to grasp and effec-tively incorporate the fundamental intermeshing of three and seven basically renders the entire enneagram of personality movement bankrupt — a "facile" diversion rather than an authentic cosmic truth. In all fairness to contemporary enneagram studies, however, it must be admitted that the classic Gurdjieff teaching never made this interconnection particularly easy to grasp either. It's not that the secret is all that hard to uncover; it's right there in Ouspen-sky if you're willing to dig for it. But once found, it is not easy to understand, partly because the Law of Seven is itself not easy to understand, partly because what is essentially a stunningly simple solution so quickly gets buried in complicated pseudomathematical arcana (the notorious "descending octaves" and "tables of hydrogens" that fill page upon page of Ouspensky's exposition). Let me see if I can give you a no-frills, nonmathematical version of the basic idea.

Conscious Shock

The crucial piece of information you need in order to crack the code of the enneagram is the notion of "discontinuous vibrations," which I introduced you to (via Jacob Needleman) in chapter 3. What this means, you recall, is that according to Gurdjieff, all vibrations (or streams of energy) intrinsically lose force at certain precise points in their development and must therefore receive an additional impulse of energy at these points in order to proceed in a straight line. These points of discontinuous vibration correspond to the *mi-fa* and *si-do* intervals on the diatonic scale, and the additional energetic impulse needed to keep things proceeding on course is known as a *conscious shock*. (To refresh yourself on the pattern of the diatonic scale, refer back to chapter 2.)

Now follow along with me as we see what happens when we transpose this familiar diatonic scale onto our enneagram diagram.

The first step is to draw the basic outline of the triangle circumscribed by a circle. Divide the periphery of the circle into nine equally spaced points and label the three triadic points in the familiar way: 9 at the top, 3 on the right, 6 on the left.

The next step is to match the seven intervals of the scale to their corresponding positions on the enneagram beginning with *re* at 1 — but leaving points 3 and 6 blank (we will find out why in a minute). This gives us the diagram that we find in Ouspensky, page 289 (figure 48). The note *do*, which sets the basic vibrational gamut for the entire octave, is assigned to point 9.

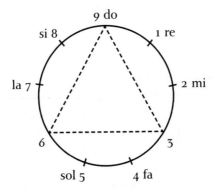

Why did we leave the other two triadic points blank? If you think back to what we have learned about the Law of Seven, the mystery begins to resolve itself. For those "lesser stopinders" or half steps are not at full strength, energetically speaking; they require the supplementation of their respective conscious shocks to keep the process on course. In this sense, then, conscious shocks are essentially "intervals" — they represent an additional vibrational packet, which properly belongs to the whole of the octave. And if you add these two shocks in, suddenly our seven-step scale expands to nine steps, arranged as follows.

do re mi x fa sol la si x (do)

Now if you look at our diagram, you'll see that our first alignment is perfect. Point 3, between *mi* and *fa*, corresponds exactly to the place where the first energy shortfall occurs and the first conscious shock must be received.

But what about the second point? It clearly does *not* occur at the correct place. For our second blank space falls at point 6, whereas the true second conscious shock actually comes between *si* and *do*, between points 8 and 9 on the enneagram. So our initial hopes are quickly dashed. The first point matches, but the second point doesn't.

Or does it? And it is exactly here that we enter the eye of the needle of our riddle. As Ouspensky slyly observes: "The apparent placing of the interval in its wrong place itself shows for those who are able to read the symbol what kind of 'shock' is required for the passage of SI to DO."[12] That secret, once discovered, allows this tool to be consciously wielded as an instrument of cosmic transformation.

Ouspensky makes us wait nearly a hundred pages (until page 377) before he divulges the secret. He does finally do so, but by then the discussion has become so embroiled in Gurdjieffian cosmological complexity that the stunning brilliance of what he is revealing may not actually register.

The secret is essentially this: *that first conscious shock is also simultaneously a new* do; while keeping things on track in its immediate octave, it simultaneously inaugurates a new line of development in a whole new octave.

Once you make this transposition, the pieces all fall into place. If you set a new *do* at point 3, it will reach its own *mi-fa* passage exactly at point 6, which is not the second conscious shock in the original octave but the first conscious shock *in the second octave of development!* (Read that statement a second time if you need to; it may sound complicated at first, but actually it's pretty straightforward.) And point 6 simultaneously becomes the new *do* for yet a third octave of development. Once this point is realized, the difficulties resolve themselves.

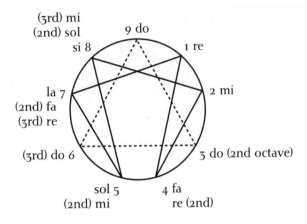

Thus, the secret of the enneagram is that it is not a "closed circuit" diagram. It bears within itself, for those who have learned to read its mysteries, its own coiled spring that inevitably propels its expansion into new octaves, each one representing a more subtle level of realization of that initial thrust. This is why the Law of Seven is also known in the Work as the "Law of Octaves." Essentially, when the "linear" progression of points along the six lines generated by the Law of Seven crosses and interacts with the "verticalizing" dimension of the three triadic points, then "the intersection of the timeless with time" explodes into reality and a whole new octave of possibility opens up. The enneagram turns out to be a jack-in-the-box!

This is admittedly an extremely quick sketch. Those who feel inspired to dig into the teaching more deeply and give it the time and reflection it deserves are heartily encouraged to do so. My quick summary here is only to help you better understand the horror that longtime students of the Work feel at what appears to be a desecration of their sacred symbol. For the contemporary enneagram of personality inadvertently collapses the diagram (and the possibilities it contains) into a set of two closed circles, repeating their 1-4-2-8-5-7 and 3-6-9 dances continuously, mechanically, on the same plane, like a dog chasing its tail. The original Gurdjieffian enneagram, by contrast, is inherently open-ended, stretching out to invoke and receive the cosmic processes binding life in time to life beyond time. That is why, for a seasoned Gurdjieffian, constricting the enneagram to a personality-typing device is tantamount to harnessing "the love that moves the sun and the stars" to drive a toy electric train around a track.

Third Force

So why, then, does the enneagram work so well as a personality-typing device? This remains a mystery to be solved, but my own best guess would be that this psychometric feature is a felicitous hitchhiker on the back of a powerful cosmic law. Because the law itself is so profound and comprehensive, the subsidiary patterns that nest within it will tend to hold together. And if you ask why Gurdjieff himself did not seem to notice this pattern, my answer would be "because his attention was elsewhere." He was in search of far bigger cosmic game.

As a participant in the Gurdjieff Work for more than a decade, I know only too keenly what depth has been lost in the present enneagram of personality movement. Yet I do not share the same negative assessment of so many Fourth Way regulars. I think that this new species of enneagram teaching is unquestionably a positive development and carries a powerful new transformative impetus. It also displays enough of those signature earmarks of third force — surprise, elegance, new energy — that we need to be paying serious attention to what might be unfolding through it.

The classic enneagram teaching of the Gurdjieff Work is magnificent indeed — *provided* it can be understood and practically applied. But in the seven or eight decades that the Work has maintained its below-the-radar presence as an esoteric school, one can hardly say that it has fully tapped the potential of the magnificent arcanum at its core. The teaching has tended to remain intellectual, speculative, and secretive, with little concern for imparting this tool as a moral force in society as a whole. By its own self-understanding, the Work has chosen to remain elitist and hidden, more attuned to individual spiritual striving than to launching mass "human potential" movements, which in any case would sound like an oxymoron.

The enneagram of personality has captured the popular imagination, that's for sure. And you have to admit that there is something brilliant and even damnably strategic in its design. Using that classic ego bait — "let me learn my type, some interesting new thing about *me*" — it draws people in, only to put in their hands basic tools for self-observation and nonidentification that classic psychotherapeutic models have generally failed to deliver.[13] Progressing enneagram students rapidly develop the capacity to see that they are in fact *not* their type; it is simply an impersonal, mechanical pattern that plays out within them. A shift in the sense of selfhood begins to occur, so that they reside less and less in their outer personality manifestations and more and more in their inner witnessing presence. Fixation upon the personality begins to wane as the deeper roots of identity emerge. Thus, the teaching has the possibility of moving people to a new level of interior freedom and encourages them to develop precisely those spiritual skills that Gurdjieff himself identified as essential to conscious transformation but that his own cumbersome spiritual system so often wound up sabotaging. *Something* is clearly working here, and the enneagram of personality movement seems to be manifesting the fruits of conscious inner work in ways that are both personally authentic and statistically significant. Perhaps Gurdjieff should, indeed, have been paying more attention to that hitchhiker on the back of his cherished cosmic symbol.

At any rate, in a signature "third force" sort of way, the new movement has created a bridge between contemporary exoteric psychological models and the classic esoteric teachings of the Western inner tradition, wherein lie both the spiritual skills and the visionary road map needed to help recover a true sense of our human vocation and destiny in a vastly expanded and multidimensional cosmos. And this will be of paramount importance to my own concerns in this book. For you can see that the shortcoming I find in our classic theological model of the Trinity is exactly the same shortcoming that seasoned Gurdjieffians find in the enneagram of personality: the flattening into one dimension of a symbol whose full cosmic wisdom can only be read in three dimensions, from within the dynamism itself. The knowledge of how to do this (both for the enneagram and for the Trinity) is there to be found in Gurdjieff, but until recently there has been no popular access point. While the complete Gurdjieff system may remain a specialized discipline, there are ideas in his teaching that definitely deserve a wider circulation, for they point the way out of theological logjams that have too long been holding the Christian visionary imagination captive. The contemporary enneagram movement, whose ranks include not only therapists and counselors but also spiritual directors, clergy, and monastics, has succeeded in opening a gate through which significant numbers of people can begin to enter. My hope is that the Work will be able to rise above itself and go out to meet them halfway.

Part Two

METAPHYSICS IN
TWO AND THREE

5

Blueshift

IN PART 1 we spent a good deal of time familiarizing ourselves with the basic workings of the Law of Three. I trust that this has been an interesting inquiry in its own right. But however intriguing and even practical this law may be, what makes me think that an obscure esoteric principle, articulated only in the early twentieth century and unknown to both classical theology and classical metaphysics, should have anything to do with the Holy Trinity? How can it be seen as useful, or even *admissible*, to the contemporary theological conversation?

As I indicated in the introduction, I am not going to try to argue the case on historical grounds. Doing so would require me to demonstrate that the Cappadocian fathers, principal theological architects of the Trinity, were explicitly aware of the Law of Three and intentionally embedded it in their formulation of the doctrine. The supporting evidence for such a claim is simply not there — and frankly, I do not believe that it actually exists. And while Gurdjieff's innuendo that knowledge of the Law of Three was transmitted through monastic oral tradition may or may not have some truth, I simply do not see how it can be verified given the limited resources available to me as a non-Orthodox, nonmonastic, non-Greek-speaking woman.

Imaginal Causality

But historical causality is not the only way of determining the truth of a situation, (although it is certainly the preferred mode in our literal-minded culture). From time immemorial mystics, artists, prophets, and visionary theologians (such as the Cappadocians) have gravitated to what has been classically known in the inner traditions of the West as *imaginal causality*, or the preeminence of archetypal pattern over historical facticity. According to this mode of seeing, the patterns that generate and organize the energy field of our visible world originate beyond time (on a higher plane of reality) and are transmitted largely through images (hence *imaginal*) impressed upon the still mirror of the contemplative imagination. (In fact, in the classic Greek meaning of the term, *contemplation* does not refer to an absence of thinking but to the presence of visionary seeing.) Jung's celebrated rediscovery early in the twentieth century of the archetypes of the collective unconscious was merely a reawakening to what had long been the dominant hermeneutical method of the Western mystical and esoteric traditions, in use virtually universally in Christendom until it was swept away in the thirteenth century in the rising tide of Scholasticism.

In imaginal causality, the overarching pattern determines the field in which linear causality plays itself out. If a pattern can be shown to make sense of the data, to give energy and coherence to the field it is organizing, and to offer intelligent and useful directives for future action, then it is deemed to be true, whether or not it is, strictly speaking, historical. Once a basic fit has been established, the rest of the pieces will tend to fall into place, and the arrangement will typically prove itself to be not nearly as illogical as first expected once one understands that the organizing principle looks more like chiasm (concentric rings of action fanning out symmetrically from a causal epicenter) than like linear causality as we are accustomed to it. But if there is a basic mismatch at the imaginal level, then nothing will quite work.

That is essentially the case I am going to try to build. To paraphrase that well-loved fairy tale, I believe that Christianity has from the start been a ternary swan in a binary duck pond. And this imaginal mismatch — unrecognized because there was no way it *could* be recognized in the prevailing intellectual and spiritual culture of the times — has been largely responsible for the erratic and even schizophrenic trajectory that the religion has carved in its two-thousand-year course over history, causing it in periodic paroxysms to disown its mystical and contemplative traditions, demonize its own transformative Wisdom as "gnosticism," and consign more than half of its once extraordinary treasury of sacred texts to the theological scrap heap[1] rather than run the risk that something utterly precious but completely unnamable—its ternary essence—might be contaminated or lost. Against an underlying backdrop of ternary metaphysics, all of this begins to make sense.

Furthermore, once the duckling has been correctly identified as a baby swan, we begin to see valuable clues for healing the schism between theology and metaphysics that has sapped Christianity's energy almost from the start and for tapping into a ternary system's inherent aptitude for dynamism, change, and process in order to set a more confident course toward the future. That, I believe, is the real inducement for paying more serious attention to this theoretically obscure esoteric principle.

The Perennial Philosophy

In my original article on feminizing the Trinity, I noted that most traditional cosmologies are based on a binary system, and it is the nature of binary systems to be stable. They swing like a pendulum between the great cosmic polarities—light and darkness, yin and yang, male and female—but eventually come to equilibrium. Their stability lies in the symmetry of the paired opposites. Within such systems, time tends to take on a static quality characterized by cyclical patterns of repletion and recurrence, and completion is achieved by integrating the opposites.

The grand dowager of all the great binary systems is unquestionably that magnificent metaphysical edifice now widely known as the perennial philosophy. The term was first coined in the early twentieth century by Aldous Huxley, but the system itself is ancient; in fact, Huxley named it as such because he saw it as a universal metaphysics at the root of all the world's great sacred traditions.

While claims sometimes made on its behalf that it faithfully mirrors the deep structure of reality itself may prove to be exaggerated, it *does* mirror with near-perfect accuracy the evolutionary advance in human consciousness that launched what is now widely known as the Axial Age. In a remarkably compressed period of time (generally dated as 800–200 B.C.E.), human beings seemed to awaken universally to a newfound sense of personal destiny and responsibility, and the great spiritual traditions of the world were either born or catapulted to a new level of maturity. This was the great age of the Buddha, Lao Tzu, Zoroaster, the Old Testament prophets, Plato, and Pythagoras. The roots of world civilization as we know it today reach deep into the fertile ground of the perennial philosophy.

When Christianity first came of age intellectually and began to tackle its own identity formation, the perennial philosophy was already flowing strongly through the thought structures of both the Greek and the Semitic worlds. In Greece it was carried mainly in the pervasive Platonic influence that would emerge as early as the third century as Christian Neoplatonism, brilliantly articulated by Origen (d. 254) and passed down in an unbroken lineage of patristic intellectual speculation and devotional practice. Contemporary church historians have often talked about this as the hellenization of Christianity and lamented that a certain swashbuckling Semitic reality seemed to fade beneath the heavily Platonic philosophical categories all too readily available for its theological processing. But the Semitic thought forms were equally under the sway of the perennial philosophy, albeit with a different center of gravity. Jesus himself came of age in the spiritually charged environment of Merkavah (chariot) mysticism, emphasizing a personal ascent to a higher spiritual realm through purification and self-denial, and his subtle but decisive variation from this pattern went largely unnoticed not only in his own era but even down into our own. The perennial philosophy is, as I have said, built into the hardwiring of the axial brain itself. It cannot be spotted by the usual structures of the mind; the frame too closely matches the vision itself. It takes a new kind of consciousness before one can stop looking *through* the frame and begin to look directly *at* it.

Tellingly, the contemporary philosopher Ken Wilber, while more than ready to scrap the term *metaphysics* itself, winds up validating the core tenets of the perennial philosophy and extrapolating them virtually unchanged into his new "postmetaphysical" road map. While Wilber's thinking continues to evolve on this subject, it is still essentially summarized in the description he offers in his 1997 book *The Eye of Spirit*:

> Central to the perennial philosophy is the notion of the Great Chain of Being. The idea itself is fairly simple. Reality, according to the perennial philosophy, is not one-dimensional; it is not a flatland of uniform substance stretching monotonously before the eye. Rather, reality is composed of several *different* but *continuous* dimensions. Manifest reality, that is, consists of different grades or levels, reaching from the lowest and most dense to the highest and most subtle and most conscious. At one end of the continuum of being or spectrum of consciousness is what we in the West would call "matter" or the insentient or non-conscious. And at the other end is "spirit" or "godhead" or the "superconscious" (which is also said to be the all-pervading ground of the entire sequence as we shall see). Arrayed in between are other dimensions of being according to their individual degree of reality....The central claim of the perennial philosophy is that *men and women can grow and develop (or evolve) all the way up the hierarchy to Spirit itself.*[2]

If we examine this description more closely, we discover that the perennial philosophy sets forth three basic premises, which together define its metaphysical milieu. I will now describe each of these in my own words.

Cosmological Redshift

What Wilber terms the Great Chain of Being (following Arthur Lovejoy),[3] I would describe as "cosmological redshift." This is a variant way of naming the same basic item, but I think you will quickly see the point I am driving at. Redshift (alias the Doppler effect) is a basic law of physics stating that as sound waves or light waves move away from their source, their wavelength appears to lengthen, moving toward the "red" end of the visible spectrum (or, with sound waves, to a slower vibration). That's why the ambulance siren drops to a lower pitch as the ambulance hurtles past you and on down the street.

The prevailing scientific cosmological model in use today essentially sees the history of the universe as a vast cosmic redshift. By measuring the Doppler effect in the light emanating from distant galaxies, scientists have observed that the universe is expanding — that is, moving away from its source. And as it does so, there is a decided frequency drop, not merely from the perspective of a passing bystander, but objectively real and measurable. From its point of origin in a hypothetical "big bang," the universe hurtling out through time and space has steadily lost energy, grown colder and more dense. The molten energy of that initial explosion gradually "cooled off" to become quarks, particles, atoms, molecules, rocks, cells, amoebas, people. In a redshift universe, as energy travels outward from the source, its frequency diminishes. Things grow more solid, cooler, less like the source itself.

Interestingly, that's exactly what the perennial philosophy has been saying all along as well — only it has been saying it in the realm of spiritual cosmology rather than scientific cosmology. Underlying that great hierarchical procession of realms traditionally known as the great chain of being, it is not hard to spot as the real operative principle what might picturesquely be described as *spiritual redshift*. With the Godhead, or Source, envisioned as the initial "big bang" of the great chain of being, creation inevitably presents itself as a *descent* — a vast cosmic Doppler effect. The energies of the Godhead stream outward, losing frequency in the process and giving rise to a series of embedded universes, each one progressively more dense and coarse than its predecessor.

Sara Sviri, a contemporary writer in the Naqshbandi Sufi tradition, whose metaphysics are rooted firmly in the perennial philosophy, succinctly describes this basic redshift cosmology in her book *The Taste of Hidden Things*:

> The cosmos was envisaged as a series of concentric spheres, one within the other, all *emanating* in a descending order from the One, the Source, the Eternal. The One, in His overflowing dark and hidden luminosity, produced a "sphere," an "other." …This sphere, in turn, out of its own effulgence, produced another sphere, lower than itself, less luminous. Other spheres of existence *emanated* in the same way. These are the spheres of planets and fixed stars. The spheres became denser and dimmer as their distance from the Source increased. The lowest sphere was identified with the moon. Beneath the moon, in what came to be known as "the sublunar world," lay our universe — the plane of Nature, which became populated by man and other living creatures. This was considered the densest, darkest plane of being.[4]

In essence, Sviri has encapsulated here the Neoplatonic principle of *emanation*, at the heart of the mystical and visionary cosmology of the West.[5] And here the basic cosmic principle, both energetically and morally, is that to be created — particularly as a flesh-and-blood human being — means to descend to a lower state, a more coarse and "corrupt" mode of being, subject to the laws of entropy and decay. So it follows inevitably that the return to God must entail some form of *ascent:* working one's way back up the ray of creation like a salmon working its way upstream. These are the second and third of the three core tenets of the perennial philosophy, to which we will now turn.

The Corruption of Matter

It is only in the past century that we have come to understand definitively that spirit and matter are not fundamentally different. Thanks to Einstein, we now know that matter is merely a more condensed form of energy, and what we have traditionally called spirit would presumably be merely a much more subtle form of energy. But until the beginning of the twentieth century (a mere drop in the bucket of the overall life span of the perennial philosophy), that continuum was unsuspected, and in the pervasively redshift modality of traditional Wisdom metaphysics, there is a virtually unanimous tendency to identify density (that is, the increasingly concentrated presence of matter) as the opponent of spirit and the root cause of all human misery. Situated on "the densest, darkest plane" of existence, at the tail end of the great chain of being, our human sphere is deemed to be virtually at the maximum distance from God, from whom we differ not only in degree but in substance as well. And the very density that confers our human form (traditionally known as "flesh") is seen as the primary corruption that must be overcome in order to reclaim our true spiritual identity.

Along with a tendency to regard matter (density) as the primary source of our human exile comes the tendency to identify God with the top of the great chain of being only, not with the whole chain. Ken Wilber himself falls prey to this deeply entrenched metaphysical proclivity when he writes (in the passage we looked at earlier): "At one end of this continuum of being or spectrum of consciousness is what we in the West would call 'matter' or the insentient or nonconscious. And at the other end is 'spirit' or 'godhead' or the 'superconscious.'" And while he seems to catch himself in the metaphysical act here and hastily adds a parenthesis (that this "superconscious" can also be seen to be "the all-pervading ground of the entire sequence"), he is still regularly blindsided by his tendency to identify the godhead with the top of the pyramid only and to see "matter" as "insentient or non-conscious," hence far removed from Spirit. Even his foundational teaching on the five "states of consciousness" that comprise the ladder of spiritual evolution (gross, subtle, causal, witnessing, nondual)[6] still heavily favors the association of spirit with consciousness and matter with insentiency, a metaphysical habit imported lock, stock, and barrel from the perennial philosophy. While the "gross" realm may on the one hand appear to be merely a technical term to describe the physical density of the realm we humans know only too well, as every good Valley girl can tell you, gross is *"gross!"* It is an all-too-convenient (and now scientifically invalidated) shorthand to see flesh itself as the chief impediment to spiritualization.

Spiritualization as Ascent

Given the first two tenets, the third follows inescapably. If we have "fallen" into matter and density, then the way home must inevitably entail an ascent. And since in the spiritual realm as well as the material one to ascend requires energy, most spiritual technologies in the classic Wisdom traditions are built on some form of "conservation of energy." Through celibacy, meditation, recollection, attention, one "collects" and "deepens" the reserve of energy so that spirit can rise to its home in Spirit.

Earlier in this chapter I described the perennial philosophy as "the grand dowager of all the great binary systems." By now it is perhaps more clear why I have characterized it in such a way. For all of its claims to metaphysical preeminence, it reveals itself as a binary system because of the foundational dualisms on which it rests — between matter and spirit, descent and ascent — and because of its tendency to seek its stability in a symmetrical balancing of the opposites. In a spiritual journey unfolding according to the perennial philosophy road map, one will be working with three basic operating assumptions: (1) the identification of the divine Source with the subtle, (2) the identification of the subtle with the highest energetic frequency, and (3) the conclusion that spiritual evolution (or "return") means to ascend the frequency scale, a transformation sometimes referred to as subtilization. The journey into form and back out of it will thus tend to configure itself as a vast *exitus et reditus* (exit and return), the return always being to the eternal changelessness of Spirit. The journey through density contributes little or nothing to the return itself; it merely offers the milieu in which awakening may occur as "men and women evolve all the way up the hierarchy to Spirit itself."

A San Andreas Fault in the Country of the Heart

Somewhat perversely, perhaps, given the sheer weight of spiritual authority behind this road map, Christian orthodoxy has always rested uneasily within it. That is not to say the perennial philosophy has been without influence in Christianity; it has in fact exerted enormous influence. Open any textbook on Christian spirituality or mysticism and you will find it prominently represented: from the Christian Neoplatonism of Origen to the sixth-century writings of Pseudo-Dionysius that so profoundly impacted the mysticism of the West to the imagery of the ladder popularized by John Climacus in the seventh century, which framed the monastic praxis of both Christian East and Christian West. It takes a well-practiced theological eye to spot the San Andreas fault running through this magnificent body of spiritual teaching. And yet the fault line is there, and once you see it, a lot of the early history of Christianity makes a good deal more sense. I am not talking here about those obvious theological conundrums such as Augustine's "grace versus works" but something much more fundamental: an uneasy intuition, just below the surface of the collective theological imagination, that there is something fundamentally askew in the metaphysics themselves.

We have just spent several pages exploring the core metaphysical building blocks of the perennial philosophy, and from this exploration it is not hard to see where the fundamental points of tension will arise. First and most significant, the tendency to equate physical density with corruption and to picture the journey to God as an ascent to a more spiritualized plane of reality directly clashes with that foundational datum of Christian lived experience: that in Jesus, God had drawn very close and, in fact, "became flesh and dwelt among us" (John 1:14). At the very epicenter of Christian identity — in direct challenge to the perennial road map — is the lived experience that *God does not lose energy by plunging into form.* If anything, the thrust is in the opposite direction, toward a kind of spiritual "blueshift" in which Jesus, like a great magnifying glass, makes more concentrated and vivid the accessible presence of divine Spirit itself. While Christian-

ity has often lost its nerve around extending this magnifying capacity to anyone other than Jesus himself, still, the core theological proclamation at stake in the statement "God was in Christ reconciling the world to himself (2 Cor. 5:19) is that God can be fully present in the physical world without form being an impediment to divinity—or to put it another way, that things do not lose spirit simply because they inhabit form. This blueshift modality of Christian lived experience is in direct tension with the redshift thrust of the grand perennial road map. Even more against the metaphysical grain is that stunning Johannine intimation that the reason for Jesus's mission is that "God so loved the world" (John 3:16). There is something more than just a rescue operation going on here; the created world is infinitely precious and valuable in its own right.

Following from this intuition, then—and in contrast to the dominant upward thrust of the perennial road map—is that corollary tenet, again rooted in lived Christian experience, that the way to God is not up but down. The essence of this intuition is brilliantly expressed in that great Pauline hymn of Philippians 2:6–11, which captures in a highly condensed and compelling form the energy field pervading the entire gospel tradition. At the very heart of that original Christian vision, tugging against the Neoplatonic undercurrents that would eventually overwhelm it, is the staunch intuition that the Jesus mystery is ultimately not about ascent but about descent; its epicenter lies not in subtilization but in kenosis, self-emptying:

Though his state was that of God,
yet he did not claim equality with God
something he should cling to.

Rather, he emptied himself,[7]
and, assuming the state of a slave,
he was born in human likeness.

He being known as one of us,
humbled himself obedient unto death,
even to death on a cross.

For this God raised him on high
and bestowed on him the name
which is above every other name.

So that, at the name of Jesus,
every knee should bend
in heaven, on earth, and under the earth.

And so every tongue shall proclaim,
"Jesus Christ is Lord!"
to God the Father's Glory.

Theologians have had a heyday with this passage, of course, emphasizing the spiritual virtues of humility and obedience, but *metaphysically* it again reinforces that counterintuitive wisdom that one does not lose force or Godhood — one does not move away from God — by entering the realm of form; quite to the contrary, descent seems to be the chief operative in making the fullness of the divine manifestation happen.

If the truth be told, I do not actually think that *descent* is the right term here, and the theological polarization that has grown up around this issue is more than a little unfortunate. "Descent" is merely the closest theological approximation traditionally available for describing that corkscrewing motion into new manifestations that is characteristic of ternary metaphysics. The thrust is actually outward, not downward, and what we are in fact dealing with here is not descent but third force. In fact, the entire Paschal Mystery can be seen to play itself out as a fairly straightforward configuration of the Law of Three. If you assign *affirming* as Jesus the human teacher of the path of love; *denying* as the crucifixion and the forces of hatred driving it; and *reconciling* as the principle of self-emptying, or kenotic love willingly engaged, then the *Fourth*, which is inescapably revealed through this weaving, is the Kingdom of Heaven, visibly manifest in the very midst of all the human cruelty and brokenness. I realize that this is getting ahead of the game, but I wanted to make sure that you stay in practice with your Law of Three triads, and also to plant a few seeds as to where all of this may be headed.

For now, to return to the topic immediately at hand, it is enough to observe that these two areas of direct collision leave Christianity in a fundamental quandary about its metaphysical underpinnings. Perhaps that is the meaning of Jesus's cryptic warning in Luke 12:52 (and the Gospel of Thomas 16) that "the household will be divided, three against two and two against three." A basically ternary theology erected on the foundations of a binary metaphysics is bound to result in cognitive dissonance. And while this dissonance is never named for what it is, it makes its presence known in those periodic theological upheavals and course corrections that so dominate the early centuries of Christian history.

I was particularly gratified to see Father Bruno Barnhart, in his recent book *The Future of Wisdom*, finally naming this issue that has been for so long the unmentionable elephant in the parlor. In a section titled "Limitations of Monastic Wisdom" — or in other words, influences that have pulled the innate Christian sapiential compass off course — he specifically flags "a very strong Platonic influence which supports the vertical and interiorizing monastic options and sanctions an ascending crystal tower of spiritual theology."[8] Even ten years earlier, in his 1999 book *Second Simplicity*, Barnhart had begun to voice his concerns about the propriety of simply subsuming Christian metaphysics into the perennial philosophy. His deep monastic listening had already attuned his ear to the subtle dissonance between the Neoplatonic road map and the gospel kerygma:

> The perennial philosophy, unsurpassable in its own direction of simplicity and profundity, and in the authority of unitive experience that it reflects, does not begin to give an adequate account of Christianity. New Testament expressions of the "divine Unitive" are dynamic and intensely personal; they communicate an energy that is something new in the world.[9]

I will be returning to this intuition shortly, for I believe that the intuition that "there is something new in the world" is in fact at the heart of the Christian lived experience and can really be accommodated only within a ternary system, for a ternary metaphysic is specifically set up to accommodate new arising in a way that a binary system can never be. This will be the business of our next chapter.

Many people still like to think of metaphysics (whether premodern or postmodern) as an objective science — true everywhere and for all times — rather than the art of selectively choosing the "right view" (as the Buddhists call it): the pattern that best highlights and unifies the lived reality of a particular faith tradition. I run into this prejudice all the time in my own work with attempting to reclaim an authentic Christian Wisdom tradition. It is remarkable how many people assume that since I am using the word *Wisdom*, I am teaching perennial philosophy metaphysics. This assumption leads many of my more "spiritual but not religious" acquaintances to expect that I have simply dispensed with the cranky eccentricities of Christian theology and found my Wisdom ground in the "transcendent unity of religions."[10] And it has led many more traditionally minded Christians to dismiss my work out of hand as gnostic. Both of these assumptions are equally untrue.

The transcendent unity of religions notwithstanding, in Christianity, for better or worse, we are dealing with a horse of a different metaphysical color. It is not Platonism or Neoplatonism, not Traditionalism or Gnosticism, not Jungian archetypes or anthroposophy, not the perennial philosophy. Throughout those early centuries of Christian identity formation, it seems that the Church Fathers could generally smell ternary metaphysics even if they couldn't articulate it. While patristic thinkers such as Irenaeus and Tertullian are highly in disfavor nowadays because of their relentless fulminations against heresy, it must be admitted that these early Christian patriarchs did have a strong intuitive grasp of where the metaphysical center of gravity really lay in Christianity and a sixth sense for when Christianity was wandering off its metaphysical course. Over the centuries — from those early polemicists of the second and third centuries down through the medieval inquisitors and papal bulls of more recent eras — institutional Christianity has proved itself more than willing to disown and condemn even its loftiest mystical expressions and most profound nondual teachings rather than run the risk of having the entire theological structure compromised by a metaphysical framework intuitively sensed to be alien. It is a kind of brute, intuitive courage, not pretty in its own right, but validly expressing an intimation of something here too precious to lose. Named as ternary metaphysics, it can perhaps finally be seen with less heat and more light.

Ternary metaphysics

6

Dynamism

The world is charged with the grandeur of God,
It will flame out, like shining from shook foil.
— Gerard Manley Hopkins

IN HIS MOST RECENT BOOK, *The Future of Wisdom*, Bruno Barnhart advances a daring hypothesis. He suggests that our modern Western world in all of its sprawling untidiness is not a deviation from the path of Christ but its legitimate and, in fact, inevitable trajectory. The ongoing upheavals and revolutions of modernity — the scientific revolution, secularity, global economics, the computer age — are not to be seen as a betrayal of spirit but as further creative expressions of that same dynamic Christic ground. "The apparent eclipse of Christian wisdom by history is an optical illusion," he writes — "since history is itself an unfolding of the event of Christ."[1]

It is precisely for this reason, he feels — continuing a line of thinking we began to explore in the previous chapter — that "the wisdom of Christianity does not find itself quite at home among the other sapiential traditions of the world." In contrast to that great upward spiritual thrust of the perennial philosophy, "the unitive wisdom which has become manifest in Christ disappears into — more boldly, we might say, *metamorphoses* into — an immanent historical dynamism that transforms all of created reality."[2]

This is a train of thought that Barnhart had already been pondering at least a decade before. In s striking meditation in his 1999 book, *Second Simplicity*, he reflects:

There is a secret in the heart of life that is not only the unmoving white light. It is not only the still point of the turning world, not only the light-filled empty center. It is also the lion of fire, the unceasing explosion of expansive being, of proliferating life, from the center. It is the fontal energy that demands to express itself everywhere and through every form....It is not only secret but also manifestation: the secret manifestation, the nameless, ubiquitous power that is expressed in our own restless centrifugal living.

The gospel's secret power, often hardly glimpsed by Christianity itself, is the gathering up of all our passion, our entropic centrifugal energy, our very outward thrust and vital compulsivity, secularity, and carnality, into this divine energy that ever flows out from its hidden Source.[3]

While in no way turning a blind eye to the darker manifestations of Western culture, he is still able to say, with striking affirmation, "The West occupies the unique position of being the one great civilization that has been united and formed by the Christ-event and that has mediated the unification of humanity. It is largely through the peoples and civilization of the West that the gifts of the incarnation have been distributed to the world. These gifts include not only Christian faith but — touching many more people — the human and social values, the rationality and freedom, the science and technology that gradually humanize the world and bring it together as one world."[4] Barnhart's challenging but ultimately hopeful vision of the future of Christian Wisdom is closely tied to the willingness to claim this legacy (both the shadow and the destiny) and to learn to move with the grain — not against it — following a dynamism he recognizes as emanating from the Christ event itself.

Early on in his exploration, Barnhart invokes the spirit of Teilhard de Chardin, and with good reason. As a fellow scientist, priest, and mystic, Barnhart is assuredly walking in the footsteps of that extraordinary twentieth-century Jesuit visionary. But what a difference a mere half century can make! For his brilliantly original efforts to chart a new course for Christian mysticism running *through* the world rather than away from it, Teilhard's fate was to be universally misunderstood and rejected. His Catholic superiors accused him of pantheism and forbade his works to be published, while among metaphysicians of a more traditional bent, his fascination with density as an evolutionary principle and his wholehearted embrace of modernity seemed to be going in exactly the wrong direction. You will still see his name regularly vilified in Traditionalist metaphysical circles.

But Teilhard persisted, and a half century later the tide is slowly turning in his favor. In those dark days of the cold war (he died on Easter Sunday in 1955), he prophetically saw that the increasing urbanization of humanity, the accelerating pace of technology — and challengingly, for most contemporary liberals, the discovery and harnessing of nuclear power — all augured an increasing concentration of divine energy converging rapidly on an Omega Point, which he greeted with an open-armed embrace. One can only imagine what this unabashedly "metaphysically incorrect" prophet of the future would make of the explosive acceleration of human communications in our contemporary Internet world.

What interests me most here is that Barnhart and Teilhard are both picking up on essentially the same dynamism, which they see as exploding out of the Christ event and launching the universe on a trajectory distinctly different from that stipulated by perennial wisdom. There is a different energy at work here — something about its epicenter in incarnation, perhaps — that makes it want to burst out into the world in a continuing stream of innovation and creativity. In Barnhart's words, "Spiritual reality — divinity — enters into earthly matter to initiate a new *sacramental* creation."[5] Teilhard's language is more complicated, but the gist is similar: the risen Christ enters *organically* into the physical reality of this universe as the new driveshaft of evolution. "Cosmogenesis [the continuing evolution of the planet] has become Christogenesis," Teilhard proclaims, as the world moves toward its Omega Point, in Christ, "where the consummation of God and the consummation of the world converge."[6]

It doesn't take too much of an imaginal leap to recognize that what both of these writers are actually describing — unbeknownst to them, of course — is the dynamic ground of ternary metaphysics. The dynamism itself is the giveaway.

As we have seen already, just as a binary system is by nature stable and symmetrical, a ternary system is asymmetrical and inherently innovative. Unlike a pendulum, it cannot come to equilibrium within its own orbit; it seeks its stability in a new plane, through a resolution that is at the same time a new arising. It corkscrews its way through time, matter, form — whatever plane is at hand — in a riot of uncertainty and new combinations, the whole of which (not merely the top of the pyramid) is the fullness of divine reality. With good reason Gurdjieff named it the Law of World Creation, for its mandate is to move things forward. While Barnhart and Teilhard develop their argument in traditional theological and Christocentric categories, the energy pattern they are describing belongs to the Law of Three.

In fact, in the course of their discussion, both of these Christian visionaries explicitly refer to Christ as a "third" — and in terms closely approximating third force — although again without recognizing the import of what they are doing. Explaining the "reconciling" nature of Christ as a bridge between two planes of reality, Barnhart writes: "Between the metaphysical sun and the physical sun arises a third: the embodied divine sun which is Jesus Christ — in whom the metaphysical and the physical have become one."[7] And Teilhard's extended mystical speculation on what he calls "the third nature of Christ" (the cosmic or resurrected Christ) amounts to a remarkably precise job description of third force. In her masterful summary of Teilhard's thought in *Christ in Evolution*, Ilia Delio comments:

> By using the term "third nature" Teilhard indicated that Christ is related organically, not simply juridically, to the whole cosmos....Since the cosmic Christ is the resurrected Christ, this third nature, or cosmic nature, emerges from the union of divine natures so that it is neither one nor the other but the union of both, although it exists on the side of creation. It is what allows us to see that Christ the redeemer is Christ

the Evolver, or in Teilhard's language, cosmogenesis is really Christogenesis.[8]

In a comment that presses right to the threshold of this ternary metaphysical terrain, Delio concludes this section of her discussion by commenting on a remark by fellow scholar James Lyons that Christ, in his third nature, is the organizing principle of Teilhard's evolving universe. "Whereas the Alexandrian Logos was the organizing principle of the stable [that is, *binary*] Greek cosmos, today, Lyons states, we must identify Christ with a 'new Logos': the evolutive principle of a universe in movement."[9]

Make no mistake here; I am not claiming that *ternary metaphysics* is a term these contemporary Christian visionaries, Barnhart and Teilhard, would acknowledge or even recognize. But the pattern they are both describing is, in fact, the ternary pattern, and they both rightly intuit that it is what makes Christianity so distinctly different from the other great sapiential traditions.

A New Breed of Trinity

Perhaps the most significant indicator of this dawning ternary consciousness is a new kind of awareness beginning to percolate within mainstream Trinitarian scholarship itself. As a growing number of highly respected contemporary theologians circle back for a closer look at the Trinity, the picture beginning to emerge is looking less and less like angels dancing on the head of a pin and more and more like a mandala of love in motion. Dynamism, relationality, and creativity (or cocreation) within an open-ended field are the hallmarks of this new breed of Trinitarian reflection. In this section I will look closely at three of the most influential of these voices. The new course they are charting for contemporary Trinitarian theology is, to say the least, synchronous. Once again we find ourselves at the very threshold of ternary metaphysics: not formally designated, but intuitively sensed.

Catherine LaCugna

Trinitarian studies received a major new energy boost in 1991 with the publication of Catherine Mowry LaCugna's *God for Us: The Trinity and Christian Life,* for which she deservedly won the Catholic Press Association's first-place award for theology.[10] Given the abysmally anaerobic state of Trinitarian speculation at the time, it is no small wonder that the book saw the light of day at all, but the even greater wonder is that LaCugna managed to place it with a prestigious *popular* press (HarperSanFrancisco), ensuring that its influence would quickly make itself widely known. Virtually single-handedly LaCugna managed to rescue the Trinity from the theological margins to which it had been increasingly relegated and restore it to active duty as a primary symbol of Christian life.

In the first part of her book, LaCugna rigorously traces the "defeat" of the doctrine of the Trinity over a thousand years of theological development as it moves from its starting point as a participative vision of God's redemptive love at work in all creation to an increasingly abstract speculation on the inner life of God. As early as the fourth century it had already become an established theological habit to divide the field of operations into an "economic" trinity — in Greek, *oikonomia*[11] — covering God's actions in the visible world, and a "theological" (or "immanent") Trinity concerned with relationships within the Godhead itself. Once this fundamental rupture between God *in se* (in himself) and God *pro nobis* (for us) had occurred, the drift continued to widen — in the Christian East through an exaggerated differentiation between the "essence" and "energies" of God, and in the post-Augustinian West through an increasing fixation on the substance and psychology of the divine persons. More and more the Trinity became locked up in a speculative realm all of its own, until all connection with the practical and moral reality of Christian life was lost.

Following in the footsteps of her spiritual mentor Karl Rahner, LaCugna issues a passionate call for a return to that original undivided field of gospel experience in which the inner life of God and the outer life of salvation are one and the same reality. "The economic Trinity *is* the immanent Trinity," was Rahner's celebrated bottom line,[12] and LaCugna's work both nuances that assessment and develops it more fully. As she sees it, "The biblical and pre-Nicene sense of the economy is the one dynamic movement of God....The economy is not a mirror dimly reflecting a hidden world of intradivine relations; the economy is God's concrete existence as Christ and as Spirit....[They] are two aspects of *one* reality: the mystery of divine-human communion."[13]

In fact, so intent is she upon this one lived reality that on page 222 she "unbends" those two separate circles (economic and immanent) and refashions them as a single parabolic curve sweeping from its Alpha in the hidden depths of God into historical time and space and on to its Omega in the full revelation of those hidden depths. Here is her diagram:

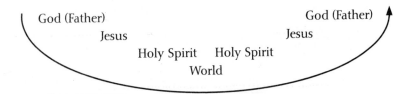

"There is neither an economic nor an immanent Trinity," she writes, "there is only the *Oikonomia* that is the concrete realization of the mystery of *theologia* in time, space, history, and personality. In this framework, the doctrine of the Trinity encompasses much more than the immanent Trinity, envisioned in static ahistorical and transeconomic terms; the subject matter of the Christian theology of God is the one dynamic movement of God, *a Patre ad Patrem*. There is no reason to stop at any one point along the curve, no reason to single out one point as if it could be fixed or frozen in time."[14]

In these lines LaCugna comes very close to anticipating exactly the parabolic flow into historical time and out of it that I will lay out in part 3 according to the Law of Three.[15]

Raimon Panikkar

One of the great pioneers of contemporary interreligious dialogue, Panikkar worked on the Trinity for most of his long and productive scholarly career. Between his early *The Holy Trinity* (1973) and his magnificent *Christophany* (2004) lie more than thirty years of increasingly subtle scholarship as he, too, comes to see the Trinity more and more as a dynamic mandala, entrusted in a particular way to Christianity but universal in its scope, illumining the "dynamism of the real."

Cosmotheandric is the term Panikkar invents to describe this dynamic relational ground. The word itself is a fusion of *cosmos* (world), *theos* (God), and *andros* (man) and suggests a continuous intercirculation among these three distinct planes of existence in a single motion of self-communicating love. The gist of this idea is already fully there in those profound images that cascade from Jesus's mouth in the farewell discourses of John 13–17: "I am the vine, you are the branches; abide in me as I in you (John 15:4); "As you, Father, are in me and I am in you, may they also be in us....I in them and you in me, that they may be completely one" (John 17: 21–23). The vision is of a dynamic, interabiding oneness whose "substance" is inseparable from the motion itself. Panikkar is emphatic that "being is a verb, not a substance,"[16] and the Trinity is the indivisible expression of the mode of this beingness. All speculation on the "substance" of the individual divine persons (as has dominated Western metaphysics for more than fifteen hundred years) thus starts off on a fundamental misperception; for, as Panikkar sees it, "the Trinity is pure relationality."[17]

As I have already insinuated, Panikkar sees the basic template of the Trinity arising directly from the mind of Christ. This is a striking example of what I referred to in the last chapter as imaginal causality in action. While the fully articulated doctrine of the Trinity came into existence only much later in historical time, Panikkar argues that its real roots lie in the lived reality of Jesus's own relationship with God. It holds the pieces of that lived relationship together in a way that is faithful to the experience itself and opens the relational dynamism at the heart of it to all of his followers. In a fascinating and closely argued section of *Christophany* entitled "The Mysticism of Jesus the Christ," Panikkar builds his case that the Trinity is essentially an icon of the mind of Christ and extends that mind outward as a cosmic principle. Between the pole of maximum unity of being (conveyed in Jesus's powerful exclamation, "The Father and I are one") and maximum differentiation (captured in his shockingly tender "*Abba*, Father") flows an unbroken current of kenotic love through which all things are invited into that great cosmotheandric intercirculation. For Panikkar, the Trinity is not a theological add-on; it is a manifesting principle of the first order, linking the visible and invisible realms together according to a single relational dynamism that he summarizes as follows: "I am one with the source insofar as I too act as a source by making everything I have received flow again — just like Jesus."[18]

While Panikkar displays no formal awareness of the Law of Three, his metaphysics are definitely prototernary, and in a couple of instances he comes right to the threshold of an explicitly ternary understanding. He intuitively recognizes — and at one point even explicitly states — that the Spirit functions as a "placeholder," so that the trajectory of divine love does not collapse back into itself: "It is not an *amor curvus*, as the Middle Ages would say, a love that folds back in on itself, but a Trinitarian love."[19] While he does not further develop this observation, he is clearly thinking spatially here, envisioning that triadic model in which three points are necessary to keep an action open and flowing. With that same spatial intuitiveness, he also begins to push gently against Saint Augustine's celebrated dictum, unchallenged in the West for more than fifteen hundred years, that "the Spirit is the love between the Father and the Son." While not quite directly challenging that formulation, he seems to be subliminally aware of a certain solipsism at work here (that amor curvus, or love folding back in upon itself) and states firmly — though again without offering any substantiation — that "this relationship, in which the whole universe is involved, does not result in a final monism; it is not closed because it is the Sprit that keeps it open."[20] Transposed to an explicitly ternary paradigm, everything that Panikkar is correctly intuiting here would find its clear and obvious validation.

Beatrice Bruteau

One of the most striking recent contributions to the evolution of Trinitarian thought is Beatrice Bruteau's 1997 book *God's Ecstasy: The Creation of a Self-Creating World*. A mathematician and philosopher as well as one of this century's most respected contemplative theologians, Bruteau brings all of her skills to bear on this exploration, and while less known than some of her other writings, this book is in many ways her boldest and most prophetic. In it she comes within a hair's breadth of reinventing the Law of Three out of her own philosophical and mathematical resources. She depicts the Trinity (again, completely unsuspectingly) along almost exactly the same lines as Gurdjieff: as a necessarily threefold embodiment of the fundamental cosmic Law of World Creation.

For Bruteau the Trinity is first and foremost an image of *symbiotic unity* — in fact, it is "the original symbiotic Unity."[21] The three "God-Persons in Community," as she sees it, comprise the prototype *and the prerequisite* for the expression of agape love, the constituent energy of the Godhead itself. In chapter 2 she builds a detailed philosophical case for why threefoldness is a necessary precondition of agape love. She then goes on to demonstrate that threefoldness is by nature "ecstatic," or in other words, self-projective. By its very threefold-ness it "breaks symmetry" (the symmetry of the intradivine equilibrium) and projects the agape field outward, calling new forms of being into existence, each of which bears the imprint of the original symbiotic unity that created it. "It is that presence of the Trinity as a pattern repeated at every scale of the cosmic order," she feels, "that makes the universe the manifestation of God and itself sacred and holy."[22]

Because this Trinitarian template is built right into the dynamism of the universe itself, Bruteau sees no need to seek philosophical recourse in an extrinsic creator God, "above" and "beyond" creation itself; it is all there in the Trinitarian dynamism itself. The next several chapters of her book explore this template at work in every stage of cosmogenesis — from the original big bang through the emergence of atoms, simple chemical compounds, increasingly complex life-forms, and finally humanity itself, converging toward a critical threshold of collective consciousness. Because of this inbuilt Trinitarian dynamism, the universe itself is not only created but creative; it bears the capacity to be a "self-creating world." Freedom, innovation, open-endedness, and surprise are all built into the mix as agape love follows its inherent trajectory.

Bruteau's thinking here brings us right to the threshold of the Law of Three. More than any of the other writers we have explored here, she powerfully "gets" that the Trinity is a dynamic, generative principle stamped into the very nature of created reality; it is both cosmic law and creative template. She recognizes as well that the key to this dynamism is the inherent capacity of threefoldness to "break symmetry and let the differences interact."[23] With these two pieces in place, all that is lacking is the recognition that agape love is a not a personal attribute of God (or even "God-Persons in Community," as her theologically trained mind requires her to stipulate) but an energy field arising out of the interplay of three independent forces (affirming, denying, reconciling). If she were to make that leap, she and Gurdjieff would be on the same page.

Going the Distance

From these contemporary visionary theologians we hear a distinctly different note being sounded, a whole new resonance opening up within Trinitarian self-awareness. While stopping (just) short of any formal articulation of the Law of Three, they are all definitely intuiting a ternary metaphysics at the heart of Christian experience whose effects are fully confirmable in the oikonomia, the visible sphere. There is a new confidence emerging that the Trinity is not simply an arcane theological sideshow but an essential operational principle that somehow holds the key to a renewed Christian life. With that recognition, we are already about 90 percent of the way toward unearthing the Law of Three.

That final 10 percent is essentially the law itself, the articulation of the actual mechanics by which this dynamic, symmetry-breaking, innovative metaphysical principle is translated into action.

The interweaving of the three produces a fourth in a new dimension. So far this is the one significant aspect of the Law of Three that contemporary theology has not yet uncovered and that therefore separates the way the Law of Three is understood in the Gurdjieff Work from the increasingly keen intimations of its presence in contemporary theological circles. In this final section of the chapter I would like to suggest several ways in which the explicit acknowledgement of this important missing piece might be helpful, not only for a more complete and forceful articulation of Christianity's innate Trinitarian wisdom, but also as a corrective to certain aspects of its traditional theological articulation that have never been fully convincing.

The *first* and most important point is that linking the Trinity to the Law of Three adds predicative capacity. It explains why the inherent dynamism that Bruteau calls agape love *must* create new worlds; why it cannot simply remain locked up within a great intra-Trinitarian circulation. Even Bruteau's intricate philosophical demonstration that agape love demands "at least three persons"[24] does not explain why this love must *necessarily* jump its boundaries from there and move into the creation of new worlds (Bruteau merely stipulates that this is part of the diffusive nature of love). The "fourth in a new dimension" puts teeth in her assertion and also supplies the nuts-and-bolts confirmation for LaCugna's theologically impassioned argument that economic and immanent Trinities must never be separated—for according to the Law of Three, they cannot be separated. This predicative tool should also allow us, theoretically, to discern within the great flow of cosmic history successive and quantifiable stages unfolding according to the dictates of this law and also (once we get the math under our belts) to offer some intelligent estimates as to where the pattern seems to be headed. In other words, it allows us to become proactive (rather than merely bewildered or catatonic) in responding to the unique challenges of the era we find ourselves in as cosmogenesis accelerates toward its Omega Point. We understand better what is truly required and how to go about it.

Second, it frees us from reliance on anthropomorphic language to derive foundational metaphysical principles. Rather than grounding our ternary metaphysics in a hypothetical "God–Community" — a supposition that is unverifiable beyond the domain of Christian faith (and highly vulnerable to anthropomorphic and sentimental distortion within it) — it grounds the God–Community in the stipulations of the Law of Three itself and allows us to see the Trinitarian persons as a primordial personification of this law in action. This may be a dubious benefit for those already within the Christian belief community, but it is a huge advantage as Christianity tries to explain its Trinitarian fixation to the rest of the community of world religions. It offers a much more credible way to advance the case that Trinitarian metaphysics is not some sort of arbitrary tritheism but the "personalization" of what early Christianity authentically came to understand as the fundamental modality of God-in-creation. If the Law of Three is universally true (as Gurdjieff stipulated and I attempted to demonstrate in part 1), then the community of God–Persons coincides with that verity and puts a human face to it. It allows Christians to proclaim that the great relational field of divine consciousness is not an "it" but a "Thou" and to enter into that thouness as all lovers do, through devotion and self-giving.

Third, because the Law of Three is valid across the entire spectrum of creative operations — from the subatomic to the galactic and from the scientific to the psychological and sociological — it offers a powerful foundation on which to reunite cosmology, theology, personal spiritual transformation, and collective ethical action: those four quadrants of a coherent spiritual universe that for so long now in Christianity have been kept in separate boxes, playing by different rules. It rebuilds the bridge between spiritual cosmology and physical cosmology in a way that is respectful of both scientific and mystical truth, and it offers a simple but practical tool with which to move out into the world as skillful agents of change. This is the area of exploration closest to my own heart, which I will begin to open up in part 4.

(4) *Finally* — and this may be something of an in-house matter — it creates a set of objective criteria by which to identify and correct those places where traditional Trinitarian theology is still undeveloped or has wandered off course.

The weakest links in traditional Trinitarian theology have always been around how to incorporate the Holy Spirit. Catherine LaCugna has rightly observed that this has been a theological tension from the start as Christianity emerged only slowly from a "di-theism" ("Jesus is Lord") into a bona fide Trinitarian ground. But this Trinitarian ground has always rested on theological underpinnings only, never metaphysical ones, since there has as yet been no collective awareness that ternary metaphysics actually exists. This has allowed significant distortions to enter, particularly around the questions of how the three persons are connected to each other and the direction of flow within their love. Augustine's vision of the Spirit as the love between the Father and the Son is a classic example. It is a theological statement pure and simple, and however effectively it may function at this level, *metaphysically* it collapses the Trinity back into a ditheism (an amor curvus, as Panikkar identifies it — a closed circle). In my opinion this dictum (whose flaw is impossible to spot apart from a ternary metaphysical perspective) has been the principal culprit, at least in the Christian West, in the severing of the immanent Trinity from the economic Trinity, for it essentially sanctions a love that is fully contained within itself; it disarms the "new arising" function and renders the world irrelevant to the fullness of the Father's love. Ternary metaphysics would spot the fallacy here instantly and send the theologians back to their drawing boards with the instructions that the three forces must be independent and equal and that their intertwining must *necessarily* result in a new arising — or in other words, the oikonomia is irreducibly a part of the Trinitarian life.

There are other correctives that an explicitly ternary metaphysics might suggest as well. As I mentioned all the way back in my initial article on feminizing the Trinity, it would explain why the contemporary "spiritually correct" trend toward correcting the gender balance among the Trinitarian persons is a sincere but misguided wild goose chase. Longer range, it might encourage an upcoming generation of theologians to pay less attention to "persons" at all (understood as permanent psycho-spiritual identities) and more to *functions* they are performing at any given moment — affirming, denying, reconciling — within a fluctuating relational field. Imagine the spaciousness that would suddenly open up in Trinitarian studies if rather than starting with three fixed "persons" and asking "who?" we started with three interweaving forces and asked "how?" I am realistic enough to realize that for most of my Christian readers this will be the hardest transposition to make — so deeply engrained are our habits of tying our sense of the "personal" to these three particular persons — but I hope to be able to show how nothing is lost thereby and quite a lot is gained.

In these and other ways, a conscious appropriation of Law of Three metaphysics would furnish an important corrective to traditional Trinitarian theology and allow visionary theologians such as the ones we have met in this chapter to move forward more forcefully in the direction their hearts are already intuiting. It adds the "how" to the "why" of Christian metaphysics in a way that is precise, objectively verifiable, and universally relevant. To fully claim the Trinity as Christianity's personalized mandalic expression of the Law of Three and to commit to living consciously beneath its banner would literally open up whole new worlds. It would place the key in our hands to unlock the treasure-house of Christian mystical Wisdom and — in Teilhard's boldly prophetic words — harness the energy of love.

7

Jacob Boehme, Ternary Master

Though in many of its aspects this visible world seems formed in love,
the invisible spheres were formed in fright.
— Herman Melville, *Moby Dick*

AT THIS POINT I will officially invite Jacob Boehme into our discussion. My hope is that he will be able to provide some third force between "affirming" — my desire to show you why the Law of Three is so important and relevant to our understanding of the Holy Trinity — and "denying": your no doubt still-lingering misgivings about this contention.

Better than anyone else I can think of, Boehme bridges the gap between traditional Christian devotion and the esoteric tradition. His standing within the Christian mystical lineage (admittedly toward its outer edge) is unanimously acknowledged, and for more than four centuries now his visionary writings have been a deep well from which many of the greatest Christian mystics have drawn. But his wildly original cosmology has baffled many; it does not play by the rules of classic Christian theology, and while Christocentric to the core, it seems to get there according to its own unique trajectory. Over these next three chapters I hope to demonstrate that this trajectory is implicitly the Law of Three.

Virtually alone among Christianity's great mystical theologians, Boehme does not develop his ideas using the thought categories furnished by either monastic Neoplatonism or Scholasticism, the rising star of medieval Catholic academia. This is partly because he was not Catholic (he was a German Lutheran) but equally because he was unlettered — not illiterate, by any means, but a shoemaker by trade who lived most of his fairly brief life in the small village of Görlitz in southeastern Germany. His theology is a total original, emerging directly out of a vision that galvanized him in 1600 when he was twenty-four years old. Brooding and dreamy by nature, he was gazing at a pewter dish sparkling in the sunlight when suddenly he was swept up in such a firestorm of unitive vision that "in one quarter of an hour I saw and knew more than if I had been many years together at a university."[1] It was a direct download from the imaginal realm.

Twelve years passed before he was able to fashion his instantaneous illumination into words. At last in 1612 his first treatise, the *Aurora*, was completed, only to fall into the hands of Gregorius Richter, the chief pastor of Görlitz, who attacked Boehme for heresy and forbade him to write. But his work continued to circulate among the Görlitz intelligentsia and won him many admirers, particularly among the students of Hermetic philosophy, who plied him with additional research materials from the alchemical tradition. (This turns out to have been a mixed blessing, for it clutters the sweeping simplicity of Boehme's original vision with a complicated alchemical overlay that also introduces contradiction into his thinking.) In 1619 Boehme took up the pen again, and in the five years before his death in 1624 he completed all of his major works.

One Deep Calls to Another

My own introduction to Boehme came almost twenty years ago when my hermit teacher at Saint Benedict's Monastery in Colorado dropped off a copy of Boehme's *The Way to Christ* for my Holy Week reading. I devoured it on the spot, with the distinct feeling that Boehme was looking over my shoulder. Over the next several years I worked my way through most of the rest of the Boehme canon, including his *The Threefold Life of Man*, *The Forty Questions of the Soul*, and *The Three Principles of the Divine Essence*, his most substantial works. (A word of forewarning here to potential new Boehme readers: since there is as yet no complete modern English-language version of his major works, one is still forced to rely principally on the seventeenth-century translation of John Sparrow, Boehme's first English devotee, with its archaic verb forms and sometimes quaint phraseology. In the Boehme quotations you will be encountering in this chapter, I have removed the second person singular and modernized the verbs accordingly.)[2]

While Boehme is notoriously difficult when approached through the rational intellect, I early on learned that if one approaches him in the same state of mind in which he received his mystical illumination — that is, contemplative stillness — the way opens up much more easily. As a longtime student of Centering Prayer, I was comfortable with that entry point, and over the years I have introduced him to any number of spiritual seekers at contemplative retreats using that same methodology. The basic hermeneutic principle when dealing with all visionary mystics, I'm convinced, is encapsulated in that brief one-liner in Psalm 42:7: "One deep calls to another." In the contemplative depths, imaginal reality is readily accessible to every attuned heart.

Surrender as Catalytic Principle

What makes Boehme's work readily navigable, once you catch the basic principle, is the strict congruity between microcosm and macrocosm: between the inner world of personal spiritual striving and cosmogenesis on a far vaster scale. The tie-rod connecting them is a quality Boehme calls *Gelassenheit*, or "equanimity" (usually mistranslated as "resignation"). It literally means "letting-be-ness" and refers to the conscious laying down of the autonomous personal will. As Boehme puts it: "When you remain silent from the thinking and willing of self, the eternal hearing, seeing, and speaking will be revealed in you.... Your own hearing, willing and seeing hinder you so that you do not see and hear God."[3]

In modern spiritual terminology, this quality would easily be identifiable as *surrender,* and Boehme's spirituality quickly reveals itself to be operating in terrain already familiar to many modern seekers through practices such as Centering Prayer or interior witnessing.

Once this inner experiential benchmark has been established, it is a relatively small step to see that Boehme's remarkable cosmological vision is simply that same surrender process writ large. For Boehme, the laying down of the fiery, agitated personal will is not merely a pathway of personal holiness; it is also a *catalytic principle* that brings whole new worlds into existence. We shall see shortly how this is so.

I developed this whole idea at much greater length in an article called "Boehme for Beginners" published in *Gnosis* magazine in 1997 and still available for purchase through its online archive. For those who would like to spend more time with the spiritual practices themselves, I recommend your hunting it up.[4] The strict correspondence between inner and outer realms is not only a valuable experiential access point to Boehme, it is an additional confirmation that the Law of Three (which, as we have seen, remains consistent in every arena of application) is indeed lurking in the back of his mind.

For our present purposes, however, I want to stay focused on Boehme's cosmology, for it is on this foundation that I will construct my own model of the unfolding Trinity in part 3 of this book. As I stated earlier, I am convinced that Boehme's cosmogenetic revelation is intuitively ternary — and in fact, with a small bit of tweaking, can be brought into full alignment with the Law of Three and shown to unfold according to its dictates. If this is indeed the case, then Boehme is not only one of Christianity's greatest mystical geniuses, he is also its first ternary theologian and thus sets the cornerstones on which all subsequent expositions must rest. In this chapter I will present the vision "as is," in Boehme's own terms and as you will find it explicated by any number of Boehme scholars, medieval and contemporary. Then in the following chapter I will attempt to connect it explicitly to the Law of Three.

The Impressure of Nothing into Something

The words of the subheading above come from the next-to-last page of *Clavis* as Boehme offers his final summary, and in a single phrase they summarize the essence of his elaborate cosmology.[5] In the intricate brilliance of his mind, Boehme begins with a question that few have even conceived: How does one move from God at rest, from the "eternal, immense, incomprehensible Unity,"[6] to God the author of the multiplicity and diversity that is our created universe? For most, it is simple: God "spoke," and the world came to be. For Boehme it is not so simple. What had to happen internally, in the depths of the Godhead, before that first Fiat could be spoken? In Boehme's own words, how does "the Endless Unity bring itself into somethingness?"[7] In answer to that question, Boehme will lead us through three principles, subdivided into seven properties (sometimes also called forms), which bridge the gap between inaccessible and accessible light.

The First Principle

First property. Before anything can come into being, Boehme postulates, there must be movement ("outflow") in the "Endless Unity" of Divinity. This is accomplished by creating an "unequal pressure" in the equilibrium of the divine will through the *concentration* of desire. As he explains: "The first property is a desirousness, like the magnet, viz., the compression of the [divine] will; the will desires to be something, and yet it has nothing of which it may make something to itself; and therefore it brings itself into a receivingness of itself, and compresses itself to something; and that something is nothing but a magnetical hunger, a harshness."[8]

Boehme variously calls the first property "hardness," "harshness," "sharpness," "sourness." The core component is yearning, "magnetical hunger."

Second property. Where there is unequal pressure, things start to flow, as one can observe in siphoning water or in wind or weather systems. Boehme identifies this "drawing or motion in the sharpness"[9] as the second property, which he calls the "motion," the "stirring," and sometimes also the "sting" or the "astringency."

It is important to pay careful attention to what Boehme is saying here. I have read several spiritual commentators who tend rather glibly to equate these first two properties with the classic spiritual dualism of affirming and denying (whether Gurdjieffian or Hegelian). But Boehme's thinking is a bit more nuanced. The second property is not, strictly speaking, a contrary motion, such as in a tug-of-war. Rather, it comes closer to an inflammation, an *agitation created in and through the very insatiability of the desiring*. This is a subtle point but an important one. In Boehme the second property is not so much opposing the first as rushing toward it, like a whirlpool being sucked down a drain. The whirlpool is the motion, the second property.

   Third property. This leads directly to the third property, which Boehme calls "anguish." He explains: "For when there is a motion in the sharpness, then the property is the aching [or anguish], and this is also the cause of sensibility and pain, for if there were no sharpness and motion, there would be no sensibility."[10]

You have probably noticed by now how precipitously Boehme jumps between physical description and its emotional counterpart. In the first property "compressure" and "desire" are essentially the same motion playing in two different fields; in the second, "stirring" on a physical level registers as "stinging" on an emotional one. Now, in his great third associative leap, what would be "friction" on a physical level is immediately translated as "aching" or "anguish." Whether this associative tendency of his thinking intrigues or merely irritates you, it is nonetheless one mainstay of his integrative genius,[11] and the insight he has captured through this leap is really the key to his entire cosmology. What is born out of the struggle between desire and its insatiability is, to be sure, anguish. But this anguish is simultaneously *sensibility*, the capacity for self-reflective awareness. Boehme's explanation of how this happens is a stroke of pure genius:

> No thing may be revealed to itself without contrariety. If it has no thing that resists it, it always goes out from itself and does not go into itself again. If it does not go into itself again, as into that out of which it originally came, it knows nothing of its cause.[12]

In this third property divine nature becomes perceptible to itself; it goes "into that out of which it originally came" and knows itself from within. This is really *the* critical breakthrough, as we will see shortly.

These first three properties — shortly to explode into the fourth, fire — compose Boehme's First Principle. He calls it the "fiery" or "wrathful" principle and asserts that it belongs to the eternal nature of God.

This assertion has caused bewilderment and distress to many, who see Boehme straying here into a kind of ontological dualism in which good and evil are eternally pitted against each other in the very marrow of divine being. But Boehme's thinking is more subtle than that. To his mind the First Principle and the Second (the "light principle," which we will meet shortly) are not symmetrically balanced opposites. They are more like successive stages in the unfolding of a process whose final goal, you remember, is "the impressure of nothing into something." In order for outward and visible creation to emerge, the divine must undergo *a compression into somethingness,* and this entails a passage through the "fiery" matrix of desire and its frustration; hence Boehme's core cosmological principle: "Pain is the ground of motion."[13]

Boehme's First Principle is a catalytic process, not a permanent moral outcome. One commentator has perceptively argued that this "dark underbelly" of the divine process was never intended to be manifested in the visible world. In a creation untouched by the Fall, it would have remained hidden, safely locked up within divine love.[14]

Boehme reminds us, picturesquely, that "God has withstood his own anger, and with the center of his Heart, which fills all eternity…has broke the sting of the fierce wrath."[15]

From the perspective of the Law of Three, the thing that should most capture our attention here is that Boehme is thinking process, not ontology. "The impressure of nothing into something" is intrinsically a trajectory of new arising, and that is exactly how Boehme is seeing it.

The Second Principle

Boehme calls the Second Principle "the light principle." It is wrath transfigured by love. From the anguish (third property) we move directly to the *fourth property*, which Boehme calls "fire." He has two different sets of metaphors for describing this critical transition. The more accessible set pictures this property beginning as a spark ignited by friction — the friction being precisely the anguished striving on the wheel of contending set in motion by the first three properties. "For so," Boehme writes, "the eternal delight becomes perceivable, and this perceiving of the Unity is called love."[16]

I find this one of the most extraordinary sentences ever penned. While for many Christians the statement "God is love" is little more than a theological cliché, Boehme sees this love as the fruit of a dramatic, even outrageous, transformative process. Through the audacity of compressing desire into the friction of anguish, the flint is struck by which God's nature can manifest outwardly in the dimension of love, which becomes the *fifth property*. Boehme's love is not a preexistent divine attribute but more like a new alchemical compound that arises out of the interaction of the first four properties. It can come into manifestation in no other way.

As it emerges from its fiery ground, this love is a perfect image or mirror (or "counterstroke," Boehme's own preferred term) of the original Unity, only now in the dimension of perceptivity and "motion" — or in other words, with a newfound capacity to manifest itself through the myriad and diverse forms of individual createdness "so that there might be eternal play in the endless unity."[17] Thus, the appropriate divine matrix is established in which all creation will come to be. The fifth property quickly gives rise to the *sixth property*, "sound" (the divinely generative Word, or Logos, with which the familiar biblical narrative begins), and the *seventh property*, which Boehme calls "substance," or "nature," the primordial building block out of which the created universe is fashioned. Interestingly for Boehme, this "substance" is not simply a material but an active template that can reproduce itself. He makes it clear that this final property recapitulates all the others within itself. In modern terminology, we might characterize it as something like a "cosmogenetic DNA." It is a both a hologram of the original sevenfold emergence and a creative principle in itself.

The Third Principle

The Third Principle is the outward and visible universe. Boehme sees this visible world as a constant interplay between the First Principle and the Second Principle, and he reminds us that "the inward eternal working is hidden in the visible world"[18] and is always operative throughout it.

Superficially this may look like a Law of Three triad, but upon closer inspection we see that it is not quite so simple. While the First and Second Principles clearly function in a manner closely analogous to first and second force, the outer world is not in and of itself holy reconciling. For Boehme, that catalytic role is played by the spiritual property we met up with earlier in this chapter: Gelassenheit, or "equanimity"—that is, the surrendered will. The untransformed human soul, or egoic self, has its origins, according to Boehme, in the fire principle. If, during the time of its earthly life, it continues to remain in that principle, living exclusively by its own disordered desiring, it essentially fails to germinate and ends exactly where it began. By bringing its fiery beginnings (first force) into interplay with the transformed light (second force) by means of the surrendered will (third force), it essentially emerges itself as that "fourth in a new dimension": a whole new creation. Our task—actually our supreme invitation as human beings—is to forge this counterstroke of ourselves: to give birth to true Self, the child of both First and Second principles, who alone can carry back to God "the wonders you have wrought and found out here."[19]

As I remarked earlier, the significance of Boehme's work lies in the perfect melding of the macrocosm and the microcosm, the cosmic process and one's own spiritual path. In both, the journey passes through the same narrow spot: the transformation of anguish. Boehme's deep humanity, as well as his spiritual genius, lies in his implicitly ternary understanding that will, desire, and pain are not obstacles to spiritual perfection but rather the raw materials out of which something yet more wondrous will be fashioned. Thus, these things are not to be feared, denied, or eradicated; they are to be *transformed*. Boehme's practical spiritual teaching falls effortlessly into a classic Law of Three configuration in which *soul* (the fire principle; first force) and *spirit* (the light principle; second force), mediated by *conscious surrender* (third force) calls into being Self, "the bush that burns but is not consumed." It is a counterstroke of its old fiery self but now manifesting in the dimension of light. Boehme's Third Principle, the visible universe, must thus be seen not as an artifact but as an ongoing dynamism, Like that burning bush, it manifests only as long as it remains actively connected to its dual generative principles.

The Threefold Source in Everything

For an ostensibly ternary thinker, Boehme's Trinitarian theology per se falls curiously flat. My own suspicion is that it was not a part of his original 1600 revelation but belongs to later levels of overlay as he attempts to connect his vision to known theological reference points. Like most Western Christians, he makes a beeline for the "persons" understood as psycho-spiritual entities and exerts much effort, only semisuccessfully, in trying to match up their traditional spiritual "personalities" with the dynamically interweaving forces he is already perceiving as the true driveshaft of cosmogenesis.

Every so often, however, something of a different order emerges as he returns to his own visionary ground. In *The Forty Questions of the Soul*, for example, in the midst of a lengthy discussion of the fifth property of the divine will, he abruptly states:

> As there is a threefold source in everything, and each is always the glass [image], begetter, and cause of the other, nothing excepted, all things are according to the essence of the Ternary.[20]

Gurdjieff himself could not have put it more precisely.

Beneath Boehme's often fluctuating grasp of how the three persons of the Trinity correlate with the "threefold working" of God, he never loses touch with his basic insight that the Trinity is somehow the manifesting principle that enables the "Eternal Unity" to project itself outwardly and to bring everything else into existence. As he succinctly expresses it toward the end of *Clavis:* "God is the eternal, immense, incomprehensible Unity, which manifests itself in itself from eternity in eternity by the Trinity."[21]

It is in Boehme's "three principles, seven properties" rather than in his Trinitarian theology per se that he most clearly reveals himself to be on a closing course with the Law of Three. First and most obvious is his attunement to the dynamism itself: his awareness that "the impressure of nothing into something" is a process with stages, not simply an instantaneous divine fiat. As I have clarified already, Boehme's First, or "wrathful," Principle is not ontological dualism; rather, it functions exactly in accordance with the Law of Three as one of the legitimate forces required for a new arising to occur. It is a necessary precondition for the manifestation of love, "the perceiving of the Unity" — or in other words, the Unity imbued with self-reflective awareness and the capacity to express itself in diversity and motion. A knowledge of the Law of Three allows us to grasp more firmly the extremely nuanced nature of what Boehme is unfolding here. His idea of creation as a self-unfolding process, bringing itself forth out of a recombination of its essential working properties, is at least three centuries ahead of his time and unparalleled anywhere else in mystical cosmology.

If we examine his "three principles, seven properties" more closely, we notice that he has also implicitly designated three stages of what we might call "protocreation" before the visible world comes into existence; in fact, his entire cosmological vision essentially unfolds entirely within this protodomain. In the *first stage,* properties one, two, and three interact to produce the fourth, fire. In the *second stage,* fire undergoes its own virtually instantaneous transformation to emerge as light/love, the fifth property; this in turn catalyzes the *third stage,* in which the two remaining properties, sound and substance, are generated, the latter containing the template for recapitulating the entire sequence. Only after this full set of prop-erties has run its gamut can the Third Principle, the visible world, actually come into existence; in Boehme's vision, what the Bible calls "in the beginning" is actually the fourth stage of an already ongoing cosmic process.

That, of course, got me intrigued. If there is indeed a process going on here whose outcome seems to be successive new arisings, could these properties, in fact, be combining according to the Law of Three? What if Boehme's seven properties are not simply an a priori numerical sequence but in fact arise one out of another according to that now-familiar principle *the interweaving of three produces a fourth in a new dimension?* In other words, what if the first four properties somehow take on the roles of affirming, denying, and reconciling among themselves to give birth to the fifth property, and if it, in turn, becomes the new holy reconciling for the sixth, and the sixth for the seventh? What if Boehme's vast cosmogenetic vision is in fact unfolding according to the Law of Three?

Boehme does not seem to notice this; it is not on his radar screen. But if it could be demonstrated, without doing violence to his think-ing, that the process he is describing through his intuitive vision-ary brilliance is actually subsumed within the Law of Three, then we might see, behind this great Christian ternary metaphysician, an even greater hand moving the pen.

8

Seven Properties, Three Forces

MY LONG-STANDING HUNCH that the Law of Three might, in fact, prove to be the underlying operative in Boehme's complex cosmology was triggered by more than just the superficial coincidence of the numbers seven and three. It emerged from a deeper intuition that if Boehme's visionary download indeed originated from the level of Objective Truth (as Gurdjieff would call it), and if Gurdjieff's dual laws of World Creation and World Maintenance also belong to that same causal plane, then they must necessarily confirm each other — at least, they cannot directly contradict.

Obviously we are again talking about imaginal causality here, since Boehme predated Gurdjieff by a good three hundred years and in the linear stream the two systems appear to be apples and oranges. The challenge is further compounded by the fact that Boehme himself is not consistent in his description of the sevenfold cosmogonic process or in his presentation of how the Trinity actually functions as a ternary principle. His *Clavis, Forty Questions of the Soul*, and *Three Principles of the Divine Essence* all record slightly variant interpretive maps, with the tension always emerging at the clash point between Boehme's own intuition of a divine dynamism and the much more static categories available to him in traditional esoteric and theological thought.

And yet, at the risk of forcing the fit, I believe it is worth pursuing this imaginal connection to see whether Boehme's boldly original and at first glance idiosyncratic cosmology can, in fact, be brought into conformance with the Law of Three. What's really at stake here — aside from simply strengthening my own case about ternary metaphysics — is that I believe the Law of Three can help clarify what Boehme is instinctively groping toward and make his teaching both more accessible and more coherent. Simply put, Boehme's account of "the impressure of nothing into something" is already far and away the best creation story available to us in the West, the only one to account successfully for the origin of evil without setting up a cosmological dualism or else transferring the blame onto humanity (under the guise of free will). His process-oriented cosmology, in which wrath is not a permanent ontological principle but simply the first step toward the alchemical emergence of "somethingness," is a profound theological achievement, and against the backdrop of the Law of Three it rings even more true. With this law in place as a primary interpretive frame, it would be much easier to rescue Boehme from the aura of esotericism that is so intimidating to many readers and resituate him as the rightful patriarch of Christian ternary metaphysics, where his contribution is sorely needed.

Toward the end of this book I will comment further on how this connection also builds a bridge between Boehme and some of the conversation currently under way at the leading edge of theoretical physics, where the question "What conditions would have had to preexist in order to bring about the big bang?" is yielding calculations remarkably congruent with Boehme's three-stage "proto-creation" described briefly in the previous chapter and about to be fleshed out more fully here. While the importance of this may not fully register yet, I am personally convinced that it holds a significant piece of the puzzle toward healing the schism between biblical and scientific cosmology that has crippled the Christian religious imagination for more than five hundred years.

My objective in this chapter, then, is to demonstrate that the sevenfold progression by which Boehme unfolds his impressure of nothing into something is not simply a mathematical sequence but bears the signature "braiding" pattern of the Law of Three. To accomplish this, I will first need to show that his fifth property (his "Light- World," or "Love") is a genuine new arising created by the interweaving of the first four properties. With this piece in place, the next task is to show how the two remaining properties — sound and substance — also emerge as successive Law of Three arisings.

What I am about to share with you here is still in some ways a work in progress. When I first recognized that the Trinity could be "unfolded" according to the Law of Three, Boehme's cosmology was instinctively in the back of my head as a prototype, but it took a long while for a feedback loop to emerge between them. As I gradually learned (largely by trial and error) how to wrestle Boehme's seven properties into three successive new arisings according to the Law of Three, I was also discovering the basic principles that would govern my own metaphysical expansion of the Trinity in part 3. So this chapter is not just a summary of how I solved the riddle but will also introduce some of the basic conventions I will be using in part 3 and will give us our first run-up on "turning" the Trinity according to the Law of Three.

Setting Up the Triangle

Let me begin by introducing our basic visual: a triangle with the three forces — affirming, denying, reconciling — assigned to the triadic points as follows:

This convention is substantially but not entirely arbitrary. It is the format I will be using throughout part 3, and my reason for placing *denying* at the peak will become clear shortly. When I worked through this material with my Wisdom School students, many of them preferred to invert the triangle (peak down), and this is fine as well, though personally I prefer the solidity and balance of the triangle right side up.

In the center is the new arising created by the interaction of the three forces.

The numbers you will shortly see in parentheses at each of these three triadic points (and in the center) refer to Boehme's seven properties, which are, as you recall:

1. Desiring (attraction)
2. Agitation (stinging, breaking)
3. Anguish
4. Fire
5. Light
6. Sound
7. Substance

From here on, it is simply a matter of filling in the blanks, the respective points of each triangle.

FIRST STAGE

AGITATION (2) *denying*

LIGHT
(5)

re concealing

ANGUISH/
FIRE (3, 4)

Density

DESIRING
(*ATTRACTION*) (1)

In this initial triad the matching of properties to triadic corners comes straight out of Boehme's own narrative. Desire, or *attraction* — the "compressure of the Divine Will" — takes the role of first force. *Agitation* (my summary of Boehme's descriptors of "stinging, breaking, dividing") takes the role of second force. We saw in the last chapter how it is not strictly an *opposing* holy denying but more an aggravating and intensifying holy denying, which renders the attraction all the more insatiable. The result, nevertheless, is oppositional: what is wanted cannot be attained.

The third, or reconciling force, then, becomes Boehme's third property: *anguish* — which for him, remember, is also the headwaters of "perceptibility and feelingness." As he explains in *Clavis*:

> The third property of the eternal nature is the anguish, viz. that will which has brought itself into the receivingness to nature and somethingness: when the own will stands in the sharp motion, then it comes into anguish, that is into sensibility.... For if the feeling were not, the will could know nothing.[1]

The all-important point here, you recall, is that for Boehme anguish is not just an emotion, a physical turmoil. It contains within it the actual headwaters of reflective consciousness; *anguish is a primordial state of self-awareness.* It is for this reason that this third is not merely a sequential third but a third force mediating between two things locked in an unbreakable impasse at the purely physical level.

Or, rather, anguish *becomes* a primordial state of awareness. There is a before-and-after component to Boehme's presentation: a "before," when the anguish is merely physical friction, and an "after," when it explodes into authentic perceptivity. In his various renditions Boehme refers to this moment as a "cracking noise" or "flash," analogous to a spark cast off by rubbing two stones together.[2] What happens next is pretty much an unbroken explosion or *whoosh* — Boehme's own version of the cosmological big bang — as physical friction awakening to itself as anguish ignites a spark that leads to *fire* (the fourth property) and immediately on to *light* (the fifth).

The challenge in Boehme's schematic, at least in terms of wrestling it into alignment with the Law of Three, is that the third, forth, and fifth properties are essentially a single trajectory. The spark that ignites the fire emerges from within the anguish and proceeds directly to light. Thus, to decide where one property leaves off and the next begins is in some sense arbitrary. Nor is Boehme himself entirely consistent on the matter. While his narrative explanation apportions the properties as I have just described, the accompanying diagram (*Clavis*, p. 32) slices the deck in a slightly different way. Here desiring (attraction) and stinging (agitation) are combined into a single first property (affirming);[3] anguish becomes the second property (denying), and fire moves into the role of third force, continuing to "burn rapidly" through a combined third/fourth property to land us at light, which is again our first new arising.

This alternative first triad would thus look like this:

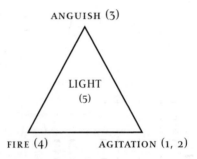

ANGUISH (3)

LIGHT
(5)

FIRE (4)   AGITATION (1, 2)

Since both variations originate with Boehme himself, we will keep them both on the table for a while. In either case, they wind up in the same place. The new arising is Light. It is his Second Principle, that which has emerged out of the alchemical transformation of the First or "Fire" Principle, which he also names "Wrath."

In Boehme's own terminology, this new arising (which he also variously describes as "the Light–World," "Light/Love," "Wisdom," and "Love") is a *counterstroke*: an authentic double of the Original — the Unity or "Endless Liberty" or God — only now manifesting in the dimension of separability and perceptivity. I will have more to say about counterstroke in the next chapter.

The Seven Forms of Spirits, mentioned Revel. Chap. 1.

♄	The First	Harsh Desiring Will
☽	Second	Bitter or Stinging
♃	Third	Anguish, till the Flash of Fire
♀	Fourth } Form	Fire { Dark-Fire / Light-Fire
☉	Fifth	Light or Love, whence the water of Eternal Life floweth
♂	Sixth	Noise, Sound, or Mercury
♀	Seventh	Substance or Nature
♃		
☽		
♄		

1. Dark-World; a similitude of it is a candle.

2. Fire-World; a similitude of it is the fire of a candle.

3. Light-World; a similitude of it is the light of a candle.

The First Principle.

The Dark-World: hence God the Father is called an Angry, Zealous, and a Jealous God, and a Consuming Fire.

Dark or Fire of Wrath

The Second Principle.

The Light-World: hence God the Son, the Word, the Heart of God, is called a Loving and Merciful God.

Light or Fire of Love

The Third Principle.

This World of four Elements, which is produced out of the two Inward Worlds, and is a Glass of them; wherein Light and Darkness, Good and Evil are mixed, it is not Eternal, but hath a Beginning and an End.

SECOND STAGE

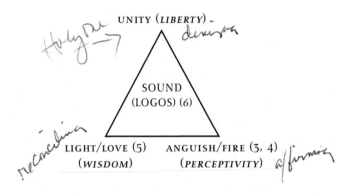

This second triad may surprise you. Our task here is to demonstrate how sound, Boehme's sixth property, emerges as the next
Law of Three arising out of the ingredients already on hand. But
you will immediately notice a discrepancy. The base of the triangle does indeed give us 3-4 (anguish/fire, alias perceptivity) as the
new affirming, and 5 (light/love) as the new reconciling. But 1-2
(attraction/agitation) seems to have disappeared from the equation
altogether, and in the role of denying I have placed the term *Unity*
(*Liberty*), which is not one of the seven properties at all but rather
the undifferentiated ground out of which the whole sequence has
emerged. What am I thinking here?

The answer is simple. From my work with the Trinity material, I learned that in order to make the calculations come out right
both theologically and mathematically, it was necessary to portray
clearly that the Holy One — Boehme's Endless Unity or Eternal Liberty — continues to *participate directly* in every new cosmogenetic arising. Failing to make this corrective, one quickly falls into a kind of
emanationist schematic, where with every new procession from the
Source, the Source itself gets further and further removed from the
field of action, until gradually it is written out of the equation altogether. The theology wanders off the mark, and the theorum itself (A
opposed to B, mediated by C, yields D in a new dimension) ceases to
yield up meaningful statements.

It took me a long while to come to this discovery, but when I did, the pieces quickly fell into place. As soon as the Endless Unity was introduced directly back into the formula as a kind of divine "Planck's constant," the picture cleared up; Boehme's sevenfold cosmology fell into line with the Law of Three, and the rest of the pattern emerged.[4]

You may wonder why I placed this "Planck's constant" at the denying pole (why not affirming or reconciling?). The reason, which you can no doubt ground-truth in your heart, is that the tug toward the endless infinite — back to Source — is always at work in everything, quietly eroding its illusory permanence. Hence denying seemed to be the correct positioning.[5]

Translated into a Law of Three proposition then, this second triad reveals that the Fire-world (anguish, God's *utfus*, or "out-eager," will), in tension with the Unity (the drawing back toward that primordial oneness) but now mediated through the Light-world (reflective consciousness, wisdom, and love), gives rise to what Boehme calls "sound": a Logos or fundamental ordering principle from which all will be created. And that does indeed seem to be a valid statement both theologically and experientially.

THIRD STAGE

As the pattern settles in, Unity continues to hold its place as the ever-present denying. Sound, the new arising from the former triad,

moves into the role of reconciling, while light, the former reconciling, now moves into the affirming position. (We will discover what
happens to the former affirming — "anguish/perceptivity" — in due
course.) This is again in accordance with one of the basic conventions I came upon while working with the Trinity, which you will
meet directly (and with a fuller explanation) in part 3.

This third stage then, when read according to the Law of Three,
makes the following, rather extraordinary, prediction. It suggests
that when *Inaccessible Light* (another way of describing the Endless
Unity, or undifferentiated Oneness) and *Reflected Light* (another way
of describing Wisdom, that basic mirroring awareness created in our
first triad) are brought together through a fundamental ordering
principle (Sound, or Logos), the result is Substance, the headwaters
of "somethingness." Out of this final property, Boehme makes clear,
the visible world (his Third Principle) will come into being. That is a
remarkable statement in its own right — well worth taking the time
to wrap your mind around — but even more, it is a remarkably con-
cise summary of Boehme's complex cosmological calculations. For
in essence, he is saying exactly this: that Oneness must first project
itself into twoness ("take perceptivity and divisibility" is his specific wording)[6] in order for anything to come into being. But having
undergone that initial separation, it must then bridge the gap in a
way that respects the integrity of both states and relieves the tension
of their inherent contrariety through the dynamism of new arisings.
That is Boehme in a nutshell. It is also the Law of Three in a nutshell.

I will have more to say about these first three triads in part 3. You
will notice at that point that with only the smallest of modifications
I have essentially imported them as the first three stages of my own
seven-stage Trinitarian unfolding. This at least gives me some sense
of having a foundation beneath me: while Boehme is not exactly
what you'd call mainstream Christian orthodoxy, at least I am not
simply building castles in the air. While you may have to move back
and forth a few times between this chapter and my presentation in
part 3 before deciding whether this attempt to reframe Boehme's
cosmology according to the Law of Three really holds water, I think

it can at least be established that there is enough energy flowing between these two visionary streams to warrant a continuing conversation. Boehme may not have known the Law of Three, but in some way it seems to have known him, and in the very allusiveness of that connection, a whole new world of imaginal insight opens up.

9

Counterstroke

AS MENTIONED EARLIER, Jacob Boehme was a shoemaker by trade, and it was not through theological reflection but from the directly embodied act of punching his awl through leather to fashion a pair of shoes that he came to grasp the principle he called *Gegenwurf*. The word literally means "counterstroke," or "counter throw," and the usual scholarly translations of this word as "figure" or "similitude" do little more than render Boehme's meaning largely unintelligible.

Perhaps not many of us nowadays have worked with an awl and punch, but if you've ever sewn a hem, you've essentially had the same experience. As you move your needle through the cloth, you'll notice that there is an initial downstroke to push the thread through to the underside of the cloth, then an upstroke to bring it back through again to the upper side (or if you're a more experienced seamstress than I, you'll start on the underside, where the loose ends are hidden). This second stroke is the Gegenwurf, the counterstroke, and Boehme's remarkable metaphysical principle is fundamentally no more complex than that.

It's the same thing, of course, in drawing a violin bow or adjusting the pistons in a race car. The full cycle consists of a downstroke and an upstroke, which are simply two different phases of one unified motion. But the sewing (or shoemaking) metaphor adds an important additional element: the cloth. And if we focus our attention here, we'll notice a couple of things about this downstroke/upstroke motion that may escape the attention of the violinist or auto mechanic: (1) the thread remains the same whether it's on the topside or the underside, (2) but as thread goes through cloth, it creates distinctly different patterns on top and bottom: a truism humorously captured in an anonymous piece of folk wisdom known as The Weaver's Prayer:

> Dear Lord, my life looks like a mess of tangled knots and loose threads. But that's because I only see the underside.[1]

Once you get this into your fingers, you have everything you need to crack the principle of Gegenwurf, Boehme's stunning metaphysical alternative to the classic Neoplatonic principle of emanationism.

In the Neoplatonic model, you recall, the original of a thing — its ideal form or archetype — exists on a higher plane, and as one moves downward along the great chain of being, the reflections become more and more distant mirrors of the original (this according to the principle of redshift we explored earlier). The reflective principle is essentially passive, and with each successive iteration, something of the original vibrancy is lost. This is the classic "visual" understanding of the relationship between the original and its "figure" or "image" in traditional metaphysics.

While the name of Black Elk would hardly come to mind as a primary exemplar of traditional metaphysics, I have never seen this reflective principle more vividly described than in his following haunting vignette:

> I looked about me and saw that what we were doing just then was like a shadow cast on earth from yonder vision in the heaven, so bright it was, so clear. I saw that the real was yonder and the darkened dream of it was here.[2]

In Boehme's model, by contrast, stroke and counterstroke are symmetrical phases of a single, unbroken cycle whose active agent, the thread, remains constant throughout. But the same thread operating successively on two different planes (topside and underside) does in fact create two strikingly different visual patterns on the cloth. Both authentically replicate their phase of the motion, *but they are not replicas of each other.* That is why the words *similitude* and *figure* by which Gegenwurf is typically translated are misleading, for they suggest a copy or mirror image of the original (like the reflection of the moon in a still pond), while one would be hard put to say that the erratic pattern one finds on the underside of the cloth looks anything at all like the orderly row of stitches on the top. There is a connection between them, of course, but to see it you have to stay with the thread.

Counterstroke and the Law of Three

The introduction of the cloth, or *plane of manifestation*, into the equation adds a distinct ternary thrust to what is otherwise a solidly binary principle. Again, you can see this for yourself simply by staying with my sewing metaphor. It makes a difference whether one is on the topside or underside, whether one is passing a needle through cloth or punching through leather with an awl, whether the cloth is rough or smooth, calico or gingham. The same thread will create very different results in different materials.

If this sounds to you like a setup for the Law of Three, you're right. And if you pay careful attention to what Boehme is actually saying, you can once again see his intuitive gravitation toward a ternary scenario. Fundamentally, I would say that for Boehme the plane of manifestation tends to function as third force, connecting the holy affirming of the divine yearning for form with the holy denying of the essentially formless and indivisible nature of divinity. In its role as holy reconciling, the plane of manifestation offers itself not only as a playing field for the divine action but as an essential line of force in the action itself.

Thus, when Boehme writes that Wisdom is "a subject and resemblance of the infinite and unsearchable Unity"[3] he is not thinking in terms of a visual resemblance or image (in fact, he did not use the words *subject* and *resemblance* at all; he used *Gegenwurf*). What he means is that the infinite and unsearchable Unity, *when it punches through into its initial plane of manifestation* (which, as we have seen from our earlier discussion, is "perceptivity") *will manifest as Wisdom*.

And this is, in fact, exactly the process he describes in the emergence of his Second Principle (which he variously describes as "the Light-World," "Wisdom," and "Love") out of the primordial ground of anguish/perceptivity. Wisdom is not a *copy* of the original but an altogether new arising (Boehme repeatedly calls it an "effluence" or "outflowing"). It bears witness to the original "infinite and unsearchable Unity" in the same way that topside and underside bear witness to the single trajectory of the needle, but it adds its own distinct flavor and "tincture" (as Boehme calls it) to the mix. And at the same time — in accordance with the stipulation that the interweaving of three creates a fourth in a new dimension — it presents itself not only as the *product* of this interweaving but as a new *plane* on which and through which the Law of Three can continue to play out, or in other words, as third force for yet another round of manifestation. The Wisdom that has arisen as the counterstroke to the "unsearchable Unity" will itself become the new "cloth" that the thread of the divine will "punch through," creating yet again a new manifestation and a new plane. And on and on it goes.

As you work with Boehme, it is important always to make this ternary compensation. His Gegenwurf is not a simple backstroke, the completion of a motion on a single plane; it always implies the emergence into a new dimension. Wisdom is not simply a *reflection* of the divine Unity, like a moon in a still pond. It is the actual divine Unity itself as realized in the dimension (plane) of perceptivity.

As I mentioned earlier, Boehme uses a variety of terms more or less interchangeably to describe this all-important first counterstroke: *Wisdom, Light, Light/Love,* or simply *Love.* Thus, he is essentially tracing the same cosmogenetic process when he makes that astonishing statement that so captured my attention earlier: "[The] perceiving of the Unity is called love." Translated into Law of Three language, it reads: "The divine Unity, when it manifests in the dimension of perceptivity (or as we would more readily say today, within the domain of consciousness) manifests as love." Same unity, different expressions.

In part 3 I will be adopting the term *counterstroke* to designate each of the successive new arisings that emerge when the Trinity is set in motion according to the Law of Three. Each one of these counter-strokes (there are seven altogether) is a new and unique realization of that original unity as it manifests itself on a succession of playing fields generated by the Law of Three. I will also introduce you to a secondary counterstroke pattern at work (between the new arising of one triad and the holy affirming of the former triad) which establishes an important second line of bearing.

Beyond Ascent and Descent

You can see how Boehme's notion of counterstroke deftly fulfills our blueshift stipulation that God does not lose energy as God moves outward and downward through the realms along the great chain of being. Like the thread, the quality and quantity of divine beingness remains always the same and always fully participatory. It does not get "more" as one travels up the chain or "less" as one travels down it. Each of these realms, which come into existence as the "law-conformable" result of the play of the Law of Three against the divine yearning for self-disclosure, is simply a field for the revelation of *the whole of God in that particular dimension*. The intrinsic dynamism of the Law of Three provides the forward motion that drives the blueshift.

In fact, you might say that the revolutionary impact of Boehme's insight here, at least as far as traditional metaphysics is concerned, is that it cuts through the notion of "up" and "down" altogether. Ascent and descent are no longer opposite spiritual directions but simply the stroke and counterstroke of a single motion, always headed in the same direction: toward an ever-fresh and inexhaustibly vibrant revelation of the divine heart. Rather than drawing all things back "up" the chain of being to a reunion with their spiritual origin, it corkscrews its way "forward" through space/time toward successively more intricate and concentrated articulations of the "wonders" (as Boehme calls them) veiled within the Endless Unity.

And that would indeed furnish the metaphysical milieu for that luminous insight from Bruno Barnhart that I quoted earlier:

There is a secret in the heart of life that is not only the unmoving white light. It is not only the still point of the turning world, not only the light-filled empty center. It is also the lion of fire, the unceasing explosion of expansive being, of proliferating life, from the center. It is the fontal energy that demands to express itself everywhere and through every form.[4]

It also furnishes the mechanics by which we can begin to get a handle on Teilhard de Chardin's challenging notion of the Omega Point. His profound — and profoundly unsettling — revelation, you recall, is that within an implicitly fontal metaphysical ground, the phenomenon of increasing density is not so much a sign of spiritual fall (into lower realms) as it is an indication of *the increasing concentration of spiritual energy as the form nears the implosion that is also its final consummation.* Within the givens of classical metaphysics, this notion simply does not compute. But with the Law of Three to demonstrate how each new arising does in turn become the plane of manifestation for a yet more articulated counterstroke of itself, the mechanics of Teilhard's mystical intuition at last become fathomable. I will be drawing on these same mechanics in my own exposition, and they do indeed appear to confirm the direction in which Teilhard was headed.

Part Three

THE UNFOLDING TRINITY

10

The Essential Ground Rules

CONSIDER THIS A GAME, if you'd like, a kind of cosmic Rubik's Cube. Using that basic stipulation of the Law of Three—the interweaving of three creates a fourth in a new dimension—I propose to "rotate" the Trinity in successive stages until by following its own intrinsic pattern it comes to its completion.

Not surprisingly, given the affinity between the Law of Three and the Law of Seven, this progression unfolds as a seven-stage pattern, an "octave" of Trinities. Within this vastly expanded Trinitarian galaxy, there is room for all of those speculative quandaries that have so long bedeviled theologians—the place of the feminine, the relationship between the human Jesus and the divine Logos, the gender of the Holy Spirit, the immanent versus the "economic" Trinity—to find their rightful place.

I began this game with a single rule: "three creates a fourth in a new dimension." By assigning each of the three triadic points not to a "person" but to a function according to the Law of Three (affirming, denying, reconciling), I was indeed able to generate a series of seven new arisings. These are Heart of God, Word, Substantiality, Jesus, Holy Spirit, Kingdom of Heaven, Oikonomia. I will explain what each one of these means in due course, but for now I can simply confirm that they each arise logically and organically out of the interweaving of their respective triadic points.

Following the further stipulation that "every triad can give rise to another triad"[1] I then began to plug these new arisings back into the mix as one of the three triadic points of the newly arisen Trinity. Although the Law of Three allows any point to assume any of the three functions, I soon discovered that the way this particular series seemed to want to work out was if the new arising from the former triad assumed the role of third force, or holy reconciling, in the new triad. The determining factor here proved to be what mathematicians call "elegance": the pattern thereby generated was simple, self-consistent, and profoundly congruent with known reference points in Christian mystical theology. So that became my second rule.

3) My third rule was a decision perhaps arbitrarily made: that the second triadic point, holy denying (or as I rename it, Unmanifest) would always be directly occupied by God: by that infinite, superessential reality that traditional mystical theology might call the "Godhead" and that Boehme alternatively names as "the Endless Unity" and "the Eternal Liberty." I have already explained my reasoning here in our earlier discussion of Boehme (page 112). The decision was made partly on theological grounds, to avoid falling into an emanationist pattern in which God becomes progressively more distant from creation. But it was also made on practical grounds: doing it that way yielded up a sequence of predicative statements about each respective Trinity that rang strong and true theologically and in fact often shed new light on long-standing theological quandaries. So that became my third rule.

The application of these three conventions yielded the basic pattern that I earlier likened to turning a Rubik's Cube: former new arising moves to holy reconciling, holy denying remains constant, former holy reconciling now moves to holy affirming. (This will be easier to visualize when we actually get into the process and the diagrams are before you.) Those of you blessed with a stronger visual imagination than my own will see immediately that this means that with every new arising, a former holy affirming will be displaced and apparently disappear out of the succeeding triad. But this is only apparently the case, for as I gradually discovered, it reemerges in the next triad as the distinctive flavor of the new arising — its "tincture," as Boehme would call it: the quality of its aliveness. Thus, the new arising becomes the counterstroke of the former (now displaced) holy affirming. This yields not only a fascinating theological counterpoint but also a second line of bearing by which it becomes possible to check the accuracy of the calculations generated by those first three rules. On page 131 I have provided a table of the counterstrokes that will allow you to glimpse this pattern as a whole as well as to keep track of where we are at any given point in the sequence.

Each new arising, then, takes its turn in the next Trinity as holy reconciling. In terms of Boehme's shoemaker metaphor, it becomes the "cloth" (or leather) on which stroke and counterstroke can carve their unique designs. While I have likened this process to turning a Rubik's Cube, it is, in fact, much more like turning a kaleidoscope, in which each turn creates stunning and intricate new patterns from the shimmering fragments of glass.

I do not claim that this is the only possible way to unfold the Trinity according to the Law of Three. On a mere seven notes, an infinite variety of melodies can be played. But it is a *good* way to do it, one that aligns particularly well with Christianity's own best self-understanding and with events observable in our own times. Taken across its sevenfold wingspan, this expansive Trinity gradually unfolds a majestic progression from Alpha to Omega, from cosmic beginnings to the ultimate regathering of all things into One. It is "the universe story" told in three dimensions: not only along a horizontal axis in space/time but also along a vertical one in the hidden purposiveness of the divine heart.

> He has made known to us his hidden purpose
> made so kindly in Christ from the beginning
> to be effected when the time was ripe
> that all heaven and earth be brought together
> in unity through Christ.
> —Ephesians 1:12

With the help of the Law of Three, that is the Trinitarian wingspan I am going to try to unfold here.

Once again I would ask you to keep in mind that we have shifted gears here; the domain I am working in is no longer systematic theology but something much more akin to metaphysical poetry. We are in the right brain now more than the left. My goal is not to enforce a particular solution upon you but to invite your own spiritual imagination to engage.

Each of the following seven chapters consists of an orientation to the particular Trinity in question, followed by a reflection on its spiritual significance. I invite you to approach them lectio divina style (analytical mind quiet, imagination attuned) and see what your heart tells you.

The Law of Seven?

Before we embark on this journey, I realize that there is one remaining aspect of my methodology that may puzzle you and that I need to address directly. What about the Law of Seven? Has it simply disappeared out of the picture? Gurdjieff made clear that there are two cosmic laws, not one, and that they are intended to intermesh. In chapter 4 I took the contemporary enneagram of personality movement to task for failing to demonstrate this intermeshing in its teaching. And yet in the entire exploration shortly to follow, you will probably notice that I seem to have set the Law of Seven aside altogether and based my calculations exclusively on the internal dynamism of the Law of Three. Do I not stand convicted of exactly the same thing I was complaining about?

True enough, and I will not deny the charges. I would simply ask you to take into consideration the following mitigating factors.

First, simply from a practical standpoint, the interweaving of three and seven makes the project I am taking on here so mindbogglingly complex that it runs the risk of the whole thing's collapsing. For my primary audience — whom I take to be predominantly Christian-based readers seeking to explore a wider metaphysical universe — the most important goal is to demonstrate that the model can work at all: that the Trinity can indeed "expand" and "turn." Since the time of Augustine, we have been so stuck in substance theology — in our fixation upon three eternal and changeless "persons" with specific identities and functions — that it is very difficult to begin to think in terms of movement, particularly three-dimensional movement. As we saw in chapter 6, I believe that a number of modern theologians are now well on their way toward intuiting the basic dynamism but have lacked a metaphysical framework in which to carry their insights forward. My main goal here has simply been to "connect the dots," calling upon the Law of Three to fill in the basic mechanics that indeed support the vision of the Trinity as a dynamic template of divine love stamped into a self-creating world. That is itself a tall order, and I do not want to risk losing the forest for the trees.

The full Gurdjieffian system is extraordinary, but it is also extremely complicated, with its own formidable jargon and a pronounced tendency to draw its devotees down an intellectual rabbit hole. It simply does not open itself outwardly, and most people do not have the patience to find their way inside — particularly people whose goal is not to master the entire Gurdjieff corpus but only to learn what leverage this body of teaching might bring to bear on some difficult logjams in contemporary Christian thought. To insist on an all-or-nothing approach to the two cosmic laws would most likely bring the entire inquiry to a screeching halt. I knew that working with the Law of Three in isolation would inevitably be a simplification, but it was a risk that had to be taken in order to engage a discussion at all.

As I worked with the materials, however, my confidence grew that this simplification is not necessarily falsification. I have now begun to see it more as what philosophers call a "heuristic": a shorthand solution that nevertheless gives an accurate approximation of the full resolution. "The interweaving of three creates a fourth in a new dimension" turns out to be a pretty effective heuristic. It allows people to get an immediate handle on the Law of Three and to begin working with it practically in their lives. And frankly — though I realize that an argument from silence is always less than fully persuasive — Gurdjieff never said that the Law of Three could *not* be used this way. While the bulk of his recorded teaching concentrates on the interweaving of Three and Seven, each law has its valid internal rhythm and its own domain of application. The domain of the Law of Seven is to explain how temporal process unfolds once a new arising has occurred. The domain of the Law of Three is to show how new arisings occur in the first place. Thus, it seemed defensible to explore this law separately, particularly since the domain I am investigating in these reflections is cosmogenesis, which is entirely about new arising.

One question you may find yourself asking as my seven-stage Trinity unfolds over the course of these pages is *What determines the length of a stage?* Some of these trinities seem to stretch for timeless aeons. Others — my fourth and fifth, for example — are extremely brief, encompassed entirely within the gestation and human life of Jesus. While I have not developed the idea systematically, my immediate answer would be "The Law of Seven!" Once a new *do* is struck — once the newly arisen counterstroke turns the kaleidoscope to a new configuration — I suspect that the process thereby set in motion plays out according to the Law of Seven, with the duration of each new configuration determined by the vibrational quality and strength of that initial new *do*. In each of these Trinitarian "octaves," the Law of Three and the Law of Seven are no doubt interplaying in exactly the same way as stipulated in the full Gurdjieffian teaching, and the various stages can no doubt be demonstrated. But I leave that to better heads than my own.

Finally, though, I developed my material the way I did because the master symbol of Christianity is the Trinity, not the enneagram. Gurdjieff himself indicated this much in his teaching on "Holy God, Holy the Firm, Holy the Immortal" in *Beelzebub's Tales*,[2] and I can only trust that there is not only truth but much practical wisdom in this self-limitation. It is the Trinity, not the enneagram, that Panikkar and others have discerned as the metaphysical cornerstone of the mind of Christ and in whose interpretive light the teachings of Christianity come together and make compelling sense on all levels at once — mythological, historical, devotional, aesthetic. With this key alone Christianity can open the door of its long-locked mystical treasure house and reconnect with the full breadth and depth of its original cosmological vision. It may as yet be only a ham radio that I am finding in this tea cupboard, not a full GPS satellite system. But the important point is to turn it on and get it broadcasting.

THE FOUR GROUND RULES IN SUMMARY

1. The interweaving of three produces a fourth in a new dimension.
2. New arising from the former triad becomes holy reconciling in the new triad.
3. Holy denying (second force) will always be played by the divine Unmanifest.
4. New arising in any triad is a counterstroke of the now-displaced holy affirming from the former triad.

TABLE OF COUNTERSTROKES

New arising	is the counterstroke of	in the dimension of
1. Heart of God	Endless Unity	(separability/motion)
2. Word	Desire	Heart of God
3. Substantiality	Perceptivity	Word
4. Jesus	Heart of God	Substantiality
5. Holy Spirit	Word	Jesus
6. Kingdom of Heaven	Substantiality	Holy Spirit
7. Oikonomia	Jesus	Kingdom of Heaven

What is the dimension? where does it come from?

11

STAGE 1:
The Proto-Trinity

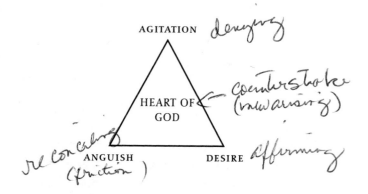

AGITATION *denying*

HEART OF GOD ← *counterstroke (inwavising)*

re concealing (friction) ANGUISH   DESIRE *affirming*

At first there was neither Being nor non-Being
  no kingdom of air, no sky beyond it.
Who straddled what, and where? Who gave shelter?
  was water there, unfathomed depth of water?
There was no death then, nor immortality,
  no sign of stirring, no curtain of day or night.
Only one thing, Breath, breathed, breathing without breath,
  nothing else, nothing whatsoever.
Also there was Darkness, darkness within darkness
  the darkness of undiscriminated chaos…
Then rose desire, primal Desire,
  the primal seed, the germ of Spirit.
The searching sages looked in their hearts, and knew:
  Being was a manner of non-Being.
And a line cut Being from non-Being transversely:
  What was above it and what below it?
  —Rigveda

TO VENTURE INTO THIS FIRST TRINITY is to embark on a journey into a world very few have dared to enter: into the innermost workings of God, many, many inner worlds before the first speaking of "Let there be light." This first triad — and the two that follow it — unfolds in the gap between the eternal silence and the divine outspeaking. While it is safe to say that for vast stretches of mainstream Christianity no such gap is perceived to exist — God simply "spoke" and the world tumbled into being — most of the world's great cosmological and mystical traditions (including our own Western traditions) recognize implicitly a huge inner distance to be traversed before the "Endless Unity" (as Boehme calls it; the inaccessible light) can turn outward to manifest as accessible light, visible creation. These triads recognize as well that somehow this gap holds the key to what ensues in time and form.

In our Western traditions, this is the world of Boehme and Meister Eckhart, of the Kabbalah, and of the entire Pseudo-Dionysian mystical stream. It is also, as Catherine LaCugna has properly forewarned, a notorious philosophical cul-de-sac in which the forward and outward thrust of Trinitarian theology can easily lose its way in endless speculations on angels dancing on the head of a pin. But as I have already intimated, I believe that the real cul-de-sac is not the exploration of intradivine relations per se but the failure to recognize that the Trinity is a dynamic trajectory — a moving target as it were. When the theological Trinity (God in Godself) and the economic Trinity (God for us) are viewed as reified categories, distortion will result whether one is "inside" or "outside." The purpose here is not to shrink back in fear and trembling from the starting point but to prepare oneself to stay aboard for the full ride.

But this is also, ultimately, the world of direct revelation; and it is to this source that I, too, will make my final appeals. For those readers who may properly feel some reticence at prying into the innermost mysteries of God, the dispensation lies in the fact that such glimpses are occasionally directly given; in fact, they come flooding in with a force that overcomes all resistance. Bidden or unbidden, the Mystery suddenly appears, and one simply stares into its face and *sees*. Whether we consider ourselves mystics or not, there is a light of recognition that shines in each of us, deeper than our intellect and our conditioning, for it draws from that same deeper aquifer that we are about to explore.

Let's proceed, then, to the exploration.

Setting Up the Triangle

As I stated earlier, the first three of these Trinitarian triads will recapitulate Jacob Boehme. In chapter 8, you recall, I worked hard to wrestle his Three Principles and seven properties into a Law of Three configuration in order to build a bridge between his extraordinary cosmology and my own presentation of an unfolding Trinity. The calculations will remain identical with those already presented, but in my commentary I will begin to introduce a slightly different nomenclature for the properties occupying each of the cardinal points.

The first step is to set up the triad itself. While there are two options for arranging a triangle visually on the page (pointing up or pointing down), I have opted for the up version because this is the presentation Christians will be most familiar with from the standard symbolic portrayals of Father, Son, and Holy Spirit. I think you will see the utility of this in due course. For reasons that will also begin to make themselves clear, I will adopt the convention of placing first force (holy affirming) at the lower right, second force (holy denying) at the peak, and third force (holy reconciling) at the lower left. The new arising, or counterstroke, will appear in the middle of the triangle.

Holy Affirming

At the bottom right, then, we find desire, Boehme's first property. As we have seen already, Boehme's visionary insight into the question of how the Endless Unity brings itself into somethingness lies in the mystery of self-contraction followed by an explosion outward from that divine self-tensioning. In this initial step, the will "compresses itself to something," Boehme states picturesquely[1] — but "that something is nothing but a magnetical hunger, a harshness like a hardness."

Holy Denying

At the top of the triangle, in the role of holy denying, I place the word *agitation*. This is probably the most accessible of a complex of terms Boehme uses to describe this somewhat nuanced second property: "bitter," "stinging," "breaking," "sharpness." The idea here is that at this prototypic stage in the journey toward somethingness, the activation of desire leads inevitably to frustration, because desire seeks an object and there is as yet nothing upon which the Endless Unity can affix itself and slake its thirst. The result is an inner uproar—"a continual strife in itself"[2] — in which the frustration of desire serves only to inflame its intensity and escalate the whole process. It is this frenetic, agitated quality that Boehme has in mind when he describes it in words like *breaking* or *sharpness* and that I attempt to convey in the term *agitation*. It is still second force, but its oppositional nature expresses itself in an intensification of the turmoil, not just a frustration of the desire.

Holy Reconciling

Third force is the place where the other two meet, and the name I have used to describe it is exactly Boehme's third property: *anguish* — or specifically, "anguish, till the flash of fire."[3] As noted during my initial discussion of this passage in chapter 8, the movement through Boehme's third, fourth, and fifth properties (anguish, fire, light/love) occurs as a single unbroken motion, an explosion out of the spark or flash of fire kindled in the escalating intensity of desire and its frustration. Anguish is the third and catalytic element in this triumvirate of agitation. It is a mounting interior friction, like sticks rubbing together, which, to relieve itself, will ultimately cast off a spark. At the third triadic point this spark (or flash, as Boehme calls it) will emerge as primordial third force, calling into existence both the Law of Three and all that flows out of it.

What is this spark, then? If we follow the metaphor at a physical level, we at least know how it is generated: through friction caused by the tug of contrary motions within the divine equilibrium. But the name Boehme gives to this friction, "anguish," is both fascinating in its own right and crucial to an appreciation of what is really at stake at point three. Part of the genius of Boehme's allusive cosmology is the way he moves back and forth seamlessly between physical forces and their emotional counterparts. Friction in the domain of physical sensation becomes anguish in the domain of emotion. And this anguish, as Boehme intuits in his own great flash of illumination, contains within it what he calls sensibility, or perceptivity — the means by which the Endless Unity becomes perceptible to itself.

Today we would more likely use the word *consciousness* — the means by which the Endless Unity *becomes conscious of itself*. Pursuing with precocious clarity an intuition well known in the *Rigveda*, but hundreds of years ahead of his time as a Western Christian, Boehme senses that in undifferentiated unity there is no self-awareness, no reflective principle or mirroring, which is the crucial touchstone for the journey into full manifestation. He intuits that this yearning for full divine self-awareness is the real driveshaft of the impetus toward outward manifestation and summarizes his conviction in that beautifully portentous passage: "The Unity longs for sensibility …For so the eternal delight becomes perceivable, and this perceiving of the Unity is called love."[4]

More than three centuries later, the Christian hermeticist Valentin Tomberg, one of Boehme's greatest spiritual descendants, would affirm this same point when he wrote in *Meditations on the Tarot:* "The pure act in itself cannot be grasped, or in other words, it is by virtue of the reflection that we become conscious of it."[5] Boehme's mysterious spark or flash — the primordial big bang from which the worlds emerge — *is the flash of pure consciousness. Rigpa*, the Buddhists would call it: pure awareness. It is the light by which we see light, suddenly exploding out of the pressure of compressed desiring. Boehme describes it as "the light of the fire, wherein the Unity comes into mobility and joy."[6] In that flash divine being sees itself as it is—"and this perceiving of the Unity is called love." But the flash emerges not "from above" but "from below"; for Boehme the capacity for reflective consciousness is born on the rack of desire and its frustration. This crucial point has not only cosmological implications but profound psychological ones, too, as we ponder our own personal and human emergence into full consciousness.

Arising: Heart of God

According to the dictates of the Law of Three, the interweaving of three results inevitably in a new arising from the previously arisen—or in simpler language, that fourth in a new dimension. When we looked at this newly arisen ("outflown," in Boehme's terms) entity in our earlier discussion, you recall, there were two ways of "getting from here to there," but in either case "there" turned out to be Boehme's fifth property, which he describes as "light or love." Note that while he uses the conjunction "or," what he really seems to have in mind is light *and* love. To his way of thinking, the two are not alternative candidates for the fifth property slot; they are a single indivisible reality whose original is the fire itself. And in fact, Boehme's fourth (fire) and fifth (light) are not really two different "properties" at all, but successive stages of a single trajectory, and Boehme's Light-World shines forth from the flames like the three young Israelites of Biblical fame dancing in Nebuchadnezzar's fiery furnace.

In my earlier discussion of this first new arising, I simply adopted Boehme's terminology and called it light/love. But now, and particularly in recognition of its fiery arising, I propose that we call it Heart of God. For the heart is both fire and light, both passion and equanimity, and in fact, it is precisely in making the two become one that the heart realizes its true sovereignty and attains in actuality what it already is at its source: the first counterstroke of the "endless unity" of God. Heart signifies what is innermost and most essential about something—"the heart of the matter," its deepest core or nature. But also, since in all the great spiritual traditions the heart is the seat of love, the phrase *Heart of God* gives a foreshadowing of what this revealed nature might be. It brings us into exact alignment with Boehme's statement: the "perceiving of the Unity is called love." In fact, from the standpoint of the Law of Three, it is a remarkably precise encapsulation of the principle of counterstroke itself.

Please remember what we learned earlier about the workings of counterstroke. This love Boehme has in mind is not an *image* of God, a reflection of a prototype whose "real" substance is elsewhere. Nor is it a quality that God possesses already and is simply projecting outward (as Christians typically assume when they say, "God is love"). It is, rather, *God's very self*—the Endless Unity, the Eternal Liberty—now moving in the dimension of perceptivity, or consciousness. Love is what God looks like, what God actually is, once the divine consciousness has awakened to itself—or as Boehme expresses it, has brought itself into "mobility and joy."

In the traditional language of Christian devotion, the phrase *Heart of God* might immediately call to mind Jesus Christ, and that familiar association was indeed in the back of my mind when I put forth my suggestion. Using the traditional language, we could thus say that the outcome, or new arising, from this first "procession" of the Law of Three is that God generates his eternal Son. Understood in a limited, allusive way, this statement is correct, but I do not want to pin things down quite so tightly yet. I will merely acknowledge that the words I am introducing at each triadic point have been carefully chosen with a view to the long range. Like snowballs, they will begin to pick up layers as they roll along.

For now, it is more productive to stay focused on the intuition of Boehme (and Eckhart's as well, and in fact, that of many of the great Christian mystics) that the real business of this first stage of Trinitarian unfolding is to generate the Trinity itself—the Trinity here understood as the inner dynamism through which everything else will come to be. In a word, the Law of Three. The Trinity, Boehme claims, is "God knowing himself in divisibility"—which is, of course, the flip side of the "knowing himself in community" so cherished in traditional depictions of the Trinity. This kind of self-knowing is the "anguishing" but necessary foundation for any outward manifestation whatsoever. Without it both awareness and being are impossible. With it, they are inevitable.

12

STAGE 2:
The Primordial Trinity

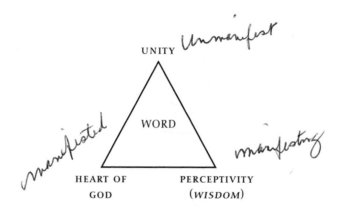

UNITY *Unmanifest*

WORD

manifested

manifesting

HEART OF
GOD

PERCEPTIVITY
(*WISDOM*)

AS WE STAND at the beginning of this second procession out of
the Law of Three, the territory may look somewhat familiar. It is, in
fact, the eternal, uncreated Trinity. With a mere transposition to the
familiar terms *Father* (in place of Unity), *Son* (in place of Heart), and
Spirit (in place of Perceptivity), we are back in the familiar configuration of Trinitarian belief. But it is in resisting this transposition that
the real possibilities begin to open up.

This second triad also dovetails with the second of those three
Boehmian triads I described in chapter 8, in this case the one in
which the property that Boehme calls sound (the sixth property)
emerges out of the interplay of fire and light. With a slight adjustment of terminology ("Word" is for all intents and purposes simply a
more theologically recognizable synonym for "sound"), the correlation between them continues to hold.

Setting Up the Triangle

We will stay with the basic configuration already introduced: affirming is bottom right, denying is at the peak, and reconciling is bottom left. But now, for reasons that will shortly become apparent, I am proposing a slightly different way of naming these three corners. In order to distance ourselves still further from the unconscious association that affirming means "active" or "good" and that denying means "negative" or "passive," let's call first force *manifesting*, second force *Unmanifest*, and third force *manifested*. The Law of Three is, after all, the Law of World Creation, and this adjustment to the terminology keeps our attention focused on the creative, self-communicating nature of this entire divine odyssey.

If we agree, then, that the top of the triangle is *Unmanifest*, bottom right corresponds to *manifesting*, and bottom left to *manifested*, we can now begin to apply those conventions I introduced earlier as establishing our four rules of the game. The new arising from the former triad — Heart of God — now moves into the position of third force, or manifested, in the new triad. Our former manifested (anguish/perceptivity) takes over the role of manifesting. Meanwhile, the one that is bumped out of the manifesting position (desire) will apparently go underground, only to emerge as the unseen "stroke" for which our new arising (Word) will furnish the counterstroke.

Unmanifest: Endless Unity

As I announced earlier, I have chosen to leave *Unmanifest* always the same: always the nonreducible, unknowable Endless Unity and Eternal Liberty of God. This is, as I explained, partly to counter any suggestion of emanationism: the implication that the superessential Godhead interacts with creation only through intermediary realms and that each new arising is a reciprocal distancing of God from direct involvement in creation. It is not so. The unknown, formless Presence always participates directly in every new cosmological arising.[1] To abide within the rules of Christian orthodoxy means that one simply cannot write God out of the equation. But if theological considerations do not alone provide a sufficient rationale for this judgment call, additional weight is supplied by the stipulations of counterstroke itself (Gegenwurf, recall — the shoemaker's trade) that the thread in all cases remains the same, no matter whether it is manifesting topside or bottom side. God is the thread running through all the worlds.

Does this not, in fact, collapse the Law of Three back into a Hegelian binary (thesis/antithesis/synthesis)? Surprisingly, no. This is primarily due to the fact that each new arising (which, in toto, comprise a series of counterstrokes of the Endless Unity in successive fields of action) introduces enough variety into the mix to ensure that Holy Unmanifest will be a real player, not a mere placeholder. In this second force, or denying positioning, it will always be pointing toward that infinite potentiality and fecundity (Boehme refers to it as the "Magnum Mysterium") that breaks all of our human molds and ensures that the playing field will remain perpetually open-ended.

Manifesting: Perceptivity

Remember the rapid train of events in the former triad that brought us to this point: there was anguish...the flash...and the light of pure awareness (or perceptivity, as Boehme calls it). The friction caused by the compression of the divine will leads to an explosion that is in the same instant both fire and light, both energy and illumination.

I have hesitated on the naming of this triadic point. Since Boehme himself waffles on where to draw the line between fire and light, my own choice as to whether the real operative here is anguish/perceptivity (our former holy reconciling) or fire is to some degree arbitrary. Once the spark is struck on that hard flint of anguish, it is fire all the way, so in that sense fire seems to be the right choice. But in accentuating fire, we run the risk of losing sight of perceptivity, which seems to me the far greater loss. For we have seen already

how perceptivity is linked to the emergence of reflective consciousness and is therefore a core element in what will soon begin to
unfold as the Wisdom strand of this weaving. In the end, I relied on
the second line of bearing provided by our fourth ground rule to
confirm that perceptivity is indeed the right choice.

Perhaps it is not an either/or but a both/and. Here at the triadic
point that Christianity will eventually come to identify with the Holy
Spirit, we are already at the headwaters of what will subsequently
develop as those two distinctly different modalities of spirit's presence: spirit as sheer energy, outward force, and spirit as pure awareness or reflection. Contemporary pneumatology sometimes tends
to discount this difference ("It's all immanence!" Bruno Barnhart
remarks), but these two distinct "faces" of spirit have been extensively commented on throughout esoteric and mystical tradition,
particularly in Boehme and the Kabbalah. Explosion, energy, and
outward force correspond to the more yang, or masculine, expression of spirit; reflection, pure awareness, to the more yin, or feminine. Throughout the ensuing progressions we will follow the dance
of these two complementary aspects as they move apart and come
together again with each new turn of the kaleidoscope.

Manifested: Heart of God

Heart of God now moves into the role of third force; it offers itself
as the meeting ground on which that divine yearning to know itself
in "mobility and joy" comes face to face with an absolute Unity that
can admit no separation. How this encounter will play out we shall
see shortly. The designation "Heart of God," you recall, was my own
suggestion as an alternative way of naming Boehme's fifth property,
which he simply calls "Light/Love." It aims to unite these two aspects
in a single symbol that conveys the essence of both: the yin of clarity and the yang of warmth.

Tellingly, in his description of this property Boehme draws on
both masculine and feminine imagery. This "true spiritual angeli-
cal world of divine joy"[2] is his Second Principle, the transformed or

Light-World, "wherein all the properties of the fiery nature burn in love."[3] But if fire predominates in this first description, it's light that pervades his second. In *Forty Questions of the Soul* he personifies this angelic presence as "an image of God, a virgin full of purity and chastity" — a virgin who is at the same time "God's wisdom, wherein the spirit discerns itself."[4] His imagery here reverberates with the powerful portrait of the primordial Sophia in the Old Testament book of Wisdom:

> She is the breath of God,
> a clear emanation of Divine Glory
> No impurity can stain Her.
> She is God's spotless mirror
> reflecting eternal light
> And the image of divine goodness.
> — Ws. 7: 24–25)[5]

In my earlier discussion I acknowledged that the term *Heart of God* implants a suggestion of Jesus Christ, God's only and eternal Son, but I cautioned against making that leap too quickly. Boehme himself has a better suggestion. He offers us his own term *Christosophia:* the cosmic Heart of God, uniting fire and light, male and female, the "only begotten Son" we know as Christ, and the "virgin full of purity and chastity" we know as Sophia.

The Christosophia is perhaps the most underutilized insight in all of Christian mysticism. The idea itself was not entirely unknown before Boehme; already in the fourteenth century Julian of Norwich had caught the gist of it with her usual succinctness: "Jesus Christ is our true mother."[6] But Boehme's profound development of this idea deserves a far wider audience, for here he accomplishes what for contemporary feminist hermeneutics is such an earnest desideratum: the recognition that in the divine archetype of Christ (which is what this triadic point is really all about), the functions that will later be arbitrarily divided into Logos and Sophia, ordering word and reflecting wisdom, are here seamlessly joined. Just as at our manifesting triadic point it is virtually impossible to separate the explosion from the light, so here it is impossible to separate the outward force from the inward yielding, the heart that bears the secret of the divine hiddenness from the heart that is the fountainhead of the divine outpouring. At this primordial holy reconciling, the two are one.

The Headwaters of Gender

In my opening reflections on this second trinity, I commented on its superficial resemblance to the Father–Son–Holy Spirit configuration of our familiar Trinity but suggested that if we could resist this transposition, the real possibilities would open up. Now it is perhaps more clear what I meant. For at each of these triadic points we have uncovered a feminine double for the masculine imagery. Even the Unmanifest, the Eternal Liberty, has its feminine double in the Magnum Mysterium, the eternal fecundity. At each of these points, we encounter in prototypic form the archetypal divine feminine: as matrix, infinite fecundity, abyss, pure reflection, wisdom, perceptivity, energy. The headwaters of the great river of the feminine arise here.

And what is all the more striking, they arise in an androgynous form. There is no question here of an archetypal goddess figure who will later be displaced by an archetypal god; rather, at each triadic point the dual aspects of masculine and feminine are so interwoven as to be virtually indistinguishable. The divine apophatic is the abyss of all creativity; the explosion is the light; the *Christos*, the anointed (that is, manifested) Heart of God is the Christosophia, the heart of the mother. They are indivisibly one. In this second trinity we encounter the eternal template of gender. Each triadic point encapsulates and prefigures what we will later know as masculine and feminine, while at the same time revealing that they are at root one.

Arising: Word

"As truly as God is our Father, so truly is God our Mother, and he revealed that in everything," writes Julian of Norwich — "I am he, the power and goodness of fatherhood; I am he, the wisdom and lovingness of motherhood; I am he, the light and grace which is all blessed love; I am he, the Trinity; I am he, the unity; I am he, the supreme goodness of every kind of thing; I am he who makes you to love; I am he who makes you to long; I am he, the endless fulfilling of all true desires."[7]

But as the Law of Three dictates, the "endless fulfilling of all true desires" does not lie at the level at which the desire arose; rather, it calls into being a new arising, which will in turn become the new field for continued exploration and manifestation. I have chosen to call this second procession out of the Law of Three by its Johannine name: Word. In its multivalent dimensions of form and force, the Word will be our touchstone for the descent into time, into matter, and into constraint.

13

STAGE 3:
The Sophianic Trinity

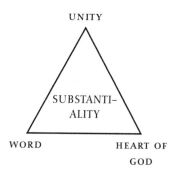

UNITY

SUBSTANTI-
ALITY

WORD   HEART OF
GOD

IN THIS THIRD TRINITY, the divine trajectory toward self–communication crosses a crucial watershed. The emergence of some–thingness out of nothing is no longer simply a hidden perturbation within the divine will; it will end exactly at the point where our modern scientific cosmology begins: with that primordial explosion which catapults us into the realm of energy and substance, the birth of the cosmos in physical space/time.

This Trinity also corresponds with that final Boehmian triad, which also arrives at this same point: with the emergence of what Boehme calls "substance" or "nature." This is the mysterious seventh property that recapitulates all the others and, in completing that intradivine template for "the impressure of nothing into something," makes it possible for that same template to project itself outwardly in the calling into being of the visible world. The gradual unveiling of the true identity and tincture of this Holy Substantiality is the real revelation awaiting us in this triad.

Manifested: Word

As the second procession out of the Law of Three, Word is supremely well poised to move into the position of holy reconciling. Boehme, you recall, designates this sixth property as simply sound, but what he means by this is essentially the same as what the author of the Gospel of John is trying to convey by his *Word* or *Logos*: in both cases the emphasis is on intelligibility, understanding, design, and action. Word furnishes the template through which the Endless Unity will make another quantum leap into solidarity and particularity.

Word's lineage flows through the "fire" side of Boehme's genealogy (if you crosscheck this in the table on page 131, it turns out to be the counterstroke of desire, that original activating agent). It aligns us with that more restless, willful, self-positing aspect of the divine nature that Boehme picturesquely describes as utfus, "out-eager." In contrast to the more feminine energy of pure awareness and reflection, this Word resonates with the masculine forces of shaping and crafting. It emerges akin to the "intelligible universe" of the Greek patristic fathers or the realm of eternal idea in Platonic thought. But it adds to these the crucial element of *sound* (for what is Word if not intention joined to vibration?) whereby the eternal idea will have the means to project itself outwardly.

Manifesting: Heart of God

Heart of God now moves into the role of holy affirming. This is of unparalleled importance, for it underscores that in this next and crucial stage in the unfolding of the Law of Three, the active principle is love. The impulse that will call everything into being — the only impulse of sufficient frequency, magnitude, and virginity (!) to leap from the realm of pure consciousness into the world of energy, as this triad does — is love.

Remember that this triadic point is also a counterstroke — in fact, our very first counterstroke: of the Unity itself. We call to mind once again Boehme's extraordinary dictum: the "perceiving of the Unity is called Love." What flows down to us through this triadic point is the lineage of the light world: perceptivity, clarity, purity, "the bush that burns but it not consumed." Heart of God is the innermost radiance of the Unity, now manifesting itself in "perceptivity and divisibility" (as Boehme calls it).[1]

Arising: Holy Substantiality

Unfathomable Unity, activating Love, reconciling Word: what emerges from the interplay of these three forces is perhaps the most extraordinary of all quantum leaps. We are standing at the threshold of that pivotal moment when divine consciousness jumps the fence, as it were, and condenses into the root energy that will birth and sustain the created order.

In describing it in this way, I am deliberately drawing on a remarkable passage from *Meditations on the Tarot* that almost from the start has framed my understanding of this process. Tomberg writes:

> Modern science has come to the understanding that matter is only condensed energy — which, moreover, was known by alchemists and hermeticists thousands of years ago. Sooner or later science will discover that what it calls "energy" is only condensed psychic force — which discovery will lead in the end to the establishment of the fact that all psychic force is the "condensation," purely simply, of consciousness, i.e. spirit.[2]

We need to "calibrate" this insight, of course, to banish any lurking traces of redshift metaphysics. In the blueshift cosmology I have been unfolding here, the quality and quantity of divine presence remains the same at any point on the ray of creation. *Con-densation* (literally: "with density") does not imply a diminishing intensity of spirit but merely an intensifying concentration of spirit within physicality. With that adjustment made, Tomberg's schematic does indeed offer a compelling way of picturing the outward (not downward) thrust of the divine energetic trajectory.

In pondering how to name this new arising, I have found once again that two candidates present themselves, two complementary threads of meaning. Boehme calls this seventh property "substance," or "Holy Substantiality," and that does indeed name its function. But when we go back to his original German, we discover that the word he is actually using is *Barmherzigkeit*, or "warmheartedness," which in German is a synonym for *mercy*. So the actual physical composition of this "substance" — its tincture or intrinsic nature — turns out to be *mercy*! And mercy, by this same linguistic stroke, reveals its essential tincture to be warmheartedness — not pity or condescension.

What are we to make of this? Boehme is certainly not alone in this insight. With remarkable consistency "mercy" is the name chosen by the Western mystical tradition to describe this innermost quality of the Heart of God, most emphatically so among those who have been my own most important guides along the way: Boehme, Julian of Norwich, Helen Luke, and Thomas Merton.

Make no mistake: it *is* a substance. It actually exists. But it exists at a vibration so high, a frequency so intense, as to be barely contained within the created order; in fact, it often appears from our creaturely perspective to be a "nothing" (a favorite paradox of the mystics). It is the most intense and subtle energy that can exist within createdness. It is at the core of all things, the wellspring of being, and is what Merton is describing when he writes: "The core of life that exists in all things is tenderness, mercy, virginity, the light."[3]

It is also in us, as the foundation of our own souls. In one of his most illumined passages, Merton beautifully captures this *point vierge*, as he calls it (virgin point), in both its intensity and its apparent nothingness:

Again, that expression, *le point vierge*, (I cannot translate it) comes in here. At the center of our being is a point of pure nothingness which is untouched by sin and illusion, a point of pure truth, a point or spark that belongs entirely to God, which is never at our disposal, from which God disposes of our lives, which is inaccessible to the fantasies of our own mind or the brutalities of our own will. This little point of nothingness and of *absolute poverty* is the pure glory of God written in us. It is so to speak His name written in us, as our poverty, as our indigence, as our dependence, as our sonship. It is like a pure diamond blazing with the invisible light of heaven. It is in everybody, and if we could see it we would see these billions of points of light coming together in the face and blaze of a sun that would make all the darkness and cruelty of life vanish completely.[4]

The mystics have intuitively understood this: that we live grounded, rooted in this great "electromagnetic field of love."[5] Itself invisible, it is the hidden bedrock of actuality. In it, all things live and move and have their being. Nothing can fall out of it because it is the *fons et origo* of all that is.

Expressed in the more psychological language of contemporary spirituality, the all-important implication of this insight is that this field in which we live and move and have our being is *relational*. Consciousness itself is relational (*conscious*: "with knowing"). In her book *Old Age*, Helen Luke points out in a passage I have long cherished that the word *mercy* shares the same Etruscan root with such words as *commerce* and *merchant*; it's all about exchange.[6] In this great electromagnetic field of love, *everything* — from the tiniest electrons to the great three persons of the Trinity — is endlessly exchanging, giving and receiving of itself in that riot of self-communication that, in fact, constitutes the very dynamism of love. This field is not an "it" but a "Thou." And it is only in opening our own hearts to the irreducibly personal and relational nature of this Thou in whom we are rooted that we ever come to discover who we truly are.

Holy Wisdom

But there is yet one more hidden treasure to be revealed, and again we will find it by calling on that surreptitious little fourth ground rule. Calculating that the present new arising will be the counterstroke of the now–displaced former manifesting, we discover that this Holy Substantiality is indeed the counterstroke of perceptivity, which we have already begun to identify with Wisdom, the primordial feminine. So it is Wisdom, then, who is actually establishing the tincture of this entire triad. What a truly wondrous idea! Wisdom, pure awareness and pure reflection, turns out to be the hidden operative as the Heart of God moves into the realm of substantiality. Creation does not come into being from beyond but from within as Wisdom suffuses the whole operation and becomes the mirroring presence — in fact, the very personification — of that holy Barmherzigkeit.

This is why I have named this triad the Sophianic Trinity. Beneath the more extraverted motion of the shaping and ordering Logos lies the nearly invisible radiance so remarkably personified in that passage already alluded to in the book of Wisdom:

> She is the mobility of all movement;
> She is the transparent nothing that pervades all things.
> She is the breath of God,
> a clear emanation of Divine Glory,
> No impurity can stain Her.
>
> She is God's spotless mirror
> reflecting eternal light,
> and the image of divine goodness.
> Although She is one,
> She does all things.
> Without leaving Herself
> She renews all things.[7]
> — Ws. 7: 24–26)

Thomas Merton is intuiting along much these same lines in his remarkable prose poem *Hagia Sophia* (Holy Wisdom). With precocious mystical insight he captures the subtle connections between wisdom, mercy, and divine creativity. The "infinite light unmanifest," he writes, "...speaks to us gently in ten thousand things, in which His light is one fulness and one Wisdom. Thus he shines not on them, but from within them.... The diffuse shining of God is called Hagia Sophia. We call her His 'glory.' In Sophia his power is experienced only as mercy and as love.

"Sophia, the feminine child," Merton continues, "is playing in the world, obvious and unseen, playing at all times before the Creator. ... Hagia Sophia in all things is the Divine Life reflected in them. She is in all things like the air receiving sunlight....The feminine principle in the world is the inexhaustible source of creative realizations of the Father's glory....

"Sophia is the mercy of God in us. She is the tenderness with which the infinitely mysterious power of pardon turns the darkness of our sins into the light of grace...."[8]

I can include here only brief excerpts of a magnificent piece of visionary seeing that deserves to be pondered at far greater depth. In a substantial recent scholarly contribution to that exploration, Christopher Pramuk recognizes Sophia as Merton's "hidden Christ": the modality in which Christ's healing presence becomes powerfully immanent in the created world.[9] Again, that allusive image of the Christosophia hovers just beyond the event horizon of our imagination. We will be encountering it yet again in much more concrete form two Trinities hence.

For now, suffice it to say that it is here in the realm of Holy Substantiality that Wisdom comes into her true home and dominion, and the language of the feminine seems both natural and rich with meaning. And as that "diffuse shining of God" holds all things in readiness, this third Trinity converges upon its own Omega Point, when the inner big bang will become one with the outer big bang. There are still myriad realms of subtle energy — "many mansions in my Father's house," as Jesus expresses it — that span the gap between pure consciousness and the explosion into form of our physical universe. But as the tumbler locks click into place guided by the unseen hand of the Law of Three, all is poised on the cusp of that thunderclap moment when Word as eternal idea will become Word as outspoken sound.

And God spoke, "Let there be light." And photons, galaxies, suns, trees, time, history, waves, tumbled into existence.

14

STAGE 4:
The Incarnational Trinity

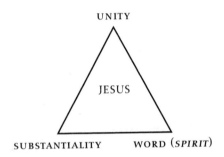

And the Word became flesh, and dwelled among us, and we beheld
his glory.
    —John 1:14

IN THIS FOURTH TRIAD we are in time; in fact, as Christians we are
right at the heart of it. The fourth new arising out of the Law of Three
will be the earthly Jesus: the counterstroke, now in the domain of
substantiality, of the Heart of God, the eternal "perceiving of the
Unity" that is love. This is the Trinity of his annunciation and birth.

The Three Triadic Points

Unity remains at the peak of the triangle, in its permanent role as
eternal Unmanifest. Since Jesus during the course of his earthly life

consistently refers to this eternal Unmanifest as "my Father," it is appropriate to introduce this terminology here — particularly, as we will see, since the theme of lineage will prove to be a pivotal issue for this entire triad.

Word now moves into the position of manifesting (displacing Heart of God, which, following the well-established pattern, resurfaces as the touchstone for the new arising, conveying the essential nature of the personhood of Jesus. As activating agent, Word will draw heavily on its roots in the explosion side of that original "light of the fire wherein the Unity comes into mobility and joy." For this new arising, it will serve as spark, seed, and outward force. From this point on we can call it by the name with which it is known in this incarnational Trinity and in all subsequent unfoldings: Spirit.

At the third, or manifested, point, we now have Substantiality. We saw in the former unfolding how Holy Substantiality is essentially synonymous with the Mercy of God, for not only is this Mercy the *cause* of created being, it is in fact its innermost nature — the root vibration of Being itself.

Now, however, our gospel heralds a new gamut of meaning for this substantiality: "And the Word became *flesh*." Flesh means createdness. Even more specifically, it means *temporal* createdness, the span of an earthly life, lived in a body as an individual person. This is a level of density formerly unencountered in the subtle and fluid realms of the first three triads. And so here in this Trinity, freedom and constraint will meet head-on: the *fluidity* of divine potentiality and the *solidity* that is the narrow channel through which it must flow in order to reach its full actualization. The drama is intense and poignant.

The playing out of this drama lends itself with touching precision to the configuration of the annunciation story (Luke 2:26–38); in fact, this story might be considered the paradigm for this entire fourth triad. An angel appears, announces a divine conception to a young woman; she gives her consent, and a child is born of equally divine and human lineage. But the presence of the Law of Three as the underlying operative in this story is at first not easy to detect. "Angel–Mary–Jesus" is a simple dialectic, as all human births would (at first) appear to be.[1] Where do we find in this annunciation story the presence of *three* independent sources?

We find them in the part that is hidden from sight in this dialogue: the underlying tension between Unity and Spirit — holy denying and holy affirming — that culminates in the angelic appearance.

We know this tension well by now. It is the same one we encountered back in the first Trinity, the Proto-Trinity, the one that called both divine outwardness and the Law of Three into being. "For the Unity longs for the sensibility, and the sensibility longs for the Unity," writes Boehme;[2] consciousness demands a mirror, but the mirror creates a twofoldness that bisects the original Unity. It is the fundamental divine paradox, the fault line in the Unity ground, which apparently goes "all the way down." There is in God that which presses outward, toward full expression and actualization, and there is in God that which draws inward, toward the equilibrium of complete stasis. And the tension of these opposites, as Boehme rightfully named it, is anguish.

But unlike that first triad, in which nothing yet existed through which the divine desiring could slake its thirst, now there is a somethingness. The primordial spark has matured into a stable middle ground, a permanently constituted strand in this interweaving of the Law of Three. It has a lineage now of new resultants that have issued forth from it: Heart of God–Word–Mercy; and it has substantiality, flesh. Now, if ever, the time is at hand to see if this flesh has acquired the heft to bear the tension of the divine opposites.

Third force in this drama is not just generic flesh, not just typological humanity, but a very specific human vessel. Mary, the young woman who will become known as the Mother of God, is holy reconciling in this triad, just as her son will become in the next; and her "Fiat" ("Let it be to me according to your will") rings with the same cosmic portentousness as the divine "Fiat ("Let there be light"), which resounded through the former Trinity. The impossible is about to be attempted: the tempering of the divine anguish in a nurturing human love.

Denise Levertov exquisitely captures the import of Mary's "astounding ministry" in her poem "The Annunciation":

to bear in her womb
Infinite weight and lightness; to carry
in hidden, finite inwardness,
nine months of Eternity; to contain
in slender vase of being,
the sum of power —
in narrow flesh,
the sum of light.
    Then bring to birth,
push out into air, a Man-child
needing, like any other,
milk and love —
but who was God.[3]

The profound conjunction of the opposites sealed in this moment
is suggested even in the multiple resonances of the wordplay. In her
willingness to "bear," that is, carry, the weight of divinity "in slender
vase of being," she also "bears," that is, brings forth, the next and pivotal unfolding in our Trinitarian progression.

Gender and Personhood

This fourth triad is supremely and unabashedly the world of personhood — and personhood implies gender. As Jesus becomes "son," so,
inevitably, does God become "father." And Mary becomes "mother."
Within the context of this Trinity, it is inappropriate to refer to God
as Mother; such a designation blurs the essential mystery of what
has just come to pass. The traditional language is here both historically correct and symbolically accurate.
    This is also the triad in which it is technically correct to say the
Father and the Spirit (*Spirit* here understood as formative principle
and engendering energy) give birth to the Son. Rather than the *filioque* (that is, *qui ex patre filioque procedit*: "who proceeds from the Father
and the Son"), we have here the *"spiritoque"* (*qui ex patre spiritoque procedit*: "who proceeds from the Father and the Spirit"), and throughout

Jesus's earthly life, this remains the configuration. The spirit which descends on him in his baptism and fills him in his moments of great strength and great need, which animates his life, and which he renders back to God at the hour of his death, is the same spirit at work in all of us insofar as we are created human beings. For not only in Jesus of Nazareth but in each of us as well, there seems to be a mysterious otherness at work in our lives, shaping our lives to its own end, and what is known of our lineage and parenthood is always offset by this mysterious unknown that seems to call us forth and drive us along toward our destiny. We are all, ultimately, children of the Mystery, and what was said of Jesus by an ancient Anglo Saxon poet applies in a deeper sense to all of us:

Come now, Guardian of victory
Maker of mankind, and manifest here
Your gracious mildness. It is needful to us all
That we may know Your mother's kin,
The true mysteries, since we can explain
Your paternity not one whit further.[4]

And yet there is one decisive difference. All the rest of us have two human parents, and this mysterious "other" is the third force in our arising. In Jesus, as we have seen, it is exactly the opposite: first force and second force are contributed by divinity itself, and it is the human vessel, Mary, who bears third force. This reversal of the pattern is of paramount significance. From its earliest centuries, Christian tradition has insisted that Jesus is a singularity — not merely a prophet, not even an avatar as the term is typically understood in the Asian traditions, but a unique and pivotal cosmic event — and that his singularity has everything to do with the circumstances of his lineage and conception. This insistence, which confounds the literal mind and remains obscure even at the level of allegory, finds its real explanation at the metaphysical level. An arising in the usual fashion, of purely human parentage, would still be under "the old order" — that is, operating within the laws and conditions governing material existence as provided through the logoic triad.

This new configuration (Father and Spirit as second force and first force, respectively; Substantiality as third) fulfills the required next sequence in the progression of the Law of Three, and hence drives the process inevitably forward. As Christian tradition has accurately intuited, Jesus, the new arising from this fourth triad, becomes the cornerstone of the New Creation.

15

STAGE 5:
The Messianic Trinity

UNITY

HOLY
SPIRIT

JESUS   SUBSTANTIALITY
(*FLESH*)

THE FIFTH TRINITY assumes the "proper" filioque configuration of the traditional creedal formula: "I believe in the Holy Spirit, who proceeds from the Father and the Son." It contains both the how and the why of that transmission: how the Holy Spirit is both the truth and the power of the risen Christ, and why the filioque phrase — "who proceeds from the Father *and* the Son" (not just from the Father alone) — is in fact correct and causally necessary according to the Law of Three.

This triad corresponds to the human life span of Jesus, beginning with his birth; encompassing his public ministry, crucifixion, death, resurrection, and ascension; and culminating in the descent of the Spirit upon the disciples in that tumultuous Pentecostal uprising:

> While the day of Pentecost was running its course, they were all together in one place, when suddenly there came from the

sky a great noise like that of a strong, driving wind, which filled the whole house where they were sitting. And there appeared to them tongues like flames of fire, dispersed among them and resting on each one. And they were all filled with the Holy Spirit and began to talk in other tongues, and the Spirit gave them power of utterance.

— Acts 2:1–4

Particularly in those final forty-three days of Jesus's earthly life (crucifixion to ascension), when what looks like certain defeat and death erupts suddenly into a series of mysterious resurrection appearances and then an even more mysterious final disappearance upward, this Trinity, the Messianic Trinity, shifts suddenly into the supernatural mode, acquiring in the process an incandescent intensity. It seems to be unfolding in two realms at once, and the breathtaking beauty is also, in the words of the poet Rilke, "nothing but beginning of Terror we're still just able to bear."[1] And this perception is indeed correct; in the inner traditions of the West this realm is often named "the imaginal realm," which does not mean imaginary but *hyper-real*, bearing witness to this higher and transfigured reality like the bush that burns but is not consumed. In the interest of brevity, and because so much of what is pivotal in Jesus's human ministry with regard to the Law of Three can be seen best (and, in fact, *only*) in the light of these final events, I will focus my discussion here.

Manifested: Jesus

Following our established convention, Jesus, the new arising of the former triad, moves into the position of manifested in this new triad. "Holy reconciling" is the name traditionally given to this point, and it is uncanny how well this coincides with the early church's deepest understanding of Jesus's mission and identity as the cosmic reconciler — as, for example, in Paul's succinct statement, "For God was in Christ reconciling the world to himself (2 Cor. 5:19); or in the more elaborate presentations of this same idea in Ephesians and Colossians:

> He has made known to us His hidden purpose, made so kindly in Christ from the beginning, to be effected when the time was ripe; that all heaven and earth be brought together in unity through Christ.
> — Eph. 1:9–10

> Through him God chose to reconcile the whole universe to himself, everything in heaven and everything on earth, when he made peace by his death on the cross.
> — Col. 1:20

Manifesting: Substantiality

Our new manifesting becomes Substantiality, which we have already seen by this time has acquired a remarkable set of aggregates. Substantiality is flesh, for sure; the solidity of corporeal being. But more fundamentally, arising from its wellsprings in the third triad, Substantiality is the Mercy of God, God's Barmherzigkeit. And as we have seen through the wonderful insights of Thomas Merton, this Mercy proves to be none other than Sophia, the hidden ground of Wisdom. As "the diffuse shining of God" (in Merton's imagery), "the Divine Life reflected in [all things]," she is the invisible foundation of all that exists and the invisible force that bonds the created and uncreated realms. Now in the human life of Jesus, this hidden ground of Wisdom has become fully visible, and in his "obedience unto death," she has become fully empowered.

My own thinking has progressed here since I first wrote these words more than a decade ago. To this beautiful linked chain of increasingly feminine presence I would now add one more link — Mary Magdalene — whose substantiality, at least for the duration of this triad, is of the same order as Jesus's own. Long demonized by the church as a repentant prostitute, she is finally gaining the recognition rightfully due her as Jesus's most precocious disciple and his expressly designated heir apparent.[2] She is a worthy addition to the sophianic lineage, but even more important, she is *woman*, not merely an archetype. Her human flesh is made of the same stuff as Jesus's human flesh. And since flesh is the active agent in this triad, their solidarity at this level will not prove to be inconsequential.

The Diffuse Shining of God

It is evident that the transfigured light is already shining very brightly in Jesus in those various resurrection appearances that dot the landscape of the final chapters of Luke's and John's gospels. Solid to the touch and yet moving completely evanescently — walking through closed doors, simultaneously appearing and disappearing — he seems to belong now more to spirit than to flesh, as if operating under the laws of a new and incomparably higher realm of being. He is at one with the energy of pure truth and love, and it is this energy that pours through those final days of his earthly life and into the hands and hearts of his disciples.

From well before his crucifixion, Jesus has already been laying the groundwork for his disciples to be able to recognize and receive him in a more subtle form. In metaphor upon metaphor tumbling from the Farewell Discourses of John 13–17, he unfolds before them his vision of a new and deeper kind of intimacy entwining them — the energy of pure, indwelling presence — that will enable him to walk through the walls and doors of their separate selfhoods as easily as he will walk through the walls and doors of buildings. "I am the vine; you are the branches." "Dwell in me, as I in you." "I will not leave you orphans." "Father, the glory you gave to me, I give to them, that they may be one as we are one." And as the instantiation of this covenant, he leaves them the bread and the wine, to be sacramentally activated through his impending death as his own body and blood, through which they will always be able to find their way to him. There they will indeed continue to meet him — not in mournful solemnity, a fading memory of "what once was," but in the fullness of his living presence apprehended at this more subtle level. This is the authentic meaning of the term *anamnesis* — "living remembrance" — of which Jesus was indisputably a living master.

"Unless a Grain of Wheat Falls into the Ground and Dies…"

I mentioned a few pages earlier that in Jesus's death the hidden ground of Wisdom has become fully empowered. It is beyond the scope of this brief exploration to explain fully why. And in fact, there is no need to do so, for it has already been brilliantly done by Ladislaus Boros in *The Mystery of Death*,[3] to which I would refer readers who want to pursue this question more systematically. But for the sake of clarity, let me at least offer a brief overview here.

Boros, too, like Jacob Boehme, came to what he knew largely through visionary experience. A rising star in the Jesuit theological world during the 1950s, he was essentially stopped dead in his tracks by a powerful mystical vision in the early 1960s in which he grasped with overwhelming clarity what he would subsequently describe as his "hypothesis of a final decision" — namely, that "death gives man the opportunity of posing his first completely personal act: death is, therefore, by reason of its very being the moment above all others for the awakening of consciousness, for freedom, for the encounter with God, for the final decision about his eternal destiny."[4] The core of his *Mystery of Death* was written in a white heat of inspiration in about six weeks and bears those unmistakable earmarks of an understanding "which flesh and blood hath not revealed." Not long after its completion, Boros left the Jesuit Order, married, and fathered four children before his brief and fateful life came to an end in 1982 at the age of fifty-three.

Central to Boros's metaphysics is a vision very much like what I myself was trying to unfold in our third Trinity. He sees the physical world as pouring forth from a place of "root unity" (I have named it Holy Substantiality or Mercy) to which one becomes totally present in death. "The soul's freeing from the body in death does not mean a withdrawal from matter," he proposes; "rather does it signify the entering into a closer proximity with matter, into a relation with the world extended to cosmic proportions."[5] Thus, when Jesus's fully divine humanity was planted, in death, right at the heart of that root unity, it followed this same pattern and *became itself the new root unity*: "the real ontological ground of a new universal scheme of salvation embracing the whole human race."[6] This bold assertion accords well with the traditional Christian understanding that it is Jesus's *death* that effects our salvation (not just any virtuous act of obedience, nor even, surprisingly, his resurrection), while also offering an explanation as to why in those postresurrection appearances his physical materiality seems so much lighter and more intimate, for it really does now belong to a different order of being. Boros explains:

> Free of all the "fleshly" constraints of time and place, Christ is able to reach the men of all times and places and make them members of his transfigured body, i.e. enable them to participate in his "pneumatic" corporeity.[7]

This idea of Christ's "pneumatic corporeity" will return in force when we move into the sixth triad, and I will have more to say about it then. Immediately at hand, however, we can see that the most obvious accomplishment of Jesus's death and resurrection is the demonstration of the continuity of personhood beyond physical death. Whoever Jesus *was*, he still *is* — and the power of that assurance sparkles through this season of Eastertide as individually and/or together the disciples discover that their wildest hopes have come true. Whether in denser or lighter corporeity, he is still indisputably Jesus — and that is the touchstone they seem to need to activate their own interior compasses for the next leg of the journey.

Clearly there is more going on here than just reassurance; there is also *empowerment*: Mary Magdalene at the tomb…Thomas…the disciples on the road to Emmaus…Simon Peter at the Sea of Tiberias. "Did we not feel our hearts on fire as he talked with us?" (Luke 24:32) Each appearance of Jesus is also a *baraka*, a transmission of spiritual energy, as all remaining wounds and doubts are healed and the disciples are commissioned for the ministry that lies ahead: "Go and tell." "Feed my sheep." His real gift to them in those forty days he continues to sojourn with them is to show them that the fire that is in him is in them as well.

The Harrowing of Heaven

There remains, however, one final task. Jesus has promised to send the disciples an advocate: "the Spirit of Truth who will guide you into all truth" (John 16:13). And in the light of all he has taught them, and of his own explicit promise that he will not leave them orphans but will come again himself, though not in a form visible to human eyes (John 14:18), it seems only reasonable to assume that this spirit of truth could not be anything less than the most intimate personal encounter with Jesus himself. Not simply a "generic" guide, a legate from the higher realms, which would never satisfy their human hearts, but the invincible certainty that their beloved is actually present among them.

The fulfillment of this promise — bringing to term the unfolding of the fifth triad — I believe is accomplished in the ten-day hiatus between the final departure of Jesus from human form and the descent of the Holy Spirit on Pentecost.

Again, I am feeling my way here more by instinct than by theological precedent. For many years now something has prompted me to keep the ten days of this Ascensiontide fast (as I have come to think of it) as one of the holiest and most liminal seasons of the church year. In hermit's solitude high in the Colorado mountains or in my little island cabin in Maine, I have the sense in the holy hush of these days of a parallel movement taking place in the invisible realm of spirit: a movement of such exquisite delicacy and intimacy that all of outward creation (usually by now well into spring) dresses for it — trees in white bridal veils of blossom, the earth sweetly green and golden in its flowers and buds. Could this be the nuptial banquet so long foreshadowed in Scripture?

The configuration of our triad here confirms this intuition, while relating it to the deepest levels of the archetypal imagination. For here, perfectly aligned in manifested and manifesting positions respectively, stand Christos and Sophia, shimmering in imaginal radiance through the human lineaments of Jesus and Mary Magdalene. And here in the final days before this fifth triad comes to full term, the work they must accomplish together in each of these realms — human, imaginal, archetypal — perfectly accords with the bridal mysticism at the elusive magnetic north of Christianity's own mystical heart, from the Song of Songs to the Marriage at Cana to the great apocalyptic parables of the wedding feast:

No more shall they call you "Forsaken"
Or your lands be called "Desolation;"
You will be called "My Delight,"
And your land shall be called "The Espoused."
For the Lord delights over you,
And your country will have its wedding.

Like a young man that marries a virgin,
Your rebuilder shall marry you;
As the bridegroom rejoices in his bride,
So your God will rejoice over you.
      — Isa. 62:4-5[8]

This bridal mysticism can now be celebrated fully and unabashedly; this is the season to which it belongs.

If the three days following Jesus's death are known in tradition as the Harrowing of Hell, when, according to Boros, his human reality is planted at "the heart of the earth" and becomes the new "root unity" of all physical existence, this parallel hiatus of Ascensiontide might be called the Harrowing of Heaven: the melting together, in silent ecstasy, of these two streams of divine being reunited at last: reflecting wisdom and manifesting love. The Christian version of the eternal *heirosgamos* or "sacred marriage" is the permanent impressure into the receiving substantiality of Holy Wisdom, of the face and heart of the human Jesus, so that the new arising out of this union, the Holy Spirit, is now and ever hereafter something it has never been before. More than simply energy, more than simply pure reflection, it is now the continuity of the person of Jesus beyond the flesh: his tincture, his humanity, his flesh. Ever hereafter in the realms of being, the encounter with the Holy Spirit will be a personal encounter with Jesus. It is not just wisdom, truth, energy, love; it is *his* wisdom, his energy, his truth, his love, as he himself comes to meet us.

This is one reason that, aside from the mixed metaphysical paradigms it creates, my own instinctive reaction is that it is inappropriate to envision the Holy Spirit as "she." For in doing so, we break the continuity between the person–in–the–body and the living tincture of that person beyond the body, which is the key to our resurrection faith and also to our own passage through death. The essence of us does not die when the physical body dies; it lives on in a form distinct, precious, and ever retrievable in love. For the Christian, therefore, it is not really accurate to think of the Holy Spirit merely as a generic chi, *ruach*, life force — or even as Wisdom or Sophia. These exist always, embedded in the very meaning of substantiality. But every encounter with the Holy Spirit is an encounter with the living Jesus, our master and light holder, in the dimension of pure energetic presence. Or to say the same thing in a way that accords strictly within the dictates of our paradigm, the Holy Spirit is the counterstroke of the ever–creative and ordering Word but now in the "field" of Jesus. Jesus is the ground, the dimension — the cloth, according to our Gegenwurf metaphor — upon which the divine pattern will be unfolded.

What part does Mary Magdalene play in all of this, you might ask? It is simple: human love is the touchstone. In that garden on Easter morning, as she receives Jesus's request, "Do not cling to me, for I have not yet ascended to the Father," and gently widens space, their human hearts in that instant undergo that sacred alchemy described by the great metaphysical poet John Donne as "not a breach but an expansion, like gold to airy thinness beat."[9] Without losing any of its human particularity, their love becomes vast and luminous throughout the cosmos, drawing together all of those realms visible and invisible in a single sacred embrace that indeed bears within it the fullness of the Mercy of God.

Transfigured eros is the immortal diamond fused at the very heart of the density of this world. It can be fused only here, under these extreme conditions of density and pressure. It is the purpose for which this realm was created. It is what we human beings are meant to discover here, and it is what we are required to offer back into the cosmos on the altar of our own transfigured hearts. This is the alchemy of love that Mary Magdalene came to know so well during her own paschal ordeal and why she can never be written out of the Easter equation, for she is the guardian of its Rosetta stone.

Jesus is, of course, named by Christians as "the Christ," the Anointed One; to name him thusly, in fact, comprises Christianity's earliest unofficial creed.[10] *Christos* is the Greek equivalent for what Jesus's own Semitic culture would call "the Messiah," meaning the long-awaited heir to the Davidic throne. In accepting this title (which he seems to have done with considerable ambivalence), Jesus also changes its domain from earthly kingship to sovereignty of a different order altogether. It is this latter, more interior and luminous domain I am alluding to when I name this triad the Messianic Trinity.

16

STAGE 6:
The Pentecostal Trinity

GOD (*UNITY*)

KINGDOM
OF HEAVEN

HOLY SPIRIT   SON
(*BODY OF CHRIST*)

But the temple he was speaking of was his own body.
  —John 2:22

THIS LONG EXCURSION through the triads lands us back in the familiar Trinity of nearly two millennia of Christian practice, with even the persons called by their familiar names (if we accept "Body of Christ" as equivalent with Son, a point I will be addressing shortly) and in their familiar alignment. From the larger perspective this exploration has opened up, it is perhaps easier now to understand my reluctance to break into this triad and begin willy–nilly rearranging its parts to accommodate contemporary gender sensitivities and standards of political correctness. The present configuration has been lawfully arrived at and, properly understood, precisely depicts both the task and the essential energy flow appropriate to the present stage of unfolding.

The corollary, of course, is equally true: It would be a mistake to regard this present configuration as the final state of affairs. When viewed from the longer perspective of the Law of Three, this triad suggests itself to be but another phase in a principle pushing constantly toward change and new manifestation. When the work of this stage has been completed, a new configuration will assuredly arise.

But what is the work of this stage? That question will frame our exploration in this chapter, but the pattern that emerges out of this sixth triad is neither easy nor altogether comfortable to grasp. It seems to point toward a more subtle embodiment, the discovery of an essential quality of aliveness that lives within all things as their animating principle and purpose. But more important — and far more difficult — it seems to point toward a radical transformation of consciousness that would allow one to engage with that inner aliveness directly, with less and less dependence upon the mediation of the outer form — and finally, with no mediation at all. Just as Jesus followed the path from fully enfleshed human being to lightly enfleshed human being (in those postresurrection appearances) to "pneumatic corporeity" — pure spiritual energy but unmistakably himself — so, too, this Pentecostal Trinity seems to extend the invitation to follow his path of "pure flame," as the wick and tallow of our human lives are set ablaze in love to release the imperishable fragrance of our own true selfhood. Not to flinch from the "holocaust of becoming" constitutes both the great challenge and the great possibility of this triad.

But let's see how this mandate emerges from within the inner dynamism of the Trinity itself.

Manifested: Holy Spirit

In this sixth-stage configuration, Holy Spirit moves into the position of "manifested," or holy reconciling. Our fourth guideline reveals to us that this Holy Spirit is the counterstroke of Word. It bears that same ordering, shaping intelligence of its logoic prototype but is now manifesting in the "field" of Jesus. It is not a distant reflection or mirror of the Endless Unity *but who God actually is* when refracted through (that is, deeply tempered by) the human reality of Jesus. It is God meeting God in the heart of the human experience: God touching God from the inside, from within finitude and fragility.

As such, the Holy Spirit bears within itself a dimension that is all too easily overlooked if we simply think of it as "higher spiritual energy" coming from above. The Spirit comes equally "from below." By that, I mean it bears within it the deep imprint of Jesus's human life and, because of this, a sensitivity to our human limitations and weaknesses that comes from "having been there." I mentioned at the end of the previous chapter that from ever hereafter the Holy Spirit bears the face and heart of Jesus; it is an encounter, in nonbodily form, with the imperishable aliveness of this person.

It also bears all the gentleness and delicacy we have met from its "maternal" side: its deep rootedness in the ground of Sophia. For the Holy Spirit is really neither Jesus nor Sophia but Christosophia, that primordial archetype of androgynous wholeness, now fully actualized. This gentleness is beautifully evoked by Valentin Tomberg in his final chapter of *Meditations on the Tarot*:

> As a general rule, the spiritual world does not at all resemble the surging of the sea — at work to break down the dams holding it back so as to inundate the land. No, what characterizes the spiritual world, i.e. the "sphere of the Holy Spirit," is the consideration it has for the human condition. The amount and frequency of revelation from above, destined for a human being, is measured with a lot of care, so as to avoid every possible perturbation in the moral and spiritual equilibrium of this person. What the spiritual world prefers most of all is "reasonable inspiration," i.e. a gentle flow of inspiration to the extent that the intellectual and moral forces of the recipient grow and mature. Here a succession of elements comprising a great truth are revealed little by little until the great truth in

its entirety shines within the human consciousness thus prepared. Then there will be joy, certainly, but not the perturbation of equilibrium which is intoxication.[1]

This gentleness, of course, is in contrast to the ecstatic intensity so prized and sometimes deliberately cultivated by certain segments of the Christian community. Echoing the teaching of Christianity's highest spiritual guides, including Saint Anthony, Teresa of Ávila, and the anonymous author of *The Cloud of Unknowing*, Tomberg wisely advises strict adherence to a basic principle of what he terms *spiritual hygiene* — namely, "that he who aspires to authentic spiritual experience never confounds the *intensity* of the experience with the *truth* that is revealed."[2] A better metaphysical understanding of the roots of gentleness in the "character" of the Holy Spirit might help considerably to avoid this costly mistake.

But if the Holy Spirit bears the essential stamp of Jesus's humanity, it also clearly bears it in a much lighter, more subtle form. The Holy Spirit is not an apparition, nor is it a spiritualized body of the kind Jesus walked in for those final forty days on the earth. This is not to deny that such bodily apparitions of the living Jesus do from time to time still occur; they most assuredly do. But they are not the usual mode of his ongoing connectedness to us, which is through the Holy Spirit resonating in our own innermost depths, at that place of root unity which he claimed and consecrated in his death as the ground of our being.

Throughout this book I have been using the word *imaginal* as a way of describing this lighter, more visionary realm of reality. In the original Wisdom anthropologies, as modern commentator Jean-Yves Leloup points out, this realm is neither subjective nor private but "an ontological reality entirely superior to mere possibility."[3] It objectively exists and is, in fact, more endowed with real being than our own. Recovering an authentic reconnection to the imaginal is considered by many Wisdom teachers — me among them — to be the single most important task of our present era. Because it is where this sixth stage triad is inexorably headed.

Manifesting: The Body of Christ

The movement from physical flesh and blood to its imaginal counterpart is occurring at the manifesting point as well, where I have suggested we substitute for the familiar *Son* (that is, the human person of Jesus, a term that belongs to the fourth and fifth triads) the appropriate equivalent for this stage: *the Body of Christ.*

The Body of Christ, as Christians understand the term today, has two meanings, both instituted by Jesus and both pointing toward this more spiritualized embodiment. We use it to designate the Eucharist, the sacramental meal of bread and wine that he established as the primary viaduct of his continuing presence among us. And we use it to refer to the church, the fellowship of believers who were called into being to live the life of mutual servanthood in love that he envisioned in his Farewell Discourse and modeled in his teaching and life.

In both of these usages, we can observe that the common denominator (at least in principle) is that some sort of transformation is required before the outer substance becomes one with the inner reality. In the Eucharist this occurs through the act of consecration, through which ordinary bread and wine are transformed into Christ's living body and blood. Among the fellowship of believers, a parallel force of transformation is traditionally accorded to the sacrament of baptism. Both of these foundational sacraments of Christian life are intended to activate the more subtle reality within and establish it as the new principle of spiritual growth.

That's the theory, anyhow. In practice, we know how delicate the line is between a sacrament actually *activating* that inner principle and merely symbolizing it — and in that sense *deactivating* it, replacing it with the vicarious version of itself. To what degree is conscious, personal awakening or recognition required for the power of the sacrament to be activated within? The argument has gone on for a thousand years or more and is essentially unresolvable at the level of theology. From a theological standpoint the position is unassailable: *ex opere operato,* as the principle is called — the sacrament is deemed to be efficacious without regard to the players involved. But from the standpoint of actual spiritual practice — that is, walking the path that leads to the actual transformation of one's life into a living cell in the body of Christ — the evidence suggests mightily that personal, conscious awakening is the catalytic element.

Nearly a thousand years ago an Orthodox monk by the name of Symeon the New Theologian (949–1022) pondered this conundrum and came up with yet a third meaning for the *Body of Christ* that ties the other two meanings together along this axis of awakening. This strikingly bold and intimate poem sets us down firmly upon that inner ground of transfiguration:

> We awaken in Christ's body
> as Christ awakens our bodies,
> and my poor hand is Christ. He enters
> my foot, and is infinitely me.
>
> I move my hand, and wonderfully
> my hand becomes Christ, becomes all of Him
> (for God is indivisibly
> whole, seamless in his Godhood).
>
> I move my foot, and at once
> he appears like a flash of lightning.
> Do my words seem blasphemous? — Then
> open your heart to Him.
>
> and let yourself receive the one
> who is opening to you so deeply.
> For if we genuinely love Him,
> we wake up inside Christ's body
>
> where all our body, all over
> every most hidden part of it,
> is realized in joy as Him,
> and He makes us utterly real,

and everything that is hurt, everything
that seemed to us dark, harsh, shameful,
maimed, ugly, irreparably
damaged, is in Him transformed

and recognized as whole, as lovely,
and radiant in His light.
We awaken as the Beloved
in every part of our body.[4]

In Symeon's wondrous vision, the Body of Christ is, in fact, *the body within our own body*: the mysterious divine presence that holds us in life and heals and re-creates us from within. But this indwelling "body" is also beyond us and surrounding us, for when we wake up, we find ourselves *in* it. In that moment, instantly, inside and outside disappear into a healing oneness. Or in other words, the Body of Christ is where—and who—we discover ourselves to be in the moment of our awakening.

The key word here, however, is *awaken:* we have to awaken into the Body of Christ—that is, *personally, consciously* awaken. It cannot be done without our consent and presence. The Christian inner tradition (of which Symeon the New Theologian is one of the most articulate representatives) has always insisted on this point—but so, too, have large segments of "mainstream" Christian evangelical and reform traditions. Jacob Boehme, as well, specifically referred to this act of inner awakening (and of course, commitment to the path of life it entails) as "putting on the Body of Christ" and deemed it explicitly necessary to do so while still on earth for there to be any hope of continuance beyond the grave.[5] Using very different language, G. I. Gurdjieff made exactly the same point.[6]

At any rate, whether we consider the term in its micro or its macro sense, there are consistent telltales, for those who can read the signs (beginning with those offered by Jesus himself), pointing toward inner awakening as the crucial third force that transmutes the more outer and corporeal aspects of the Body of Christ into a living reality of indwelling presence. Without its activated presence, the living fellowship of believers will inevitably be dragged into the gravitational field of a lower consciousness — that is, the institutional church — where it at best fails to actualize and at worst actively aborts the important transformative work entrusted to it.

Arising: Kingdom of Heaven

The Kingdom of Heaven is Jesus's own favored term for the transformed reality he is envisioning. But what might that be? Again, if one misses what the Body of Christ is, it will be impossible to see what the Kingdom of Heaven is. The Kingdom of Heaven will be mistaken (and often has been) for the Church Triumphant.

In fact, the Kingdom of Heaven is not an outer kingdom at all. Jesus was very specific about this, insisting: "My Kingdom is not of this world." It is not about physical buildings and institutional agendas but about *a different level of consciousness*, about consciousness transformed by awakening. It is the new arising that comes into play when the gentle light of the Holy Spirit illuminates the inner aliveness within the outer form, revealing the Body of Christ at the heart of all things.

In a recent provocative treatment of this subject, Jim Marion suggests in his book *Putting on the Mind of Christ* that this Kingdom of Heaven Jesus keeps calling us to actually means nondual consciousness, consciousness that does not revolve around an egoic center and does not view the world through the subject/object polarities inherent in egoic thinking.[7] While this view may be somewhat of a modern retrojection (and heavily influenced by the Buddhist-based metaphysics of Ken Wilber), Marion does, in fact, make a good case for his argument that the transformation of consciousness envisioned and modeled by Jesus is more functionally described by the term *nondual consciousness* than by most of the sentimental and moralizing rhetoric placed on it by Christian exegetes. Complete absence of subject/object polarity certainly is the core of Jesus's radical vision of human identity and invariably proves to be the key that unlocks his parables and other challenging teachings. "Love your neighbor as yourself," for instance: not *as much as* yourself (as this teaching is generally interpreted), but *as* yourself: those two apparently separate selfhoods interchangeably, indivisibly one. Similarly, "The first shall be last; the last first," "The one who would save his life will lose it, and the one who is willing to lose it will save it." These teachings become transparent at the moment one realizes that the fundamental illusion has all along been the notion of a separate selfhood that must be preserved and defended. While I do not think it is true that Jesus's earthly mission was fulfilled simply in the preaching of nondual consciousness, it is true that in the Kingdom of Heaven he labors in the service of something that cannot be envisioned, let alone accomplished, apart from nondual consciousness.[8]

What he is actually envisioning, however, is something slightly more subtle — and probably only visible through a Western and perhaps even specifically Christian spiritual filter, not through the Eastern unitive models that Marion tries so valiantly to superimpose. In Jesus's famous parable of the Prodigal Son, for example, the point is not simply that the generous father who forgives his repentant son displays nondual consciousness. What really happens is that the father's nondual consciousness brings into reality — *actualizes and makes manifest* — qualities of aliveness that would have no "body" otherwise: joy, forgiveness, generosity, empowerment. Through the father's action, these things that have no body flood into the world as a life-giving force. Similarly, Jesus's self-sacrifice on the cross does not just model perfected being; it *unleashes* the healing, transforming power of surrendered love that literally sets the world on a new footing.

This subtle but crucial distinction is perhaps the essence of the difference between the Western and Eastern metaphysical milieus. In the East (as well as in the classic sophia perennis model that has so heavily influenced Traditionalist metaphysics) awakening is *a return to an original unity*. One pierces through the mirages of time and separateness to the primordial unity that underlies them. In the West, particularly in the dynamic inner ground of biblical Christianity, awakening is a *creative act* that releases — that is, actualizes, or brings to full manifestation — more subtle qualities and aspects of the divine being that can be expressed in no other way. Examples of these qualities would include equanimity, gentleness, joy, forgiveness, forbearance, generosity, compassion, dignity, boundless creativity. In Christian tradition those are known as "the virtues," or "the gifts of the Spirit." The Sufi tradition describes these same virtues as "the names of God." However one describes them, the point is that in the Western mind-set, they are brought into manifestation by an active sacrifice (or surrender) of attachment at a lower, more outwardly oriented level of consciousness in order to release the higher and more subtle. In the West, the mirage of time and separateness is the means by which the light of the fire expresses itself, just as a candle is the *means* by which the light of the fire expresses itself. Awakening is something akin to striking the match.

The light of the fire latent in the wick and tallow of the world is the Kingdom of Heaven to which Jesus points us. It is, as he assures us, "in the world but not of the world."

The Meeting of Heaven and Earth

Functionally speaking, this intricate dance of "in but not of" creates a perilous tightrope upon which the Christian (and indeed, the entire Western) spiritual path must thread its way. It is easy to fall off, on the one hand, into a kind of neo-Eastern monism that denies the ultimate reality of the created order, and on the other hand, into a spiritual materialism that mistakes the outer for the inner and forgets that transformation is the gateway between them. Of these two errors, the latter has been far more prevalent during the two thousand years of the sixth-stage triadic unfolding. Even the discrepancy between the outwardly familiar form of this sixth-stage Trinity — Father, Son, and Holy Spirit, the formula routinely intoned at the beginning of most Christian worship — and the mysterious world of inner awakening we have been exploring in these past several pages speaks to how very little the church has been able to recognize, let alone ignite, the holy fire smoldering at its depths.

But it is possible to stay on that tightrope. In a compelling passage from his 1993 book, *The Bond with the Beloved,* contemporary Sufi teacher Llewellyn Vaughan-Lee describes what he sees as the emerging spiritual consciousness of our times in words resonant with this sense of inner aliveness:

> As we silently work upon ourselves, the energy of our devotion becomes a point of light within the world. At the present time a map is being unfolded made of the lights of the lovers of God. The purpose of this map is to change the inner energy structure of the planet. In previous ages this energy structure was held by sacred places, stone circles, temples, and cathedrals. In the next stage of our collective evolution it is the hearts of individuals that will hold the cosmic note of the planet. This note can be recognized as a song being infused into the hearts of seekers. It is a quality of joy that is being infused into the world. It is the heartbeat of the world and needs to be heard in our cities and towns.[9]

In this remarkable paragraph Vaughan-Lee puts his finger squarely on the essential nature of this sixth-stage configuration: the drive toward increasing *spiritualization of essence.* What was formerly contained in the heavy density of stones and buildings is now contained in a network of hearts fully open to divine love. (This certainly adds a new shade of resonance to the prophet Ezekiel's declaration "I will remove from your body the heart of stone and give you a heart of flesh" (Ezek. 36:26). In the same way that tallow and wick expire into flame when the candle is lit, so the bricks and mortar of the Church must expire into the living flame of love in order to become "pure diamond" — as Merton writes — "blazing with the invisible light of heaven."

Merton penned these words in the concluding paragraph of his essay "A Member of the Human Race."[10] We already explored the beginning of that paragraph in our consideration of the Sophianic Trinity (p. 150, where he introduces his powerful image of the *point vierge*). Now, as the paragraph comes to its end, his prophetic heart is already glimpsing that light-filled union of hearts that Vaughan-Lee has just spoken of so vividly.

"It is in everybody," Merton continues, "and if we could see it, we would see those billions of points of light coming together in the face and blaze of a sun that would make all the darkness and cruelty of life vanish completely....I have no program for such seeing. It is only given. But the gate of heaven is everywhere."[11]

"The gate of heaven is everywhere." Within the invisible breadth and depth of Christ's "pneumatic corporeity" (as Boros called it), the physical world now contains a world within a world: a world where the husk has cracked open to reveal the grain, where what sparkles in everything is the quality of its aliveness. The Kingdom of Heaven is the enlightened radiance of the eye that looks straight into being and sees that it is the Body of Christ — each bird, leaf, tree; the fullness of Being hidden in the random dots of the universe, totally transparent to the love that is its source and its destiny. Meaning dances within meaning; our human lives are set ablaze to release the root energy of love, and we discover to our amazement just how much love can be borne in human flesh.

And that is good. Because in the next and final turning of the triad, flesh itself will be left behind.

17

STAGE 7:
The Economic Trinity

UNITY

OIKONOMIA
(Soul of God)

KINGDOM
OF HEAVEN

HOLY SPIRIT

And all shall be well and
All manner of thing shall be well
When the tongues of flame are in-folded
Into the crowned knot of fire
And the fire and the rose are one.
　　—T. S. Eliot, "Little Gidding"

I USE THE WORD *Oikonomia*, or divine plan, in the fullest sense of the New Testament cosmic vision, as in Ephesians 1:9: "He has revealed to us his hidden purpose, made so kindly in Christ from the beginning, to be effected when the time was ripe, that all heaven and earth be brought together in unity through Christ." This seventh Trinity is about the fullness of time, the reunion of created and uncreated realms, the actualization of all that was potential. It is where zero and infinity converge. Other scriptural names for the reality being envisioned here would be the *pleroma,* "the fullness of time," and the *apocatastasis,* the final restoration of all things. None of these concepts is easy.

By now you may be asking — a tad nervously — how long each of these stages takes. We have seen already that these seven trinities are of very unequal temporal duration. In the first three we cannot even properly speak of temporal duration, for time does not yet exist. Triads four and five are very brief, encompassed within the earthly life span of Jesus. That sixth triad, which we are still presently slogging through, has held sway throughout these past two thousand historical years, and for virtually this entire time this question has been consistently percolating on the back burner: How much longer? When is this alleged "second coming of Christ" that will put an end to time as we know it actually going to arrive? And what then?

Our final Trinity will offer us some clues here, but not in a dramatic or apocalyptic way. The rapture is not about to descend — just yet, anyway. In each of these triads the progression across the respective terrain is determined by the Law of Seven, and the *rate* of progression — well, that is up to us as well as to factors beyond our control and perhaps even beyond divine control. The important thing to keep our eyes on is not the *when* but the *what.* In a cosmos whose innermost nature has been revealed as Mercy, we need merely rest in the goodness of that embrace and trust, in the words of the poet Philip Booth that "whatever it comes to you're bound to know."[1]

The Triadic Points

Let's start by orienting ourselves in this new terrain, whose diaphanous quality places it at the outer limits of what the human mind can comprehend. There is almost no solid matter left to get a hold on here; we are dealing entirely with the energetic world, with subtle vibrations and qualities of aliveness essentially undetectable at the purely physical level. To return to Valentin Tomberg's schematic (p. 149), in which he envisions how divine consciousness condenses into energy, and energy condenses into matter, we have now apparently arrived at the final step in this parabolic trajectory: where energy "evaporates" back into divine consciousness.

As ever, Unity — the Unmanifest, the bottomless infinity of God — continues to hold the upper corner as holy denying. The new arising from our former Trinity, Kingdom of Heaven, now moves into position as manifested. Holy Spirit becomes manifesting. Having in our last triad become intimately familiar with Spirit's lineage and with the nuptial union that has sealed its identity forever, we can thus boldly proclaim that the illuminating, active principle now in the role of holy affirming is none other than Christosophia, the fully androgynous Christ–Spirit, bearing within it the realized potential of both male and female: Wisdom, Word, Mercy. Those two streams of yin and yang, pure explosion and pure awareness, which we saw separating in the second triad, are now fully reunited as they flow back into the ocean carrying with them all that has grown along their banks.

Kingdom of Heaven, at the manifested pole, holds down the last traces of form. And appropriately so, for if we consult the table of counterstrokes illustrating our fourth ground rule, it proves to be the counterstroke of Substantiality. But what kind of "substantiality" might this be? As we have seen already, it is not a heavy physical form of stones and mortar; not a walled and barricaded New Jerusalem. Nor is it even a psychologically walled and barricaded Church Triumphant, mistaking its own institutional aims for the will of God. No, it would assuredly have to be a substantiality more akin to the burning bush Moses saw in the wilderness (Exod. 3), that powerfully archetypal image that has so transfixed the contemplative imagina-tion. It is not a "thing" at all but a dynamic aliveness, made manifest in its willingness to be set ablaze. Its "body" would be a body of almost complete imaginal essence, still unmistakable as identity though having no physical form. It would be, say, the "body" of the fragrance of a rose, the "body" of palpable sanctity in a monastic chapel where prayer has been rich and deep, the unmistakable certainty of presence as one takes in one's hand the consecrated bread, the Body of Christ.

"Consumed with that which it was nourished by"

In me thou see'st the glowing of such fire
That on the ashes of his youth doth lie,
As the death-bed whereon it must expire,
Consumed with that which it was nourished by.

In this haunting stanza from his Sonnet 73, Shakespeare poignantly describes the usual outcome of this willingness to be set ablaze: one is consumed in the holocaust. Our physical lives become the wick and tallow for the releasing of this "other," and when the wick and tallow come to their end, the blaze goes out. Such is the apparent destiny of mortal existence.

And yet, the burning bush in the wilderness burned and was not consumed. No wonder this image has had such a hold on the religious imagination from Moses's time down to our own: it speaks directly to our own deepest fears and yearning. Did this bush burn with incorporeal fire, or was it itself incorporeal? Could its burning represent the mysterious union of flesh and spirit in a substance so imperishably fine that the vessel would survive the holocaust of its own becoming? And could the fruits of that union show forth not only in the higher realms but even here in our own, as a rainbow of hope shimmering over what would appear to be a sea of total loss?

Throughout our Western spiritual tradition not only theologians but poets and mystics as well have tried to describe this substance through the mind-boggling concept of the "resurrection body" or "angelic body." The words themselves break down here. "It is a body," affirms Boehme, but not such as ours: "No gross bestial flesh, as we have in the old Adam, but subtle flesh and blood, such flesh as can pass through wood and stone, unhurt by the stone, *as Christ came in to his disciples, the door being shut* (John 2:19, 26): It is such a body as has no turba [death] or fragility; hell cannot retain it; it is like eternity, and yet it is real flesh and blood which our heavenly hands shall touch, and feel, and take hold of; also a visible body, as that is which we have here in this world."[2] According to Christian tradition, it is the body that we all wore before the fall of Adam, and its restoration signifies the end of time as we know it, and the full accomplishment of the divine purpose.

And yet, while the words break down to describe this "flesh and blood" that is *subtle* but still *real,* our Christian tradition, and specifically the Nicene Creed, has staunchly demanded that we believe in the resurrection of the body. And somehow, intuiting that these two "ends of time" — both in the microsense of our own personal existence and in the macrosense of the final accomplishment of the divine oikonomia — are in fact intimately intertwined and that the "body" that awaits us in both cases is the same, I would propose that we enter into the mystery of this final triad through the gateway of the experience of our own death.

Boros Again

For this exploration, there is perhaps no better guide than Ladislaus Boros, whose extraordinary book *The Mystery of Death* I have already mentioned earlier in regard to Jesus's death and descent into hell. But Boros is also significantly concerned here with the death of *every* human being as he presses forward with his hypothesis that "death gives man the opportunity of posing his first completely personal act." As Boros describes life's inexorable journey, with its ascending and then rapidly descending curve of outward energy and freedom, his words resonate with that Shakespearean sense of "consumed with that which it was nourished by." But moving against the tide of this outer dissolution is a countervailing current: the current of pure becoming.

"In the end," Boros writes, "the falling of the 'outer man's' curve of existence becomes plain to see.... Finally, the fact of decline makes itself felt with elemental violence and brings about the crisis of dissolution. The strength of the 'outer man' begins to ebb away. This makes possible the most decisive renewal of the 'inner man,' the deepest spiritualization of life. Overcoming this final impoverishment there emerges the old man, the wise man, the elder, whose whole strength is in spirit. Perhaps such men say little, or at any rate, little of importance, but by their simple existence they transform the complex of existence and make it transparent. Their 'act' of essential being is *the spiritual transparency of the realized meaning of existence*" (italics mine).

"Such men," Boros concludes, "have transformed all the energy of life into Person."[3] Explaining what he means by this, he adds: "From the crowded days and years of joy and sorrow something has crystallized out, the rudimentary forms of which were already present in all his experiences, his struggles, his creative work, his patience and love—namely, the inner self, the individual, supremely individual creation of a man."[4]

You will probably already recognize what Boros is driving at here from our exploration of the sixth triad: this is a very precise description of what in the previous chapter I referred to as the spiritualization of essence, the authentic work of sixth-stage unfolding (whether personal or cosmic), and the necessary catalyst for the emergence of the Kingdom of Heaven. This countervailing "something" is what I referred to earlier as blueshift, the compression of the raw materials of physical time and space into spiritual artistry—"the realized meaning of existence."

This process, begun in the second half of one's life, reaches its consummation at the moment of death, Boros insists. What was formerly the "wave" of one's life is instantly transformed into "particle," which contains the whole meaning, tincture, and virtue of that life, the imperishable essence of a person forever preserved as a realized quality of divine aliveness. (Boros does not actually use the wave/particle metaphor, but his intention is well conveyed by it.) "In death," he writes," man becomes for the first time and finally, a person, an independent and spiritualized center of being."[5]

This is the reason that some of the more intuitive streams of the Christian esoteric tradition insist that the soul is not the starting point of our human identity but the culmination; we do not *begin* our journey with a soul but end up with one, as the "particle" form of the "wave" of our life, shaped and articulated in time. Soul is not about potential but about actualization, and it is "retrievable" only as counterstroke — that is, only in alignment with that next dimension, where its real shape comes into fullness and form.[6]

Maurice Nicoll argues this position strongly in his remarkable essay "The Idea of Righteousness in the Gospels." Nicoll, you recall, was one of Gurdjieff's first-generation pupils and one of the few to remain a practicing Christian. Commenting on the gospel text "For whosoever would save his life shall lose it; and whosoever shall lose his life for my sake shall find it," (Mt 16:24–25) he observes:

> "Life" here means "Soul" in the original. . . . Translating the word "soul" by the word "life" . . . is correct if we understand . . . that the life of a man is not the outer life of his physical body, but all he thinks and desires and loves. This is a man's life, and this is his soul. . . . What a man consents to in himself makes his life, and this is his soul.[7]

"From all this we can begin to realize," he concludes, "that the soul is not something beautiful or ready-made but something that forms itself in him according to his life and that really is all his life, the image of all he has thought and felt and done."[8]

If that principle can be accepted, then it follows to say that the soul and the resurrection body are essentially the same thing. Formed in and through life by the courageous weaving together of strands of potential and time, this body is revealed fully only in the next dimension — in the imaginal realm. In imaginal embodiment we are pure tincture, the imperishable scent of the quality of our aliveness.

Remember that this next dimension is not the same thing as the afterlife. It is not later but *lighter*, a more subtle quality of aliveness that already works within us (otherwise we would not be alive at all) and has ever been the real causal ground from which we receive our life breath by breath. The only change in state imparted by physical death is that during the time we are outwardly clothed in human flesh it appears to be inside us; after the physical body has dropped away, we discover that all along we have been inside it!

While the full realization of our imaginal identity is properly the work of the next dimension, it is reassuring to realize that the higher can sometimes bleed through into the lower, illuminating physical form with a light from beyond. This was certainly the light shining in the bush that burned but was not consumed, as well as during those resurrection appearances of Jesus. Along with the generally upward thrust and lighter gravitation of the higher realms comes the reassurance that nothing of the lower is ever lost; the higher can enter and interpenetrate at will, announcing—like that rainbow over the seas of total loss mentioned earlier—that all realms and resonances of both the created and uncreated realms are bound together in love and that navigation between the worlds is no more difficult than dissolving into this root love and allowing it to flow where it will.

Valentin Tomberg speaks very strongly on this point in his chapter "The Judgment" in *Meditations on the Tarot*:

> Thus, the resurrection body will have nothing mechanical, nothing automatic about it. . . . It will not have ready-made and invariable "organs." No, the resurrection body will be absolutely mobile and will create for each action the "organ" that suits it. At one time it will be radiant light—such as Paul experienced on the way to Damascus—at another time it will be a current of warmth, or a breath of vivifying freshness, or a luminous human form, or a human form in the flesh. For the resurrection body will be a *magical will*, capable of contracting and expanding. It will be the synthesis of life and death, i.e., capable of acting here below as a living person and at the same time enjoying freedom from terrestrial links like a deceased person.[9]

This is not to say that this dissolving into the root love is easy. It requires every scrap of courage, faith, and hope the human will can muster to let go of the apparent solidity of the form and enter the deeper currents. But the realms *are* permeable, and nothing gained in solid form is ever lost to the more subtle. For the resurrection body — that is, the soul fully alive and empowered — stands as the gateway between them, equally wave and particle, gladly bearing home the harvest of all that has been gained in time and form.

In just such a way, then — moving from the microcosm to the macrocosm — we can say that the Oikonomia is the soul of God. For it is God's hidden purpose, fully revealed, fully actualized, in the weaving together of potential and time. And as Alpha converges ultimately on Omega, as the fullness of time becomes "the spiritual transparency of the realized meaning of existence," so the Trinity is revealed as the imperishable scent of God's aliveness.

18

The Reflexive Trinity

WHILE I DID NOT SET OUT to depict the series of configurations in a sevenfold schematic but only to follow the sequence to its own natural conclusion, it is perhaps inevitable that they should have wound up in this configuration. For the same esoteric tradition that gave the Law of Three also gave the Law of Seven stipulating that a seven-stage process is inherent and inescapable in every journey through time. Though I was in no sense setting out to "prove" this, the fact that the pattern happened to wind up that way provided an additional measure of assurance that I was on the right track.

Now, in the final pages of this exploration, I would like to acknowledge my indebtedness to one other significant contributor to this conversation whom I have not yet mentioned. At the same time, I will make use of his contribution to highlight yet another useful feature of this kaleidoscoping Trinitarian model: its symmetry.

The source in question is a remarkable and curiously little-known book called The Reflexive Universe, by Arthur Young, a scientist and brilliant amateur cosmologist. The book was published in 1986 with an introduction by Jacob Needleman, and it was Needleman who actually first placed a copy of it in my hands.[1] For more than a quarter of a century my now well-tattered copy has been a faithful traveling companion.

It was through Arthur Young that I first grasped what would become my own core metaphysical paradigm, which I named blueshift (though Young does not): the notion that the descent of Spirit into form is not really a descent but is, in fact, an ascent — or as Young puts it, that divine purpose "goes out into matter to obtain means to effect this purpose and finally attains its end: it actualizes the purpose that first sent it forth."[2]

When I first wrapped my mind around this idea more than twenty-five years ago, I intuitively recognized Young's insight as the missing key I had been looking for to unlock what I had long perceived as a metaphysical impasse: on the one hand the Eastern and gnostic scenarios that see the "fall" into matter as a mistake or illusion, and on the other a Judeo–Christian worldview that could intuitively recognize creation as necessary and valuable but was unable to attribute a motive to it beyond the effluent "goodness" of God and, hence, unable to develop an ethics of human planetary responsibility beyond the personal drama of repentance and redemption. Young is able to articulate a third option: that divine purpose "needs" the created world, not simply to manifest the divine attributes (such as love, beauty, steadfastness) but to *actualize* them. The journey into time, form, and constraint is also the journey from potentiality to realization and the "release" into being of qualities that cannot exist as pure potentiality — such as love and generosity — but only as realized action.

In Young's fascinating scenario — which unfolds more in the physical domain than in the metaphysical — this actualization is accomplished in a seven-stage process that follows a V-shaped trajectory (Young calls it an arc). The left side of the arc traces a "descent" into form, each of the three stages (light, nuclear particles, atoms) entailing an increasing immersion in form and a greater restriction of freedom. The arc reaches its nadir at stage four, the molecular level, and then rises on its right side to increasing degrees of freedom and power of expression. Tracing these seven "kingdoms" (as Young calls these seven stages) through an evolutionary sequence, the pattern would look like this:[3]

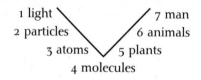

1 light
2 particles
3 atoms
4 molecules
5 plants
6 animals
7 man

The key structural element here is symmetry. With stage 4 as the fulcrum, Young shows how 3 is symmetrical with 5; 2 with 6; and 1 with

7. On either side of the axis, the ascent exactly mirrors the descent in respective degrees of freedom and mobility. Stage 4 is the point of greatest constriction. Young reminds his readers how molecules exist only in bound form: as chains of atoms held together by chemical bonds and unable either to move independently or to grow. Stages 3 and 5 are both characterized by "one degree of freedom" (plants can grow and reproduce; atoms can move at random but have a fixed nuclear mass), stages 2 and 6 by "two degrees of freedom" (animals can both grow and move; nuclear particles can appear and disappear at random, having no fixed nuclear mass), and 1 and 7 by "three degrees of freedom" (humans can move, grow, and consciously reflect; light — at least in Young's schematic — is totally unboundaried). The difference underlying these symmetries, however, is that on the left side of the arc the freedom is random and spontaneous; on the right side it is conscious and voluntary.[4] Young stresses the crucial importance of the fourth, most boundaried stage; it is "the working base that process has to reach before it can start building up again."[5]

Young's paradigm is well worth exploring in its own right, but my major point in introducing it here is that it led me to be curious as to whether the seven-stage unfolding of the Trinity I have just described displayed this same descending and ascending symmetry. My conclusion is that it does.

This is most clearly the case with triads two and six (the Primordial and Pentecostal Trinities), which are virtually mirror images:

THE PRIMORDIAL TRINITY

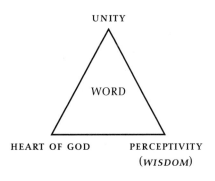

UNITY

WORD

HEART OF GOD   PERCEPTIVITY
                      (*WISDOM*)

THE PENTECOSTAL TRINITY

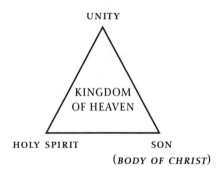

UNITY

KINGDOM
OF HEAVEN

HOLY SPIRIT   SON
(*BODY OF CHRIST*)

Both triads are so configured as to fit easily into the traditional Father–Son–Holy Spirit pattern, with the three "persons" of the Trinity arranged at the familiar three triadic points. But whereas the first of this pair is the *cosmological* Trinity (the Trinity before all time and form), the second bears the unique *historical* imprint of the human reality of Jesus Christ. In the Primordial Trinity, as we saw, all triadic points are equally male and female, and androgynous imagery is not only appropriate but unavoidable. In the Pentecostal Trinity, this imagery must be much more carefully discerned. When we have a historically male Jesus who specifically refers to the Unity as "Father," we must ask ourselves hard questions about the role that gendered language is intended to play in conveying that vivid sense of personal relatedness at the heart of Christian self-understanding. (By contrast, Creator–Redeemer–Sanctifier, the most popular of the contemporary gender–inclusive Trinitarian formulas, is completely impersonal.) And perhaps in the final analysis the most gracious solution would be simply to cut this particular triad some slack and look for our gender rebalancing elements in other Trinities.

I believe that most conundrums in present Trinitarian theologies are caused by not sufficiently distinguishing these two "lookalike" Trinities on opposite sides of the arc: cosmological and historical. While they are indeed symmetrical, they reflect different stages of process and require different ways of speaking about that process. One of my main objectives in undertaking this exploration, as you know, was to take the pressure off the Pentecostal Trinity by situating it within an expanded family of Trinities so that we would not feel obligated to lay upon it every single thing we need to say about the reality of God.

In similar ways, triads three and five (the Sophianic and Messianic Trinities) mirror each other — again, from opposite sides of the arc. Triad three has as its reconciling ground the Word, triad five the Word–made–flesh Jesus. Both have their manifesting principle in something I have named the "Heart of God." But in triad three this Heart functions as a cosmic principle (the hidden ground of love, as Merton might have called it), while in triad five it bears the stamp of Jesus's human createdness and sacrificial love; it is *his* heart, *his* substantiality. And as we compare the two new arisings from these symmetrical triads, we see that Holy Substantiality, which makes possible the descent into flesh, is balanced by Holy Spirit, which guides the way out.

Triads one and seven have a similar balance. They both unfold in realms far beyond the physical and temporal — in fact, at the outer edges of our ability even to imagine. In the first triad we see the incipient stirrings of the divine dynamism that will launch the journey into manifestation. And in the seventh we converge on that "accomplishment of purpose" that presumably stills these stirrings and restores the equilibrium of the Endless Unity. Being again dissolves into the nonbeing to which it has always belonged. But as Alpha converges on Omega (the two no longer needing to be held apart), the very first arising, Heart, and the last, the Oikonomia, or fullness of heart, are now known to be the same. The hidden, unknown, superessential Unity has "realized" its own depths.

And at the nadir point, the center of the fourth triad, stands Jesus. It is for good reason that patristic theologians intuitively referred to him as the "hinge" of salvation." (Young, who gives no evidence of having read patristic theologians, calls this point "the turn.") In this fourth configuration, aided by Young's insight, we can see new levels of resonance in the intuitive Christian insight that in Jesus, God has become man — or in other words: in Jesus, God's yearning to descend into form has reached its end point, the most dense and concentrated embeddedness in form that is divinely possible — and that precisely for this reason, creation has arrived at "the working base that process has to reach before it can start building up again." In Jesus, the love of God descending into increasingly particulate forms of createdness reaches its point of maximum densification and constriction. From here, it must inevitably be catapulted forth again on that hinge.

However, this hinge is not to be conceived of as a change of direction, as in the old *exitus et reditus* schools of emanationism. While descent and ascent may seem to be the case from our angle of vision, the reality is that there is no break in direction or velocity — simply a continued forward motion along the parabolic curve of the divine will guided by the Law of Three.

Part Four

HARNESSING THE POWER OF THREE

19

The Ham Radio in the Tea Cupboard

WHAT I HAVE BEEN UP TO IN THIS BOOK is essentially a wager, in the classic spirit of theologian Paul Ricoeur. According to Ricoeur, the proving ground for spiritual truth lies not in abstract speculation but in lived experience. You set forth a premise, and if it is correct, you will see it confirmed as you attempt to live it into action.[1]

My wager, then, is that behind the three persons of the Trinity stands the Law of Three. Starting from this initial premise, I have used that core tenet of the Law of Three — *the interweaving of three creates a fourth in a new dimension* — to expand the Trinity into a set of seven successive unfoldings spanning the gamut from Alpha to Omega, from the headwaters of creation to the fullness of time. Within this expanded Trinity, I have tried to demonstrate, there is room to experience both the scale and the dynamism of divine creativity — and more important, to participate consciously in that dynamism as our own lives become ordered around the Law of Three.

I see the work of this book as essentially supplying the mechanics by which we might enter more fully into Beatrice Bruteau's remarkable revelation: "It is the presence of the Trinity as a pattern repeated at every scale in the cosmic order that makes the universe the manifestation of God and itself sacred and holy."[2]

So what can this expanded Trinity offer that is lacking in our present model? I am sure that question will be uppermost in the minds of many of my readers as we come down the home stretch of this presentation. If the old model has served us for well more than sixteen hundred years, why do we need such a radical overhaul? Won't the relatively minor adjustments suggested by Catherine LaCugna and others suffice to get us back on course? If the greatest of Christian mystical theologians — including the Cappadocian fathers, Saint Augustine, and Saint Bernard of Clairvaux — have drawn living water from its well, who am I to suggest that the well has run dry?

But you see, that's exactly what I'm *not* saying. In contrast to what is now a growing majority in liberal theological circles, I have stated emphatically, and will continue to state emphatically, that there is nothing amiss in our familiar model. I repeat: *there is nothing amiss.* The "persons" are correctly named and configured, and nothing needs to be amended. The only problem is that it is a freeze-frame, one phase in a moving sequence, and it is the contention of this book that most of the paradigm distress besetting contemporary Trinitarian theology has arisen out of trying to bottle into particle format what is intrinsically a wave.

Or to return to the metaphor I introduced at the very beginning of this book, it's like using the Trinity as a theological tea cupboard while all along there is a metaphysical ham radio of considerable bandwidth waiting to be discovered inside. My wager is that in this expanded Trinity we will find not only the spaciousness to negotiate traditional theological impasses but also a newfound capacity to live Christianity as the dynamic and integral path it, in fact, is.

How might this play out? According to Paul Ricoeur, the proof of the hermeneutical wager lies in the pudding. The ultimate question — Is it true? — is most gracefully approached by the access route of "How is it useful to think of it in this way?" And so in this concluding chapter I would like to suggest some ways in which an expanded and dynamic Trinity, explicitly tied to a cosmic law, might be useful to a Christianity struggling to enter the twenty-first century with both its identity and its visionary imagination intact. This approach will also allow me to review some of the high points of this book and to call out what seem to be the most important directions for further reflection and conversation. By now it should come as no surprise that the number of these points works out to be seven.

The Problem of the "Missing" Feminine

For an immediate starter, this expanded model deals conclusively with the original question that launched this exploration: the problem of the Trinity's "missing" feminine representation. When we set the Trinity in motion according to the Law of Three, we find that it is not about "persons" understood as permanent, fixed identities but rather about *personifications* of flowing and intertwining energy streams — a notion that actually comes closer to what the Cappadocian fathers originally had in mind. Their term *hypostases*, traditionally translated as "persons," actually comes closer to our modern notion of "states," the multiple forms in which a single substance can exist (such as the chemical compound H_2O existing in the "persons" of water, vapor, and ice). The Law of Three affirms the flowingness implicit in the original Cappadocian Trinity and gives us powerful new ways to work with it.

In our own particular (sixth-stage) Trinity, the feminine is most clearly present in the Christosophianic energy that flows from the Holy Spirit, which is not feminine per se, you remember, but *androgynous*, the bridal union of the human Jesus and the eternal virgin, Wisdom.[3] The feminine is also strongly carried in the new arising emerging from this Trinity — Kingdom of Heaven — which as a counterstroke of the now-displaced Substantiality (see the table of counterstrokes, p. 131) bears a lineage whose headwaters lie in the primordial Sophia and whose human face is Mary. This explains why the feminine has arisen so powerfully in our own times, why Sophia is coming so universally into her own. According to the calculations of the Law of Three, it *must* be this way, for the tincture of our present age is saturated with the feminine, and its essence will emerge more and more clearly as this particular Trinitarian configuration rounds toward completion.

The contemporary concern to secure a feminine presence within the Trinity is necessary and right, but bound by the substance theology of the past, theologians have been looking for it in the wrong place. It lives not in permanently gendered "persons" holding down their respective triadic points but in the Sophianic energy upwelling from the Trinity's very heart. "She" is the fourth in a new dimension. Within the more spacious framework of the Law of Three, we are released from those endless, futile dialogues about religious gender and language and gently propelled toward our real role, as midwives and shapers of this profoundly Sophianic new arising, so that it may become a strong and true holy reconciling for the age yet to come.

Christianity Remythologized

Second, this new, expanded Trinitarian model creates a more spacious container for the rich mythological and personal language of traditional Christian understanding. I hope the exploration we have just completed in part 3 has amply demonstrated this. It is not a matter of demythologizing or neutering the language of Christianity; we simply have to assign each expression of the mystical wholeness to its proper Trinity. All of those profoundly archetypal and unitive images — the virgin birth, the mystical marriage, the resurrection of the body, Alpha and Omega, the mystical Body of Christ, the final consummation of all things in Christ — are restored to us, not simply as personal metaphors for transformation but as cosmic truths, literally grounded in a vastly expanded, biaxial reality. They resonate so profoundly in our inner imagination because they are literally grounded in a cosmic topology; creation itself has passed this way.

While the bent of modern liberal-progressive Christianity has been strongly toward demythologizing (that is, downsizing the Christian Mystery to make it fit within the domain of historical facticity), the alternative possibility being set forth in these pages is *to expand the cosmic playing field* so that it at least matches the scale of the human heart. The Law of Three gives us a way to do this, and when the Trinity is seen as its primary mandala, it conveys the knowledge of how to access the vast treasure house of Christian symbolism and reawaken its transformational power.

Reclaiming the Primacy of Christ

The importance of this knowledge becomes particularly clear when directed toward what in traditional theological language is known as "the scandal of particularity," the unique, unrepeatable, complete expression of the fullness of God made manifest in Jesus Christ. Nowadays, it is fair to say, that claim has become more of a liability than an asset. In the wake of two millennia of Christian religious imperialism, it is understandable why contemporary Christians of good conscience living in a pluralistic world would want to draw back from the cosmic singularity once claimed for Christ. Contemporary images of Christ again follow that downsizing tendency, reframing the human Jesus in more modest spiritual categories — as teacher, brother, prophet, mystic, revolutionary — while separating out "Christ consciousness" as a universal cosmic principle, accessible to all traditions.

But as Raimon Panikkar has insisted, there is no Christianity without acknowledging the centrality of Christ — not just as founder, master teacher, enlightened being, but in some sense "the icon of all reality," bearing in a particularly intense and illumined way the nature of God, the hologram of reality itself. Within the wide-angle lens of the Law of Three, this claim again becomes understandable.

The theological cornerstone of this claim was hammered out at the Council of Chalcedon (451 C.E.) in that notoriously difficult doctrine of the "two natures of Christ." This core Christological affirmation stipulates that the personhood of Jesus Christ exists in two natures fully human and fully divine, "*inconfuse, immutabiliter, indivise, inseparabiliter*" (not confused, immutable, undivided, inseparable).[4] The "how" of this mind-boggling syzygy has bedeviled the Christian rational intellect for well more than sixteen centuries, and in our own theologically timid times, it easily falls victim to the debunking tendency of the postmodern mind. Liberal-progressive Christianity's failure of nerve here, for better or worse, collapses the main pillar of the doctrinal scaffolding around that core Christian intuition that in the person of Jesus heaven and earth have been brought together in a decisive and ultimate way.

The Law of Three can help supply the mechanics of this theologically valid but perplexing doctrine. And the solution is so simple once you see it in these terms: the two natures are joined together in the dynamism of the unfolding Trinity itself. Each triad captures a different phase of that single, unified ray of divine self–disclosure. In that first Trinity, the Proto–Trinity, the Christ presence is manifest as what I termed *Heart of God*: the inmost, self–projective knowingness of God. In the second it manifests as Logos; in the third as Substantiality, the fundamental building block of our visible universe. In the fourth Trinity we meet the fully human Jesus, and in the three subsequent triads we meet successively spiritualized aspects of this same Christ presence: as Christosophia or Spirit, mystical body or Kingdom of Heaven, and Oikonomia, that realized fullness, "in whom all things hold together," so powerfully intimated in that great cosmic hymn in Colossians. They are all distinct expressions of that single Christic lineage — inconfuse, immutabiliter, indivise, inseparabiliter. But in a holographic way perhaps unimaginable to those early patristic fathers (since the concept of the hologram was still unknown in the fourth century), each carries the fullness of the entire lineage within it and is a complete instantiation of that lineage.

With the help of the Law of Three, it is possible to reclaim both the boldness and the coherence of that original Christian vision of Christ as the cornerstone of all reality without being trapped in the exclusive and triumphalistic categories of the past. The problem all along is not that the vision was too grandiose but that the map was too small.

Ternary Metaphysics Comes Into its Own

If Christ is indeed, as Panikkar intuits, the "icon of all reality," and if the Law of Three is indeed a cosmic law governing the dynamic, self–projective aspect of God (another way of describing the Law of World Creation), then it seems inevitable that the human Jesus would manifest in the highest and most intense way the dynamism of the Law of Three. As Panikkar so forcefully argues, the origin of the doctrine of the Trinity lies not in late patristic speculation but in the mind of Christ itself—a mind that the Trinity reproduces with meticulous accuracy. For those with ears to hear, it offers a luminous gateway into that mind and a comprehensive praxis for participating in the life of Christ, not through outward imitation, but through an inner appropriation of its core transformational principle.

Once this intrinsic relationship between the Trinity and the mind of Christ is identified for what it is — the evolutionary unveiling of a whole new metaphysical system based on threeness rather than twoness — so much of the puzzle falls into place. We can now understand the dynamism that Bruno Barnhart speaks about so forcefully — why the history of the West in all of its messy, centrifugal energy is not a betrayal of the path of Christ but its lawful and inevitable trajectory. We can see why orthodox Christianity (at least in the West) has tended to distrust its own rich mystical and contemplative heritage, innately suspicious of its Neoplatonic tendencies; we understand how Teilhard de Chardin so profoundly intuited the cosmic Christ as the driveshaft of evolution. They are all shadow dancing with the Law of Three — its earthiness, its evolutionary thrust, its dynamism. Once this ternary presence is recognized for what it is, the way is finally open to begin to articulate an authentic Christian Wisdom tradition founded on the threeness that is its native metaphysical ground. The ugly duckling in the binary duck pond is finally acknowledged as a swan.

This realization, in turn, provides a way to explain within the wider community of world religions Christianity's peculiar allegiance to the Trinity. It is not, as Jews and Muslims fear, an abandonment of the great tradition of Abrahamic monotheism in favor of an artificial, dogmatically driven tritheism. Once the Trinity is seen not as three divine persons to be individually worshipped but as a mandala of divine reality entrusted to Christianity in a special way, much of the problem dissolves. Esoterically understood, the threeness of the Trinity simply proclaims that flowingness is the nature of God, that relationality permeates the entire field of manifest reality, and that in every situation the optimal practical orientation is to acknowledge the threefold nature of all process and to strive for the midwifing of third force.

Of course, you don't have to be a Christian to work with the Law of Three; as a fundamental cosmic law, it is equally open to all religions and equally open to purely secular access points. But because (if my wager is correct) the headwaters of Christianity are so precisely situated in the historical unveiling of this law in the person of Jesus Christ, it follows that within the universal family of world religions, a Christian is a person called to work with the Law of Three in a very specific and intentional sort of way. And that leads us directly to our next point.

Integrating Theology and Practice

In part 1 we spent a good deal of time getting to know the Law of Three as a practical tool for inner and outer transformation. Its strength lies in its consistency and versatility as well as in its broad range of applicability. We saw that it is equally at home solving interpersonal issues, analyzing literature, computing theology, managing global economics, mediating conflicts, brainstorming solutions for a sustainable universe. Wherever there is an authentic new arising, the Law of Three is somehow involved.

To claim, therefore, that Christianity as a path has a special affinity for the Law of Three places at its disposal a powerful tool for carrying the Mystery into the marketplace. Imagine how the energies of our planet would shift if Christians en masse took seriously their obligation to work with the Law of Three as their fundamental spiritual praxis. Face to face with the vast challenges of our times — environmental, economic, political — they would abjure judgment (because according to the Law of Three, denying force is a legitimate player in every equation), set their sights higher than "winners and losers" (or even negotiated compromise), and instead strive in all situations to align their minds and hearts with third force. What a powerful new morphogenetic field would thereby be constellated!

Closer to my own immediate sphere of interest — the arena

of Christian contemplative practice — the Law of Three offers a congenial metaphysical ground on which to explore the biblical invitation to "put on the mind of Christ" — far more so than the traditional categories furnished by Christian ascetical theology. I am sure I am not the only Christian practitioner to have noticed the cognitive dissonance between Christianity's incarnation-centered theology and its body-denying praxis. Again, if my wager is correct, the cause of this dissonance can be traced to a metaphysical clash between Christianity's ternary heart and its binary head and to the fact that the dominant strain in its ascetical theology has long been carried by Christian Neoplatonism, with its upward-tending mysticism and inherent distrust of matter. Against a ternary backdrop, we can appreciate not only the deep wisdom but also the recalibrated spiritual trajectory inherent in Bruno Barnhart's powerful comment (cited earlier, p. 79):

> The gospel's secret power, often hardly glimpsed by Christianity itself, is the gathering up of all our passion, our entropic centrifugal energy, our very outward thrust and vital compulsivity, secularity, and carnality, into this divine energy that ever flows out from its hidden Source.

Practically, this suggests that the Christian contemplative needs to stop fighting the world, the body, secularity, messiness, and above all, the inevitable thrust toward the future as the self-projective nature of divine love continues to make its presence known along the horizontal axis. Teilhard de Chardin was entirely right on this point. In a twenty-first-century world rapidly evolving toward its Omega Point (more on that just ahead), spiritual praxis will want to be shifted away from subduing the body and renouncing the world and reoriented toward the acquisition of an alert and supple attentiveness that can make itself more readily available to third force. All of this, of course, has already been modeled by Jesus himself; the recovery of a ternary perspective merely restores the proper emphasis to what was there from the start.

Alpha

If the Law of Three is indeed the Law of World Creation, then it would by definition have had to be there "at the beginning" — that is, at the headwaters of space and time as we know it today. And if the Trinity is indeed our Christian connecting link to the Law of Three — as Gurdjieff himself implied — this means that it is by definition a cosmogenetic principle; in fact, it is first and foremost a cosmogenetic principle. The revolutionary implications of this statement have hardly been suspected in Christianity, let alone tapped. In this section I would like to reflect a bit more extensively on what has been an underlying theme all along: the power of the Trinity, expressly linked to the Law of Three, to heal the schism between scientific and biblical cosmology that has tormented the Western mind for more than five centuries.

For its first fifteen hundred years, Christianity lived in a unified cosmos. The biblical world was the scientific world; the creation story as told in the book of Genesis was the only "universe story" the Christian world knew. Then, in a series of disruptions beginning toward the end of the fifteenth century, that unified cosmos began to come unglued. From Columbus, Copernicus, Galileo (and many others following in their wake), we learned new and difficult truths: that the earth was not flat, that it was not the center of the universe, but only a small globe revolving in a minor solar system nested in an infinite vastness of time and space whose dimensions exceeded our wildest biblical imagination. Most of mainstream Christianity eventually got on board with the new cosmological map but at a significant cost: the disruption of that former sense of coherence. Noiselessly we bought into what I call the "Jesus theme park": an engaging but definitely smaller universe with its familiar theological rides and roller coasters. In the name of intellectual respectability we have become habituated to a hiccup between scientific reality and biblical reality, with the scientific reality being the larger, more objective, "truer," and the religious being the smaller, more personal, and subjective. This is fundamentally crazy-making and is the root,

I am convinced, of so much of the alienation and intellectual cynicism of the postmodern West.[5]

The fundamentalist approach — highly successful — is to shrink the world back to its biblical foundations and tenaciously hold it there through "faith." Coherence is again restored. But again at a high cost.

Can the Trinity, reclaimed as a cosmogonic principle whose driveshaft is the Law of Three, contribute anything to the resolution of this dilemma? That is my firm conviction and one of my main purposes in writing this book.

Throughout Christian history there have been recurrent intimations, particularly in the Christian East, that the Trinity is indeed somehow bound up in cosmogenesis; if not itself a cosmogonic principle, it is at the very least the primordial expression of such a principle. Orthodox theology has long upheld the distinction between the *ousia* of God — that ineffable, unfathomable divine essence sometimes known as the Godhead — and the *energia* of God: that self-communicating, outpouring radiance, which is knowable in and through the Trinity. While the Christian West has always rested uneasily with the idea of a "God behind God" (insisting that there is nothing of God that is not fully expressed in the Trinity), the greatest of its mystics — Meister Eckhart and Jacob Boehme among them — have similarly been drawn toward that core notion of an unknowable Godhead with the Trinity as its primary manifesting principle. We took particular note of Boehme's observation: "As there is a threefold source in everything, and each is always the glass [image], begetter, and cause of the other, nothing excepted, all things are according to the essence of the Ternary."[6]

In our own era, this vision of the Trinity as fundamentally a cosmogonic template has been powerfully rekindled by Beatrice Bruteau, who as we saw in chapter 6 comes within a hair's breadth of reconstructing the Law of Three out of her own intellectual resources. Her argument that a God-community must necessarily consist of three persons because three is the number required to sustain the dynamic and diffusive qualities of agape love is essentially the Law of Three minus the math. And her meticulous demonstration that the Trinity, understood as "the original symbiotic unity," furnishes the template for all subsequent scientific evolution in a "self-creating universe" is an eye-opening read even apart from the Law of Three. Clearly there is a huge piece of the Trinitarian dynamic that traditional Western theology has been consistently missing.

I spent a considerable amount of time with Jacob Boehme in this book because, of all Christianity's visionary geniuses, I believe he is the one who comes closest to intuiting not only the principle but the actual mechanics by which the Trinity exercises its cosmogonic agency. In chapter 8 I attempted to reformat his "Three Principles, seven properties" according to the Law of Three. When so arranged, as we saw, they yield a three-stage protocreation through which the Endless Unity establishes the essential inner conditions that will allow the outer world to manifest. The "in the beginning" of the biblical account actually corresponds to stage four in our expanded cosmogonic map.

While this notion may take some getting used to from traditional theological perspectives, it is interesting that cosmologists are now actively exploring this same speculative terrain. "What came before the big bang?" is now a legitimate and lively arena for scientific investigation, for clearly, a very specific and mathematically calculable set of conditions would have had to be in place to establish the conditions in which such a hypothetical primordial explosion could have occurred.

While I unfortunately lack the scientific training to be able to follow the complex mathematics firsthand, with the help of reliable translators such as Brian Greene and several personal acquaintances working in the field of theoretical physics,[7] I have at least been able to keep up with the gist of the conversation, and the gist suggests that there is indeed considerable overlap between current scientific calculations as to what a hypothetical protocreation might have looked like and Boehme's visionary exploration of that same turf, particularly once it is recast in Law of Three format. At the very least, there appears to be enough resonance to suggest that not only theologians but also cosmologists will need to be paying a good deal more attention to the mystical ramblings of this medieval German shoemaker. At that "beginning of all beginnings," in those first cosmic stirrings toward "the impressure of nothing into something," not only do all of those great physical forces — the strong, weak, and electromagnetic forces, plus the force of gravity — come together as one, there is reason to suspect that scientific and spiritual cosmology may also come together as one. At any rate, I suspect that it is in these visionary headwaters, made navigable by the Law of Three, that we will find the reconciling ground between the universe story as told in biblical tradition and as told by contemporary cosmology.[8]

To do so, however, we need the fully expanded cosmological map I have laid out here with the help of the Law of Three. It cannot be demonstrated on the basis of the classic freeze-frame Trinity of traditional theology. It requires the full sevenfold Trinitarian expansion, in which the first three, protocreation, stages are prominently represented. Until we can visualize the entire cosmic dynamism, we cannot see the place where the stories come together or appreciate how brilliantly the biblical story nests within the greater cosmic sweep.

Seven: Omega

Almost from the start, the anticipation of a final apocalypse has been built into the Christian worldview. First-generation Christians lived in eager expectation of the *parousia*, the Second Coming of Christ. Around the year 1000, an "end of the world" millennialist fervor swept Christianity, as it did again at our second millennial transit, still only just subsiding. From Nostradamus to the *Celestine Prophecy*, from the rapture to the Mayan calendar: the intimation of an imminent final cataclysm continues to haunt us. A sense of closure seems to be deeply embedded in the structures of the Western mind, although most of the expressions of this awareness have to date been dramatic and punitive. The expanded Trinity I have presented here gives us a new way of picturing this liminal time, rather as Teilhard de Chardin pictured it: not as a fiery Götterdämmerung but as a love come full and complete within the terms of this particular trajectory of manifestation.

Time and again we have hurled our predictions of imminent demise against the planet, and time and again we have awakened the next morning to the world still sweetly in place. Our earth seems infinitely more solid, more resilient, more forgiving than our fevered human brains. And yet the alternative is not simply to fall back to sleep proclaiming "all is well," for both the rate and the magnitude of change on even a day-to-day basis suggest that we are in a time of rapid acceleration, a dramatic jolt forward along some unknown timeline whose challenges we can no longer responsibly ignore. Wherever this planet is heading, it will require the best and deepest of our human hearts and minds to stay the course.

From the sevenfold expansion of the Trinity I have shared with you, I would suggest a slightly different way of picturing our cosmic positioning. The intimation of closure is right on target, but it is not the world that is passing — it is, rather, the sixth age, this great, two-thousand-year cycle lived under the aegis of the Pentecostal Trinity (as I have named it): Father, Son, and Holy Spirit. If there is restlessness in liberal Christendom today around the naming of the persons of the Trinity, that restlessness is well-founded, for it speaks to the much more dramatic reconfiguration as Kingdom of Heaven, the new arising as our present (and waning) Trinity moves into position as holy reconciling in a dawning seventh Trinitarian age. The emerging configuration, you recall, is as follows:

UNITY

OIKONOMIA

KINGDOM
OF HEAVEN   HOLY SPIRIT

If we can orient ourselves on this map correctly, it certainly provides the big picture that will allow us to work creatively, courageously, and skillfully with the unique challenges of our present era. We are not off the hook as far as apocalypse is concerned: the Omega Point is indeed an impending reality, and according to the calculations I have used here to guide the unfolding of the Trinity, this seventh age will complete the octave of the present sequence. (On this point Teilhard de Chardin was once again correct; against the backdrop of the Law of Three, his challenging vision is no longer anomalous but expressly predictable.) But nor is the planet going to pass away tomorrow, for we are still only standing on the threshold of a new age, and there is still a considerable distance to be traversed by conscious evolution before the business of this octave has run its course. Our seventh Trinity gives us a glimpse of where the future may be headed as well as a sense of the tasks that may be required of us.

Despite what most people think, the word *apocalypse* does not actually mean a final cataclysm (check it out in a dictionary); it means "unveiling" (literally, "uncovering"). And unveiling does indeed seem to be the agenda of this final triad, as what is gradually revealed at each of the triadic points is the oneness glowing brightly beneath the surface of multiplicity. The long journey through "perceptivity and divisibility" (as Boehme calls it) reaches its destination as the Endless Unity rejoins itself as the Oikonomia, the fullness of all things. Our human task at this stage, as we pondered it in part 3, is simply to sink our hearts more and more deeply into the Holy Substantiality of that Oneness itself and learn to live within its more diaphanous reality. What in a former age was the rare attainment of a saint is in the age at hand the new baseline for a conscious human being and a prerequisite for playing our part in the great unfolding soon to be under way as the kaleidoscope turns yet one more time and our world converges toward its Omega Point, the fullness of love.

Once again we see the confirmation of this in the world around us. We are, in fact, converging on oneness, hurtling toward it. Our global systems are already inextricably intertwined. Ecologically we know that we are one planet—no matter how much we still try to deny it. Economics and communications are already there, long since fused into a single global network. We are converging on a oneness that requires a different spirit from human beings, a different way of finding identity in collectivity; and a response to this evolutionary challenge does indeed seem to be emerging with such a heartfelt and broad-based spontaneity that many commentators are now referring to our era as the second axial period."[9] For the first time in history (so far as we know) a critical mass of people seems to be attaining the capacity for nondual consciousness — that is, the capacity to perceive from oneness, to think from the whole to the part — and they are wielding the tools of cybertechnology boldly to make their influence felt. This is exactly what Teilhard de Chardin was envisioning in his notion of "densification": an acceleration of the evolutionary process through the convergence of human energy. It is also exactly what our seventh-stage Trinity predicts, as the mature Kingdom of Heaven, or spiritualized humanity, the realized fruit of our own Trinitarian era, moves into place as the catalytic element for the unfolding — unveiling — of the Oikonomia. From this wider perspective we can perhaps find a new clarity and renewed courage that will allow us to face what lies before us in a spirit of conscious participation and not be dragged kicking and screaming into the future.

We are also in an era of deaths, as old forms die before a rising wave of new need and new understanding. But to the degree that we Christians can take hold of the tools offered us in the Law of Three, trusting its dynamism, allowing it to weave new possibilities, Christianity need not be a casualty. Intrinsically, it is a religion geared toward the future, toward new birth, toward hope. The mind of Christ, that archetypal ternary, catapults us directly into the future, and there — if we can manage not to lose our bearings but simply use the tools we have been given — we can, indeed, still participate in this astonishing new unfolding and shape this planet with spiritual intelligence and deeply transformed love as it hurtles toward fullness.

Helpful Lists

THREE FORCES (WHICH, WHEN WOVEN TOGETHER, CREATE A FOURTH IN A NEW DIMENSION):

- Affirming (first; manifesting)
- Denying (second; Unmanifest)
- Reconciling (third; manifested)
- Plus: new arising (forms the fourth in a new dimension)

THREE PRINCIPLES (BOEHME'S):

- First Principle (fire, wrath)
- Second Principle (Light–World, Light/Love, Wisdom, Love)
- Third Principle (visible world)

SEVEN PROPERTIES OF THE THREE PRINCIPLES (BOEHME'S)

1. Desiring (attraction)
2. Agitation (stinging, breaking)
3. Anguish (also perceptivity)
4. Fire
5. Light/love
6. Sound
7. Substance (nature)

FOUR GROUND RULES (CONVENTIONS)

1. The interweaving of three produces a fourth in a new dimension.
2. New arising from the former triad becomes holy reconciling in the new triad.
3. Holy denying (second force) will always be played by the divine Unmanifest.
4. New arising in any triad is a counterstroke of the now–displaced holy affirming from the former triad.

TRINITARIAN NEW ARISINGS

FIRST: Heart (of God)

SECOND: Word (Spirit)

THIRD: Substantiality (Holy Substantiality)

FOURTH: Jesus

FIFTH: Holy Spirit

SIXTH: Kingdom of Heaven

SEVENTH: Oikonomia

PARALLEL TRINITIES

FIRST: Proto–Trinity

SECOND: Primordial Trinity

THIRD: Sophianic Trinity

FOURTH: Incarnational Trinity

FIFTH: Messianic Trinity

SIXTH: Pentecostal Trinity

SEVENTH: Economic Trinity

Notes

CHAPTER 1. Why Feminizing the Trinity Won't Work

1. This argument, in approximately these terms, has been powerfully advanced by Bruno Barnhart in his *Second Simplicity: The Inner Shape of Christianity* (Mahwah, NJ: Paulist Press, 1999). I will discuss Barnhart's argument at some length later in this chapter.

2. Elizabeth Johnson, *She Who Is: The Mystery of God in Feminist Theological Discourse* (New York: Crossroad, 1992), p. 54. Her overall thesis is concisely summarized in her third chapter, pp. 42–57.

3. And, of course, "state" is the more accurate rendering of the original Greek *hypostasis*, usually translated as "person."

4. Prakriti and purusha are the Hindu polarity for God as energy and God as being. They correspond most closely with the Cappadocian fathers' concept of *energia* (prakriti) and *ousia* (purusha).

5. For a thorough study of the evolution of the Christian doctrine of the Trinity, see Catherine Mowry LaCugna, *God for Us: The Trinity and Christian Life* (San Francisco: HarperSanFrancisco, 1991). I will have more to say about this book in chapter 6.

6. Jacob Boehme, *Clavis* (Whitefish, MT: Kessinger, n.d.), p. 2.

7. Olivier Clément, *The Roots of Christian Mysticism: Text and Commentary* (New York: New York City Press, 1993), pp. 74–75.

8. For a summary of Jung's extensive writings on this subject, see Barnhart, *Second Simplicity*, pp. 149–53. Johnson's feminist critique of the Jungian argument has been noted earlier in this chapter.

9. Barnhart, *Second Simplicity*, p. 6 and pp. 90–139. The fourth pole then becomes earth, which for Barnhart incorporates elements of matter, the material world, the body, and cosmic humanity.

10. Ibid., p. 90.

11. Ibid., p. 143.

12. In identifying Christ with the second (male) pole and the Spirit/ Wisdom energy with the third (female), Barnhart has no way to establish a continuity between the historically male Jesus and his continuing personal presence as Christic energy and ground. Are we to infer that when a person leaves the physical body, he or she becomes feminine in the energetic manifestation? If this is so, then the continuity between gender and personhood must be seen as normative only in the physical/temporal realm: a position that nullifies the entire binary metaphysic as well as traditional Trinitarian theology based on the eternal hypostases of Father, Son, and Spirit. A can of worms indeed!

13. This is the ternary proposed by Elizabeth Johnson as the fully feminine equivalent of the male–imaged Father/Son/Holy Spirit.

14. This is the basic ternary of the Law of Three as set forth by Gurdjieff. See chapter 2.

15. Boehme, *Clavis*, p. 50.

16. Johnson speaks of "the fluidity of gender symbolism evidenced in biblical Christology" (*She Who Is*, p. 99), but from her fixed theological perspective she fails to see that this fluidity is a function of the metaphysical fluidity implicit in a ternary system, where the qualities affirming, denying, and reconciling are not gender linked.

CHAPTER 2. Exploring the Law of Three

1. Jacob Needleman, *What Is God?* (New York: Jeremy Tarcher/Penguin, 2009), p. 97.

2. Quoted in P. D. Ouspensky, *In Search of the Miraculous* (New York: Harcourt Brace Jovanovich, 1949), p. 128–29.

3. Ibid., p. 129.

4. Private letter, March 26, 2002.

5. In *Beelzebub's Tales to His Grandson* (New York and London: Viking Arkana, 1992), p. 689, Gurdjieff offers an alternative wording of the second invocation: instead of "Holy and Mighty," he presents the liturgical formula as "Holy God, Holy the Firm, Holy the Immortal, have mercy on us." Whether this is merely an eccentricity of trans-

lation (*firm* — that is, solid and substantial — can be seen in some ways as a rough equivalent of *mighty*) or a more deliberate allusion to an underlying esoteric meaning is a fascinating subject for conjecture. Annie Dillard fans will remember that she named her second book *Holy the Firm* (New York: Harper and Row, 1977), offering the following explanation for the term:

> Esoteric Christianity, I read, posits a substance. It is a created substance, lower than metals and minerals on a "spiritual scale," and lower than salts and earths, occurring beneath salts and earths in the waxy deepness of planets, but never on the surface of planets where men could discern it, and it is in touch with the Absolute, at base. In touch with the Absolute! At base. The name of this substance is: Holy the Firm.
>
> Holy the Firm: and is Holy the Firm in touch with metals and minerals? With salts and earths? Of course, and straight on up, till "up" ends by curving back. Does something that touched something that touched Holy the Firm in touch with the Absolute at base seep into ground water, into grain; are islands rooted in it, and trees? Of course. (pp. 72–73)

The obvious relevance of Dillard's comment to our Trinitarian inquiry leads me to suspect that Gurdjieff's insistence on "Holy the Firm" is not merely a variant translation but a deliberate allusion to the esoteric roots of the doctrine of the Trinity and a now–forgotten awareness of its cosmogenetic and hermetic applications.

CHAPTER 3. The Law of Three in Action

1. Maurice Nicoll, *Psychological Commentaries on the Teaching of Ouspensky and Gurdjieff* (Boulder, CO, and London: Shambhala Publications, 1984), p. 111.
2. See in particular my *The Wisdom Jesus* (Shambhala Publications, 2008), pp. 62–74.
3. It is my belief that Jesus's death on the cross also exhibits this more subtle Law of Three configuration. No leagues of angels arrive to snatch the beleaguered Son from the cross. And yet, when the holy

affirming of redemptive love meets the unholy denying of human hatred and fear in the reconciling ground of Jesus's surrendered heart ("Father, forgive them, for they know not what they do"), there is, indeed, a new arising, which begins right there at the foot of the cross, heralded by a new quality of presence already caught by the centurion in his hushed exclamation, "Truly, this man was the Son of God!" In the moment of Jesus's death, the innermost essence of divine love was released into the planet as a palpable force that continues to make its energetic presence directly known. That is the imaginal resurrection, the real and ongoing source of Christianity's redemptive power.

4. Needleman, *What Is God?*, p. 96.

CHAPTER 4. The Law of Three and the Enneagram

1. P. D. Ouspensky, *In Search of the Miraculous*, p. 294.

2. Oscar Ichazo is, properly speaking, the father of the contemporary enneagram of personality movement, since the original revelation of the personality system came to him as early as the 1950s. But it was Naranjo who really got the ball moving when he began to teach it at Berkeley during the 1970s. Among his early students were Helen Palmer and the Jesuit Robert Ochs. Palmer spearheaded the growth of the movement on the West Coast, while Ochs returned to Loyola University in Chicago and taught the system to twelve Jesuits; from that start the movement spread rapidly through Jesuit spiritual direction. The first books and instructional tapes appeared in the mid 1980s.

3. I am using here the typology developed by Helen Palmer, founder of one of the earliest and most influential schools of enneagram study, now known as the Narrative Tradition of enneagram teaching. Her groundbreaking 1988 book, *The Enneagram: Understanding Yourself and the Others in Your Life* (San Francisco: Harper and Row), essentially launched the enneagram as a popular movement. Types four, five, six, and eight have been renamed since that original publication, and my list here reflects the updated naming.

Other popular schools of enneagram thought include those of Don Riso and Russ Hudson (whose lineage flows through the

Jesuit side of the family tree and follows a more psychological and pathology–based model) and Kathleen Hurley and Theodore Dobson, who first began to consciously expand the enneagram into use as a kinesthetic transpersonal tool. Ichazo and Naranjo, the original founders of the movement, continued to develop their own distinctive methodologies for use of the enneagram as a diagnostic and therapeutic tool.

4. James Moore, *Gurdjieff: The Anatomy of a Myth* (Rockport, MA: Element, 1991), p. 345.

5. In the growing corpus of enneagram of personality literature, each personality type is matched to a corresponding "chief passion," which functions as its primary defensive strategy and also its primary challenge to growth. Almost from the start, these seven have been correlated to one of the seven deadly sins (or passions) of traditional Christian teaching, augmented by two additions, fear and deceit, as follows, according to type: (one) anger, (two) pride, (three) deceit, (four) envy, (five) avarice, (six) fear, (seven) gluttony, (eight) lust, (nine) sloth. Thus, for every personality type there is a fixed accompanying passion that will need to be recognized and transformed (or at least responsibly managed) if growth is to occur.

In Gurdjieff teaching, the chief feature is much more individual and specific. Sometimes it is something offbeat and even eccentric — as, for example, in Gurdjieff's celebrated assessment of one of his students: "His feature is that *he is never home*"; or of another: "He has no shame" (quoted in Ouspensky, *In Search of the Miraculous*, pp. 267–68). What makes it a chief feature is that once you spot it, you see how it controls massive sections of your behavior, imposing its self–sabotaging pattern on seemingly unrelated areas of your life. It will find a way of expressing itself in everything you do.

Once you spot it is the chief operative, however. For the all–important requirement in the Gurdjieff Work is that each person must come to a recognition of his or her chief feature *for him- or herself*. It's not a matter of learning one's typological Achilles heel from a book or even by asking one's teacher for an honest assessment. In the Gurdjieff Work the struggle to see your own blind spot is *the* initiatory passage into awakened consciousness. No one else can do it for you, and it must be approached gradually, not only through long practice in self–observation, but also through a gradually acquired self–forgiveness that will enable you to see yourself as you are and not be shattered. The fixed correlation of personality type and chief feature would strike most Gurdjieffians as not only too mechanical but also of dubious practical value, since self–awareness is conferred not by the answer itself but by the *seeing* of it.

6. This teaching is succinctly captured in one of the most famous Work epigrams: "Behind personality stands essence; behind essence stands Real I, and behind Real I stands God."

7. Ouspensky, *In Search of the Miraculous*, p. 294.

8. As I shared an early draft of this chapter with several colleagues familiar with both the Gurdjieffian enneagram and the enneagram of personality, the consensus was that comparing the two enneagrams was like comparing apples and oranges, since they are really two entirely different species. The enneagram of personality is by intention an exoteric tool whose domain is the arena of personal growth and transformation. The Gurdjieffian enneagram is an esoteric symbol intended to convey cosmic knowledge. Thus, they are not "better" and "worse," only different. But as contemporary enneagram of personality teaching continues to grow and develop, it seems inevitable that the present "parallel tracks" will at some point converge.

9. Ouspensky, *In Search of the Miraculous*, p. 294.

10. According to contemporary enneagram teaching, the direction of movement is determined for the "seven" set by the formula 1–4–2–8–5–7 (which is the decimal .142857, generated by dividing 7 into 1, the number of wholeness) and for the "three" set by the circulation around the triadic points 3, 6, and 9. Some schools of enneagram thought originally taught that one "regressed" to one's "stress point" by following the line of movement and "progressed" by moving against it (for example, a two will either "regress" to eight

or "progress" to four), but this view was never universally held and has recently come under increasing scrutiny. The main point, however, is that movement between points is contained within a three-point range — or five, if you count the two "wings" (see below, note 11).

11. In an effort to soften these boundary lines, contemporary enneagram teaching introduced the principle of "wings," which quickly gained canonical status. The idea is that each type will be influenced by either one or the other of the two numerically adjacent types. Thus, you will have "fiveish sixes," with a more paranoid streak, and "sevenish sixes," more upbeat and whimsical. This provision allows for interaction between the two patterns along the two–three, three–four, five–six, six–seven, eight–nine, and nine–one interfaces. But it still does not constitute a full circulation among the nine points, and it does not allow a specific type to "jump ship" and join the other pattern.

    For another effort by a contemporary enneagram teacher to introduce more interaction among the points, see David Daniels, "Working with the Harmony Triads," in *Talk Monthly* (online journal of the Enneagram Association in the Narrative Tradition, May 2012).

12. Ouspensky, *In Search of the Miraculous*, p. 291.

13. My own sense is that both modern psychological models and classic Christian spiritual teaching have been crippled by a loss of practical understanding about these two fundamental transformational practices of inner observation and identification. The tendency to confuse the person with the egoic self and the witnessing presence with the egoic superego has rendered much of Christian moral teaching oblivious, formatory, externally directed, and incapable of seeing where it is constantly blindsiding itself. This same confusion continues to prevail in significant sectors of contemporary depth psychology as well, where the possibility of consciousness apart from egoic selfhood is simply not understood. For an enlightened summary from a contemporary Buddhist perspective, see John Welwood, *Toward a Psychology of Awakening* (Boston: Shambhala Publications, 2000).

1. I am referring here, of course, to the forty-six early sacred texts recovered in an urn in the Egyptian desert near Nag Hammadi in 1945 and commonly (though inaccurately) known as the "gnostic gospels." Most scholars now assume they were placed in that urn for safekeeping by the monks of the nearby Pachomian monastery sometime after 367 C.E., when an edict by Bishop Athanasius determined the official "short list" of twenty-seven approved texts that would eventually become the canonical New Testament. The texts not on that list were, in a sense, "deconsecrated" and no longer approved for official use.

2. Ken Wilber, *The Eye of Spirit* (Boston: Shambhala Publications, 1997), p. 39. When I refer to Wilber's thinking having "evolved" since this description, the evolution is basically in the direction of acknowledging the whole field of reality as permeated by spirit, not just the upper echelons.

3. Arthur Lovejoy, *The Great Chain of Being* (Cambridge, Mass.: Harvard University Press, 1936, 1964).

4. Sara Sviri, *The Taste of Hidden Things* (Inverness, CA: Golden Sufi Center, 1997), pp. 196–97.

5. First articulated by the Greek secular philosopher Plotinus in the third century, the doctrine of emanationism made its way quickly into Greek intellectual speculation and from there into the Islamic world by a series of philosophers often known as the "Persian Platonists," the most prominent of whom is Suhrawardi (d. 1191). The ultimate source is the perennial philosophy. See Henry Corbin, *The Man of Light in Iranian Sufism* (Boston, Shambhala Publications, 1994).

6. Ken Wilber, *Integral Spirituality* (Boston: Shambhala Publications, 2006), pp. 74–102.

7. In Greek the word being translated as "to empty oneself" is *kenosein*, from which the term *kenosis* is derived.

8. Bruno Barnhart, *The Future of Wisdom: Toward a Rebirth of Sapiential Christianity* (New York: Continuum, 2008), p. 12.

9. Barnhart, *Second Simplicity*, p. 23.

10. This term was coined by contemporary Traditionalist metaphysician Frithjof Schuon. See his *The Transcendent Unity of Religions* (New York: Harper and Row, 1974).

CHAPTER 6. Dynamism

1. Barnhart, *The Future of Wisdom*, p. 186.
2. Ibid.
3. Barnhart, *Second Simplicity*, p. 21.
4. Barnhart, *The Future of Wisdom*, pp. 143–44.
5. Ibid., p. 32.
6. Quoted in Ilia Delio, *Christ in Evolution* (Maryknoll, NY: Orbis Books, 2008), p. 71.
7. Barnhart, *The Future of Wisdom*, p. 142.
8. Delio, *Christ in Evolution*, p. 76.
9. Ibid.
10. LaCugna's book is an expansion of a doctoral dissertation begun twenty years earlier. Her promising theological career was cut short by cancer in 1997, but the book has continued to exert a well-deserved influence. At the time of her death, she was a professor of theology at Notre Dame University.
11. The word *economic* is a translation of the Greek *oikonomia*, which in its original usage designated something akin to God's providential will as expressed in the fullness of salvation history. By the late fourth century it had been restricted to mean the human nature of Christ—"sharply distinguished from his divine nature," LaCugna writes (*God for Us*, p. 10): the first step on the slippery slope that will lead to the ultimate "defeat" of the Trinity. In part 3 I will make use of this term *oikonomia*, restoring it to its original cosmic wingspan.
12. LaCugna, *God for Us*, p. 211.
13. Ibid., p. 222.
14. Ibid., p. 224.
15. While it was perhaps inevitable—given the philosophical milieu in which it took shape—that Trinitarian theology would eventually succumb to the temptation to construct a hypothetical divine realm hermetically sealed within itself, LaCugna reminds us forcefully that "the existence of such an intradivine realm is precisely what *cannot*

be established on the basis of the economy, despite the fact that it has functioned within speculative theology ever since the late fourth century" (*God for Us*, p. 223; italics mine). What *can* be established, particularly in those earliest Trinitarian acclamations (that all things were created "*by* the Father, *through* Jesus Christ *in* the Holy Spirit") (p. 115), is the simple but profound affirmation that there is a single unbroken dynamism of love that binds together the visible and invisible realms. LaCugna's work is a powerful summons to reroot Trinitarian theology in this dynamic ground.

16. Raimon Panikkar, *Christophany: The Fullness of Man* (Maryknoll, NY: Orbis Books, 2004), p. 129.

17. Ibid., p. 173.

18. Ibid., p. 116.

19. Ibid., p. 25.

20. Ibid., p. 113.

21. Beatrice Bruteau, *God's Ecstasy: The Creation of a Self-Creating World* (New York: Crossroad, 1997), p. 14.

22. Ibid.

23. Ibid., p. 83.

24. Ibid., p. 32.

CHAPTER 7. Jacob Boehme, Ternary Master

1. Jacob Boehme, *The Confessions of Jacob Boehme*, ed. Evelyn Underhill (Whitefish, MT: Kessinger, n.d.), p. 41.

2. Perhaps the most accessible starting point for most readers is Boehme's *The Way to Christ*, in the Classics of Western Spirituality series (New York: Paulist Press, 1978). This well-edited modern translation contains Boehme's nine treatises on the spiritual life, of which the fourth, sixth, and eighth have furnished the foundational materials for my own understanding of Boehme's spirituality. From here one enters the deeper waters of John Sparrow, Boehme's indefatigable seventeenth-century English translator. I would recommend proceeding with *Clavis*, Boehme's short final summation of his most important revelations, followed by *The Three Principles of the Divine Essence*, *The Forty Questions of the Soul*, and the *Confessions*. Boehme's most famous works, *Aurora*, *The Threefold Life of Man*, and

Magnum Mysterium, are among his most difficult and will yield their insights more readily if the preceding sequence is observed. All are available in facsimile reprint from the Kessinger Publishing, POB 1404, Whitefish, MT 59937. A recent and most welcome emergence is the anthology *Genius of the Transcendent: Mystical Writings of Jakob Boehme,* translated by Michael L. Birkel and Jeff Bach (Boston: Shambhala Publications, 2010), a new translation of some of Boehme's most important writings from Shambhala Publications.

3. Boehme, *Way to Christ,* p. 171.
4. Cynthia Bourgeault, "Boehme for Beginners," *Gnosis,* no. 45 (Fall 1997), pp. 28–36. (To order, go to www.fieldsbooks.com and search for "*Gnosis* magazine."
5. Boehme, *Clavis,* p. 50.
6. Ibid., p. 46. If this seems like a prying or impertinent question, remember how visionary seeing works. Before the question is even consciously raised at a cognitive level, the "answer" is already flooding in. There is a huge difference in spiritual vibrancy between that cognitively driven theological speculation on the inner life of the Godhead we looked at in chapter 6 and Boehme's "Look out! Here it comes!!!" gratuitous revelation that fateful morning in 1600.
7. Ibid., p. 11.
8. Ibid., pp. 15–16.
9. Ibid.
10. Ibid.
11. It is also a mainstay of the allegorical mode of spiritual reflection, the primary exegetical mode in the sapiential tradition of Western Christendom until displaced by Scholasticism in the thirteenth century. This type of heart-centered associative logic is specifically trained in *lectio divina,* the foundational prayer practice of Benedictine monasticism. For more on lectio divina and the training of the unitive imagination, see my *Chanting the Psalms* (Boston: Shambhala Publications, 2005), pp. 49–58.
12. Boehme, *Way to Christ,* p. 196.
13. Ibid., p. 192.
14. George Allen, introduction to *The Threefold Life of Man,* by Jacob Boehme (Whitefish, MT: Kessinger, n.d.), p. xxv.

15. Boehme, *Confessions*, p. 164.
16. Boehme, *Clavis*, pp. 22–23.
17. Boehme, *Way to Christ*, p. 192.
18. Boehme, *Clavis*, p. 48.
19. Jacob Boehme, *The Forty Questions of the Soul* (Whitefish, MT: Kessinger, n.d.), p. 144.
20. Ibid., p. 23.
21. Boehme, *Clavis*, p. 46.

CHAPTER 8. Seven Properties, Three Forces

1. Boehme, *Clavis*, pp. 17–18.
2. See, for example, *Clavis*, p. 21.
3. In this chart and in many other places in his work, Boehme uses the word *forms* interchangeably with the word *properties*. They designate the same thing.
4. The first triad is irregular, of course, for here it seems that what is being created is the Law of Three itself, from which all further actions will emanate. But after this the pattern holds without variation. You will see more of how this works in part 3 of this book.
5. As Boehme expresses it: "The will longs earnestly for the Unity, but the Unity longs for the sensibility; thus, the one longs to get into the other" (*Clavis*, p. 21). The only stability lies in the dynamic equilibrium itself, in which all things are passing continuously from form to emptiness and from emptiness to form.
6. Boehme, *Way to Christ*, p. 192.

CHAPTER 9. Counterstroke

1. I first came across this prayer many years ago, tacked on a parish secretary's bulletin board in a small Anglican church in Campbell River, British Columbia. I have been unable to discover its authorship.
2. I discovered this text via a Christmas card sent to me in 1994. The card is still one of my cherished possessions, but I have not yet rooted through the Black Elk canon to discover its official bibliographic data.
3. *Clavis*, p. 8.

4. Barnhart, *Second Simplicity*, p. 21. I quoted this same passage earlier on page 79.

CHAPTER 10. The Essential Ground Rules

1. Nicoll, *Psychological Commentaries*, p. 109.
2. Gurdjieff, *Beelzebub's Tales*, p. 689. See also note 5, chapter 2.

CHAPTER 11. Stage 1: The Proto-Trinity

1. Boehme, *Clavis*, pp. 15–16.
2. Ibid., p. 16.
3. Ibid., p. 32.
4. Ibid., pp. 22–23.
5. Valentin Tomberg, *Meditations on the Tarot* (Rockport, MA: Element, 1993), p. 30.
6. Boehme, *Clavis*, p. 22.

CHAPTER 12. Stage 2: The Primordial Trinity

1. Jyri Paloheimo, in his letter of March 26, 2002, offers an indirect confirmation of my intuition here in his comment on Gurdjieff's teaching on "the Omnipresent Okidanokh":

> Gurdjieff maintains that everything in the Universe without exception is material (matter). The prime substance out of which everything is created is called in *Beelzebub* "etherokrilno," which is the basis of every arising and their maintenance. Gurdjieff does not say much about it.
>
> There is another substance that is perhaps more important for understanding the Law of Three. And here I might as well quote directly from *Beelzebub's Tales*:

> "You should also know that only one cosmic crystallization, known as the 'Omnipresent Okidanokh,' although also crystallized as etherokrilno, has its prime arising from the three holy sources of the sacred 'Theomertmalogos,' that is, from the emanations of the Most Holy Sun Absolute.

"Everywhere in the Universe this Omnipresent Okidanokh, or 'omnipresent active element', takes part in the formation of all arisings, both great and small, and is in general
the principal cause of most cosmic phenomena and, in particular, of those proceeding in the atmospheres."

— Gurdjieff, *Beelzebub's Tales*, p. 130

Continuing to quote from Gurdjieff's presentation of this "Omnipresent Okidanokh," Paloheimo cites the following:

When a new cosmic unit is being concentrated, the "omnipresent active element" does not blend as a whole with the new
arising, nor is it transformed as a whole in any given place in
it — it occurs with all other cosmic crystallizations in all these
cosmic formulations — but as soon as it enters as a whole into
any cosmic unit, there immediately occurs in it what is called
"djartklom," that is, it is dispersed into the three fundamental
sources from which it arose. Then these three sources, each separately, give rise to the independent concentration of three distinct new formations within the cosmic unit. And in this way
the "omnipresent active element" actualizes, at the beginning
of every such new arising, sources for the possible manifestation of its own sacred law of the Traimazikamno [The Law of
Three].

— Gurdjieff, *Beelzebub's Tales*, pp. 131–32

It seems that in some significant ways Gurdjieff's teaching on
the Omnipresent Okidanokh covers the same metaphysical bases
that I am trying to uphold in designating the Endless Unity as a
direct participant in every new cosmogonic arising.

2. Boehme, *Clavis*, p. 28.

3. Ibid., p. 25.

4. Boehme, *Forty Questions*, p. 21.

5. I am quoting from the elegant new translation by Rami Shapiro
in his *The Divine Feminine in Biblical Wisdom Literature* (Woodstock, VT:
Skylight Paths, 2005), p. 29.

6. Julian of Norwich, *Showings*, ed. Edmund Colledge, and James Walsh, Classics of Western Spirituality (Mahwah, NJ: Paulist Press, 1978), pp. 296.

7. Ibid., pp. 295–96.

CHAPTER 13. Stage 3: The Sophianic Trinity

1. Boehme, *Way to Christ*, p. 192.

2. Tomberg, *Meditations on the Tarot*, p. 574.

3. Thomas Merton, *Hagia Sophia*, in *A Thomas Merton Reader*, ed. Thomas P. McDonell (New York: Doubleday/Image Books, 1974, 1989), p. 509.

4. Merton, "A Member of the Human Race," in *A Thomas Merton Reader*, pp. 346–47.

5. This wonderful phrase comes from Kabir Helminski, *Living Presence: A Sufi Way to Mindfulness and the Essential Self* (New York: Jeremy Tarcher/Putnam, 1992).

6. Helen Luke, *Old Age* (New York: Parabola Books, 1987), p. 84.

7. Again, I am quoting from Rami Shapiro, *The Divine Feminine*, pp. 31, 33.

8. Merton, *Hagia Sophia*, pp. 508–9.

9. Christopher Pramuk, *Sophia: The Hidden Christ of Thomas Merton* (Collegeville, MN: Liturgical Press, 2009).

CHAPTER 14. Stage 4: The Incarnational Trinity

1. I say "at first" because it becomes clear on deeper reflection that there are, in fact, three factors that intertwine in all human births: the father's lineage, the mother's lineage, and the "soul" or "essence," which seems to arrive from a mysterious beyond that is never fully explained by or subsumed within linear causality. Gurdjieff always claimed that our essence comes from the stars.

2. Boehme, *Clavis*, p. 21.

3. Denise Levertov, *A Door in the Hive* (New York: New Directions, 1989), p. 87. See also *The Stream and the Sapphire: Selected Poems on Religious Themes* (New York: New Directions, 1997), pp. 59–61.

4. Robert B. Burlin, ed., *The Old English Advent: A Typological Commentary* (New Haven, CT: Yale University Press, 1968), p. 129.

CHAPTER 15. Stage 5: The Messianic Trinity

1. Rainer Maria Rilke, "The First Elegy," in *Duino Elegies* (New York: W. W. Norton, 1939), p. 21.

2. For a detailed look at Mary Magdalene, see my *The Meaning of Mary Magdalene: Discovering the Woman at the Heart of Christianity* (Boston: Shambhala Publications, 2010).

3. Ladislaus Boros, *The Mystery of Death* (New York: Seabury Press, 1973).

4. Ibid., p. ix.

5. Ibid., p. 148.

6. Ibid., p. 149.

7. Ibid., p. 157.

8. The translation I am using here comes from the service of Lauds at New Camaldoli Hermitage in Big Sur, California. I have chanted it on Wednesday mornings for nearly twenty years. It is number 250 in *Lauds and Vespers*, the Camaldolese Psalter (Big Sur, CA: Camaldolese Hermits of America, 1994).

9. John Donne, "A Valediction: Forbidding Mourning" in *The Complete Poems of John Donne*, ed. Roger E. Bennett (Chicago: Packard, 1942), pp. 32–33. This poem is also easily available online.

10. For more on this, see Panikkar, *Christophany*, pp. 148–52.

CHAPTER 16. Stage 6: The Pentecostal Trinity

1. Tomberg, *Meditations on the Tarot*, p. 644.

2. Ibid.

3. Jean-Yves Leloup, *The Gospel of Mary Magdalene* (Rochester, VT: New Traditions, 2002), p. 153.

4. Symeon the New Theologian, "We Awaken in Christ's Body," in *The Enlightened Heart: An Anthology of Sacred Poetry*, ed. Stephen Mitchell (New York: HarperCollins, 1993), p. 38.

5. On this point, see Boehme's "Sixth Treatise: On The Supersensual Life" in *Way to Christ*, particularly p.182 ff.; and *Forty Questions*, particularly the twenty-first question.

6. Gurdjieff's teaching on this point is that if one fails to develop consciously in this life, at death one's constituent material elements

dissolve back into the thin film of organic life on planet Earth, whose principal function is to provide nutrient material for the further evolution of realms subsidiary to the earth. In his celebrated phrase, we become "food for the moon."

7. Jim Marion, *Putting on the Mind of Christ* (Charlottesville, VA: Hampton Roads, 2000).

8. For more on this point, see my *The Wisdom Jesus* (Boston: Shambhala Publications, 2008), particularly chapter 3.

9. Llewellyn Vaughan-Lee, *The Bond with the Beloved* (Inverness, CA: Golden Sufi Center, 1993), p. 26.

10. Merton, "Member of the Human Race," p. 347. In his original version, these words were part of his *Conjectures of a Guilty Bystander* (New York: Doubleday, 1966), p. 158.

11. Merton, "A Member of the Human Race," p. 347.

CHAPTER 17. Stage 7: The Economic Trinity

1. Philip Booth, "Heading Out," in *Selves* (New York: Penguin Books, 1991), p. 28.

2. Boehme, *Forty Questions*, p. 264.

3. Boros, *Mystery of Death*, pp. 53–54.

4. Ibid., p. 61.

5. Ibid., p. 62.

6. This line of argument is particularly strong in the Gurdjieff tradition. Perhaps the most influential contemporary philosopher to adopt this position is Jacob Needleman, who, as we have already seen, is strongly rooted in the Gurdjieff lineage. His classic book *Lost Christianity* (New York: Doubleday, 1983) makes a particularly strong case for the need to see the soul not as a preexistent spark but as the magnum opus of a life consciously lived. The soul is formed, according to Needleman, by bringing attention and conscious presence to the raw psychological material of our lives.

7. Maurice Nicoll, *The New Man* (New York: Penguin Books, 1983), pp. 76–77.

8. Ibid., p. 78.

9. Tomberg, *Meditations on the Tarot*, p. 577.

CHAPTER 18. The Reflexive Trinity

1. Arthur M. Young, *The Reflexive Universe* (Mill Valley, CA: Robert Briggs, 1986).
2. Ibid., p. 207.
3. Ibid., p. 91.
4. Ibid., p. 42.
5. Ibid., p. 36.

CHAPTER 19. The Ham Radio in the Tea Cupboard

1. Paul Ricoeur (1913–2005) was one of the most distinguished philosophers of the twentieth century, with a long list of publications. My introduction to Ricoeur's concept of wager came much more informally, however: through my hermit-teacher, Brother Raphael Robin, who was much taken with the idea and returned to it repeatedly during our three years of working together. I believe Raphael was referring to Ricoeur's *The Symbolism of Evil*, translated by E. Buchanan (New York: Harper, 1967), although I have not personally verified this. I have more to say about Paul Ricoeur and the wager as a hermeneutical principle in my *Love Is Stronger than Death* (New York, Bell Tower, 1999), p. 167.
2. Bruteau, *God's Ecstasy*, p. 83.
3. To refresh yourself on this discussion, see chapter 15, pp. 166–69.
4. For a thoughtful summary of this difficult terrain, see Raimon Panikkar, *Christophany*, p. 150.
5. For a brilliant tracing of this San Andreas Fault running through Western Christendom, see Richard Tarnas, *The Passion of the Western Mind* (New York: Ballantine Books, 1991). Raimon Panikkar also alludes to this schism briefly but tellingly in a comment in *Christophany*, p. 146: "The Christian vision today has lost its foundation inasmuch as it lacks an adequate cosmovision."
6. Boehme, *Forty Questions*, p. 23.
7. See in particular Brian Greene, *The Elegant Universe* (New York: Vintage Books, 1999), pp. 361–63, the section entitled "Before the Beginning." I am also grateful for conversations with Dr. Tom Tiedje,

professor of physics and engineering at the University of British Columbia, and with Dr. Jyri Paloheimo at the University of Toronto.

8. There is not room in this book to follow all the implications of Boehmian cosmology recast in a Law of Three format, but here I would like to comment on one very important correlation: with that provocative comment made by hermeticist Valentin Tomberg in his *Meditations on the Tarot*, which I have already mentioned briefly in my discussion of the Sophianic Trinity (chapter 13, p. 149).

> Modern science has come to the understanding that matter is only condensed energy — which, moreover, was known by alchemists and hermeticists thousands of years ago. Sooner or later science will discover that what it calls "energy" is only condensed psychic force — which discovery will lead in the end to the establishment of the fact that all psychic force is the "condensation," purely simply, of consciousness, i.e. spirit.

Tomberg's schematic is useful because it skillfully leads us from known scientific reference points in the physical realm into the more subtle energetic realms heretofore described only in spiritual traditions. Virtually every schoolchild today knows that matter is condensed energy. And the "sooner or later" predicted by Tomberg has now become contemporary reality as science actively investigates what Tomberg calls "psychic energy," the demonstrable physical effects of those more subtle energies such as attention, will, prayer, and love. The third phase in Tomberg's scenario — from psychic energy to consciousness — is currently also the subject of intense scientific investigation in the rapidly emerging field of neurobiology, although I suspect that most scientists would hesitate a bit over Tomberg's blanket equation of consciousness with spirit. What Tomberg is essentially presenting here is a kind of spatial cosmology: describing the sequence of "condensations" culminating in our physical universe in terms of the classic spiritual realms of the great chain of being: gross (matter), subtle (energy), causal (psychic force), non-dual (consciousness).

What interests me here is how closely these stages dovetail with those first three triads of Boehme's cosmology (again, recast in Law of Three format and replicated in the first three triads of my own unfolding Trinity in part 3). Working our way back "up" the great chain of being, the "condensation" from psychic force to energy/matter is the domain of Boehme's third triad (my Sophianic Trinity); the "condensation" from consciousness to psychic force is the business of his second triad (my Primordial Trinity). What Tomberg does not seem to consider but is very much the business of Boehme's first triad (my Proto-Trinity) is the fact that consciousness itself is already a "condensation": of the Endless Unity, the pure, undifferentiated field of divine omniscience into consciousness: "knowing with" or "reflected knowing."

This second overlay (the first was Tomberg and science), between Boehme and Tomberg, further confirms that Boehme is on the right track in his intuition of a protocreation and establishes firm points of correspondence between his temporal sequencing and the classic metaphysical road map depicted in the great chain of being. If, as I will suggest shortly in the main text of this chapter, Boehme's cosmology also appears to be corroborated in some of the calculations emerging from the leading edge of theoretical physics describing the conditions that would have had to be in place to make possible a big bang, then we are very close to connecting the dots between scientific and spiritual cosmology.

9. The term *first axial period* was first coined by German philosopher Karl Jaspers to describe that remarkable six-hundred-year period between 800 B.C.E. and 200 B.C.E., when seemingly spontaneously and universally a new kind of consciousness arose to arise that laid the foundations for civilization as we know it today. In essence, what broke through for the first time was a sense of individual accountability and individual destiny before God (or divine reality). One can see this new sentiment arising spontaneously in the great masters of this era, as if passed by an imaginal torch: from Lao Tzu in China to the Buddha to the Old Testament prophets to Zoro-

aster and Pythagoras. The headwaters of the perennial philosophy certainly lie in this axial awakening. What, one might wonder, lies in store for these great spiritual traditions as a new consciousness, founded once again on collectivity but at an infinitely higher and more nuanced level — a *holographic* collectivity — begins to express itself?

Select Bibliography

This bibliography consists primarily of works actually cited in the text, augmented by a very select listing of other key readings in the pertinent areas. It does not pretend to be exhaustive, but only to offer a solid foundation for further research.

Amis, Robin. *A Different Christianity.* Albany, NY: SUNY Press, 1995.

Barnhart, Bruno. *The Future of Wisdom: Toward a Rebirth of Sapiential Christianity.* New York: Continuum, 2008.

———. *Second Simplicity: The Inner Shape of Christianity.* Mahwah, NJ: Paulist Press, 1999.

Bennett, John G. *Deeper Man.* Santa Fe, NM: Bennett Books, 1994.

———. *The Dramatic Universe.* 4 volumes. Charles Town, WV: Claymont Communications, 1987.

———. *Energies Material, Vital, Cosmic.* Charles Town, WV: Claymont Communications, 1989.

———. *Gurdjieff: Making a New World.* Santa Fe: Bennett Books, 1993.

———. *The Masters of Wisdom.* London: Turnstone Press, 1977.

———. *The Sevenfold Work.* Charles Town, WV: Claymont Communications, 1979.

Birkel, Michael L., and Jeff Bach, trans. *Genius of the Transcendent: Mystical Writings of Jakob Boehme.* Boston: Shambhala Publications, 2010.

Boehme, Jacob. *The Aurora.* Facsimile edition. Whitefish, MT: Kessinger Publishing Company.

———. *The Clavis.* Facsimile edition. Whitefish, MT: Kessinger Publishing Company, n.d.

———. *The Confessions of Jacob Boehme.* Facsimile edition. Edited by Evelyn Underhill. Whitefish, MT: Kessinger Publishing Company, n.d.

—. *The Forty Questions of the Soul.* Facsimile edition. Whitefish, MT: Kessinger Publishing Company, n.d.

—. *The Magnum Mysterium.* Facsimile edition. Whitefish, MT: Kessinger Publishing Company, n.d.

—. *The Threefold Life of Man.* Facsimile edition. Whitefish, MT: Kessinger Publishing Company, n.d.

—. *The Three Principles of the Divine Essence.* Facsimile edition. Whitefish, MT: Kessinger Publishing Company, n.d.

—. *The Way to Christ.* Edited by Peter Erb. The Classics of Western Spirituality. Mahwah, NJ: Paulist Press, 1978.

Boros, Ladislaus. *The Mystery of Death.* New York: Herder and Herder, 1965; New York: Seabury Press, 1973.

Bourgeault, Cynthia. "Boehme for Beginners." *Gnosis* Magazine no. 45 (Fall 1997), pp. 28–36.

—. *Chanting the Psalms.* Boston: Shambhala Publications, 2006.

—. *Love Is Stronger Than Death: The Mystical Union of Two Souls.* New York: Bell Tower, 1999; reissued in paperback: Telephone, TX: Praxis Publishing, 2007.

—. *The Meaning of Mary Magdalene: Discovering the Woman at the Heart of Christianity.* Boston: Shambhala Publications, 2010.

—. *The Wisdom Jesus.* Boston: Shambhala Publications, 2008.

—. *The Wisdom Way of Knowing.* San Francisco: Jossey Bass, 2003.

Bruteau, Beatrice. *God's Ecstasy: The Creation of a Self-Creating World.* New York: Crossroad, 1997.

Clément, Olivier. *The Roots of Christian Mysticism: Text and Commentary.* Hyde Park, NY: New City Press, 1993.

Corbin, Henry, *The Man of Light in Iranian Sufism.* Boston: Shambhala Publications, 1994.

Cousins, Ewert H. *Christ of the 21st Century.* Rockport, MA: Element, 1992.

Daniels, David. *The Essential Enneagram: The Definitive Personality Test and Self-Discovery Guide.* New York: HarperCollins, 2009.

—. "Working the Harmony Triads." *Talk Monthly* (online journal of the Enneagram Association in the Narrative Tradition). May 2012.

Delio, Ilia. *Christ in Evolution.* Maryknoll, NY: Orbis Books, 2008.

De Lubac, Henri. *Teilhard de Chardin: The Man and His Meaning.* Translated by René Hague. New York: Hawthorn Books, 1965.

Dillard, Annie. *Holy the Firm.* New York: Harper and Row, 1977.

Faivre, Antoine, and Jacob Needleman, editors. *Modern Esoteric Spirituality.* Vol. 21 in World Spirituality: An Encyclopedic History of the Religious Quest. New York: Crossroad, 1992.

Greene, Brian. *The Elegant Universe.* New York: Vintage Books, 1999.

Gurdjieff, G. I. *Beelzebub's Tales to His Grandson.* London: Routledge & Kegan Paul, 1950; New York and London: Viking Arkana (Triangle Editions), 1992.

——. *Life Is Real Only Then, When "I Am."* New York: Triangle Editions, 1975.

——. *Meetings with Remarkable Men.* Routledge & Kegan Paul, London, 1963; New York: Viking Arkana, 1985.

——. *Views from the Real World.* Routledge & Kegan Paul, London, 1963; New York: E. P. Dutton, 1975.

Halevi, Z'ev ben Shimon. *The Kabbalistic Tree of Life.* Kabbalah Society (Tree of Life Publishing Company), 1972, 2009.

Haught, John F. *God beyond Darwin: A Theology of Evolution.* Boulder, CO: Westview Press, 2000.

Helminski, Kabir. *Living Presence: A Sufi Way to Mindfulness and the Essential Self.* New York: Jeremy Tarcher/Putnam, 1992.

Hurley, Kathleen, and Theodore Dobson. *My Best Self: Using the Enneagram to Free the Soul.* New York: HarperOne, 1993.

Johnson, Elizabeth. *She Who Is: The Mystery of God in Feminist Theological Discourse.* New York: Crossroad, 1992.

King, Ursula. *Christ in All Things.* Maryknoll, NY: Orbis Books, 1997.

——. *Towards a New Mysticism: Teilhard de Chardin & Eastern Religions.* New York: Seabury Press, 1980.

LaCugna, Catherine Mowry. *God for Us: The Trinity and Christian Life.* San Francisco: HarperSanFrancisco, 1991.

Leloup, Jean-Yves. *The Gospel of Mary Magdalene.* Rochester, VT: New Traditions, 2002.

Lovejoy, Arthur, *The Great Chain of Being.* Cambridge, MA: Harvard University Press, 1936, 1964.

Luke, Helen. *Old Age,* New York: Parabola Books, 1987.

Maitri, Sandra. *The Spiritual Dimension of the Enneagram: Nine Faces of the Soul.* New York: Jeremy Tarcher/Penguin, 2000.

Marion, Jim. *Putting on the Mind of Christ.* Charlottesville, VA, Hampton Roads, 2000.

Merton, Thomas. *Conjectures of a Guilty Bystander.* New York: Doubleday Image, 1968.

———. "Hagia Sophia." In *A Thomas Merton Reader,* edited by Thomas P. McDonnell. New York: Doubleday Image Books, 1989.

Moore, James. *Gurdjieff: The Anatomy of a Myth.* Rockport, MA: Element, 1991.

Needleman, Jacob. *Lost Christianity.* New York: Doubleday, 1983.

———. *What Is God?* New York: Jeremy. Tarcher/Penguin, 2009.

Nicoll, Maurice. *The New Man.* New York: Penguin Books, 1983.

———. *Psychological Commentaries on the Teaching of Ouspensky and Gurdjieff.* Five volumes. London: Watkins Publishing, 1976; London and Boulder: Shambhala Publications, 1984.

O'Connor, Flannery. "Good Country People." In *Flannery O'Connor: The Complete Stories.* New York: Harcourt Brace Jovaovich, 1977.

Ouspensky, P. D. *In Search of the Miraculous: Fragments of an Unknown Teaching.* London: Routledge & Kegan Paul, 1950; New York: Harcourt Brace Jovanovich, 1976.

Palmer, Helen. *The Enneagram: Understanding Yourself and the Others in Your Life,* San Francisco: Harper and Row, 1988.

Panikkar, Raimon. *Christophany: The Fullness of Man.* Maryknoll, NY: Orbis Books, 2004.

———. *The Trinity and the Religious Experience of Man.* New York: Orbis Books, 1973.

Pramuk, Christopher. *Sophia: The Hidden Christ of Thomas Merton.* Collegeville, MN: The Liturgical Press, 2009.

Rahner, Karl. *The Trinity.* New York: Herder and Herder, 1970.

———. "Remarks on the Dogmatic Treatise 'De Trinitate.'" In *Theological Investigations,* vol. 4. New York: Crossroad, 1982.

Riso, Don Richard, and Russ Hudson. *Understanding the Ennegram.* New York: Houghton Mifflin Harcourt, 1990.

Salzmann, Jeanne de. *The Reality of Being.* Boston: Shambhala Publications, 2010.

Schuon, Frithjof. *The Transcendent Unity of Religions.* New York: Harper and Row, 1972.

Shapiro, Rami. *The Divine Feminine in Biblical Wisdom Literature.* Woodstock, VT: Skylight Paths, 2005.

Sviri, Sara. *The Taste of Hidden Things.* Inverness, CA: The Golden Sufi Center, 1997.

Tarnus, Richard. *The Passion of the Western Mind.* New York: Ballantine Books, 1991.

Teilhard de Chardin, Pierre. *Activation of Energy.* Translated by René Hague. New York: Harcourt Brace Jovanovich, 1970.

———. *Christianity and Evolution.* Translated by René Hague. New York: Harcourt Brace, Jovanovich, 1971.

———. *The Divine Milieu: An Essay on the Interior Life.* Translated by William Collins. New York: Harper and Row, 1960.

———. *The Phenomenon of Man.* Translated by Bernard Wall. New York: Harper and Row, 1959.

———. *Science and Christ.* Translated by René Hague. New York: Harper and Row, 1968.

Tomberg, Valentin. *Meditations on the Tarot.* Rockport, MA: Element, 1993.

Vaughan-Lee, Llewellyn. *The Bond with the Beloved.* Inverness, CA: The Golden Sufi Center, 1993.

Welwood, John. *Toward a Psychology of Awakening.* Boston: Shambhala Publications, 2000.

Wilber, Ken. *The Eye of the Spirit.* Boston: Shambhala Publications, 1997.

———. *Integral Spirituality.* Boston: Shambhala Publications, 2006.

Young, Arthur. *The Reflexive Universe.* Mill Valley, CA: Robert Briggs Associates, 1986.

Index

Body of Christ (*continued*)
Pentecostal Trinity and, 170,
174–77
Boehme, Jacob, 93–95, 126, 176,
210
on anguish, 156
beyond ascent and descent,
120
Gegenwurf principle, 116–19
Heart of God and, 137–38,
143–44, 149
holy affirming and, 134
holy denying and, 135
holy reconciling and, 135–37
Holy Substantiality and, 147,
150
on "the impressure of nothing into something," 20–21,
96–102
on perceptivity and divisibility, 213
"resurrection body," 185
Second Principle, 99–102
on seven properties, 97–115,
134, 135, 137, 140, 143–44, 147,
148, 150, 210
on sevenfold progression,
105–7
shoemaker metaphor, 127
and surrender as catalytic
principle, 95–96
Third Principle, 99, 101–2, 104,
111, 114
on threefold source in every-

thing, 102–4, 209
on Unity and sensibility, 156
Valentin Tomberg and, 236n8
The Way to Christ, 94
Word/Logos and, 148
See also First Principle
"Boehme for Beginners"
(Bourgeault), 96
Boros, Ladislaus, 164–65,
186–87
Bruteau, Beatrice, 87–89, 199,
209–10

catalytic principle, 96
causality, 37, 63–64
imaginal, 63–65, 85, 105
*Centering Prayer and Inner Awaken-
ing* (Bourgeault), 9
Chanting the Psalms (Bourgeault), 9
Chesterton, G. K., 9
Christ
reclaiming the primacy of,
203–4
as "third," 81
See also Jesus Christ
Christ consciousness, 203
Christ in Evolution (Delio), 81–82
Christianity, 9, 76–77
historical perspective on,
64–65
remythologized, 202
See also specific topics
Christosophia, 144, 145, 153, 172,
184, 201, 204

dynamism (*continued*)
  relational, 85–86
  of ternary systems, 18, 65
    (*see also* Three, Law of:
    dynamism of)
  Trinitarian, 87–88
  of Trinity, 138, 171

Economic Trinity, 182–83,
    186–90
  triadic points, 183–86
  See also Oikonomia
Einstein, Albert, 39, 69
emanation, 69
emanationism, 112, 117, 126, 141,
    196, 224n5
empowerment, 165
Endless Unity, 100, 134–38, 195,
    210
  becoming conscious of itself,
    136, 138
  meanings of and terminology
    for, 110, 112–14, 126, 133, 138
  movement ("outflow") in, 97
  Oikonomia and, 213
  Unmanifest and, 141–42
  Word and, 148
enemy, is never the problem
    but the opportunity, 39
enneagram, 48–51, 220–23nn2–11
  conscious shock and, 53–57
  cosmological laws and, 51–53
  Gurdjieff, Gurdjieff Work, and,
    3, 48–52, 56–58
  third force and, 57–59
equanimity, 95, 101

essence, spiritualization of, 180,
    187
Eternal Liberty, 110, 112, 126,
    138, 141, 145
Eucharist, 174
Eye of Spirit, The (Wilber), 67

Feast of the Ascension. *See*
    Ascensiontide
feminine
  Holy Spirit as, 4, 168
  Kingdom of Heaven and the,
    201
  problem of the "missing,"
    201–2
  quaternity and the, 18–19
feminine dimension of God and
    the divine feminine, 4–5
  desire to recover it within
    Christianity, 4–5
feminizing the Trinity, problems
    with, 13–14, 21
  the metaphysical corrective,
    14–15
fiery principle, 99–102, 137, 144.
    See also First Principle; wrath-
    ful principle
fire (fourth property), 100. *See
    also* Boehme, Jacob: on seven
    properties
First Principle (fire, wrath),
    97–103. *See also* fiery princi-
    ple; wrathful principle
first property, 97. *See also*
    Boehme, Jacob: on seven
    properties

"formatory" mind, 32
freedom. *See* Eternal Liberty
friction. *See* anguish

Gelassenheit, 95, 101
gender
  as binary system, 15
  personhood and, 157–59
"Gift of the Magi, The"
    (O. Henry), 44
God
  Boehme on, 103
  diffuse shining of, 163–64
  knowing himself in divisibil-
    ity, 138–39
  ousia and *energia* of, 209
  See also Heart of God; *specific*
    topics
"God behind God," 209
God-community, 90, 209
God for Us: The Trinity and Christian
    Life (LaCugna), 83
Godhead, 68, 83, 87, 97, 126, 141,
    209. *See also* superconscious
God's Ecstasy: The Creation of a Self-
    Creating World (Bruteau), 87
"Good Country People"
    (O'Connor), 41–42
great chain of being, 67–68, 70,
    117, 120, 235n8
ground rules, 125–28, 131
Gurdfieff Work, 3, 22, 35, 221n5
  enneagram and, 48, 52, 56, 57
    (*see also* enneagram)
  J. G. Bennett and, 23
  Jacob Needleman and, 24

James Moore and, 23–24, 26
Law of Three and, 4, 22, 26, 27,
    89
Maurice Nicoll and, 29
Neutralizing Force and, 41
Peter Ouspensky and, 22–23
third force and, 32, 44
Gurdjieff, George Ivanovich, 32,
    34–35, 176, 229n1
  Boehme and, 105
  on discontinuity of vibrations,
    33–34
  enneagram and, 3, 48–51,
    57–58 (*see also* enneagram)
  Law of Seven, 35
  Law of Three, 3, 4, 6, 22, 27, 28,
    33, 35, 37, 208
  Law of World Creation, 81, 87
  Peter Ouspensky and, 22–23
  on reciprocal maintenance
    (interdependent arising),
    26–27
  on third force, 26, 29, 32, 36,
    57, 58
  as trickster, 36–37
  on Trisagion, 218n5
Gurdjieff: The Anatomy of a Myth
    (Moore), 23–24
Gurdjieffian system, 129, 130

hardness/harshness (first prop-
    erty), 97. *See also* Boehme,
    Jacob: on seven properties
heart, San Andreas Fault run-
    ning through the country of
    the, 72–77

Heart of God, 195, 204
  Boehme and, 137–38, 143–44,
    149
  Incarnational Trinity and,
    154–56
  Law of Three and, 154, 156
  Primordial Trinity and, 140,
    141, 143–45, 193
  Proto-Trinity and, 132, 137–39
  Sophianic Trinity and, 147–50,
    152
  See also arising
heaven
  and earth, meeting of, 179–81
  harrowing of, 166–69
  See also Kingdom of Heaven
Hegelian dialectic, 26, 142
Henry, O., 44
Holy Spirit, 86, 168
  as androgynous, 201
  as feminine, 4, 168
Hudson, Russ, 220n3
hunger, magnetical (first prop-
    erty), 97. *See also* Boehme,
    Jacob: on seven properties
Hurley, Kathleen, 221n3
Huxley, Aldous, 65
hypostases, 20, 201

Ichazo, Oscar, 48, 220n2
imaginal causality, 63–65, 85,
    105
imaginal realm, 80, 94, 95, 161,
    167, 173, 188–89
impasses, solutions to, 31–33

incarnation, 7, 37, 79, 80, 207
Incarnational Trinity, 154
  gender and personhood,
    157–59
  three triadic points, 154–57

Jaspers, Karl, 236n9
Jesus Christ, 29, 78, 79, 144
  in Gospel of John, 73
  as human being and divine
    hypostasis, 20
  as singularity, 158
  See also Christ; *specific topics*
John, Gospel of, 72, 73, 85, 148,
    154, 163, 166, 170, 185
Johnson, Elizabeth, 14
Julian of Norwich, 144–46, 150
Jung, Carl Gustav, 18–19, 28, 64

kenosis, 7, 44, 73–74
Kingdom of Heaven, 204, 212,
    214
  Economic Trinity and, 182, 184,
    187
  and the feminine, 201
  Holy Substantiality and, 201
  Jesus Christ and, 177, 179, 181
  Law of Three and, 2, 74, 125
  Pentecostal Trinity and, 170,
    177–79, 181, 194

LaCugna, Catherine Mowry,
    83–84, 89, 91, 133, 225n10,
    225n15
Leloup, Jean-Yves, 173

Trinity (*continued*)

  origin of the doctrine of the,
    204–5

  ways Christians use, 2

  See also specific topics

Trisagion, 4, 36, 130, 218n5

twofoldness, as leading to cyclic
  recurrence, 18

unity, 212

  vs. differentiation, 86

  feminine principle of, 19

  root, 164–65, 167

  symbiotic, 87

Unity, 17, 18, 178

  counterstroke of, 100, 119,
    137–38, 142, 148

  vs. Fire-world, 113

  Heart of God and, 143

  holy denying and, 184

  Law of Three and, 120

  love as the perceiving of, 100,
    103, 119, 136–38, 149, 154

  at peak of triangle, 112, 113,
    140, 147, 154–55, 160, 170,
    182, 193, 194

  Proto-Trinity and, 156

  vs. Spirit, 156

  Wisdom as subject and resem-
    blance of the infinite and
    unsearchable, 118–19

  See also Endless Unity

Unmanifest, 126, 184

  Endless Unity and, 141–42

  Incarnational Trinity and,
    154–55

Jesus and, 154–55

Magnum Mysterium and, 145

Primordial Trinity and, 141,
  142, 145

See also denying

Vaughan-Lee, Llewellyn, 180–81

vibrations, discontinuous,
  33–34, 55

virgin point. See *point vierge*

visible world. *See* Third Principle

warm-heartedness, 150

Weaver's Prayer, 117

"Why Feminizing the Trinity Will
  Not Work" (Bourgeault), 5

Wilber, Ken, 67, 70

will, 189

Wisdom, Holy, 76, 151–53

  perceptivity and, 118, 140, 193

  as "subject and resemblance
    of the infinite and unsearch-
    able Unity," 118–19

Wisdom Jesus, The (Bourgeault), 9

Wisdom schools, 3

Word, 20, 100

  "and the Word became flesh,"
    154, 155

  Gospel of John and, 148, 154,
    155

  Holy Spirit as counterstroke
    of, 168, 171

  Incarnational Trinity and,
    154–56

  Jesus and, 154

  Law of Three and, 153